D1055434
32565

Claudel's Immortal Heroes:
A Choice of Deaths

Tête d'or

This frontispiece by André Masson was first published in Cahiers Renaud-Barrault Number 27

Claudel's Immortal Heroes: A Choice of Deaths

By Harold Watson

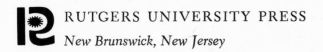

RUTGERS UNIVERSITY PRESS
New Brunswick, New Jersey

Copyright © 1971
By Rutgers University, The State University of New Jersey
Library of Congress Catalogue Number: 73-160572
ISBN: 0-8135-0695-6
Manufactured in the United States of America
By Quinn & Boden Company, Inc., Rahway, N.J.

Pour Michel

Pour Marie

Pour Madonna

Contents

Abbreviations

A   First version of *Tête d'Or* (pp. 31–167) or of *Partage de midi*
        (pp. 983–1064 in *Théâtre*, Vol. I; or of *L'Annonce faite à
        Marie* (pp. 11–114), *Théâtre*, Vol. II. Paris: Gallimard-
        Pléiade, 1956.
B   Second version of *Tête d'Or* (pp. 171–302) or *Partage de
        midi* (pp. 1065–1151) in *Théâtre*, Vol. I; or stage variant of
        Act IV of *L'Annonce faite à Marie* (pp. 115–129), *Théâtre*,
        Vol. II.
CCC   *Cahier canadien Claudel.* Vols. I–VI. Ottawa: University
        Press, 1963–69.
CPC   *Cahiers Paul Claudel.* Vols. I–VIII. Paris: Gallimard,
        1959–68.
J   *Journal.* Vols. I–II. Paris: Gallimard-Pléiade, 1968–69.
MI   *Mémoires improvisés.* Paris: Gallimard, 1961.
OC   *Oeuvres complètes.* Vols. I–XXV. Paris: Gallimard, 1950–
        65.
OP   *Oeuvre poétique.* Paris: Gallimard-Pléiade, 1957.
OPR   *Oeuvres en prose.* Paris: Gallimard-Pléiade, 1965.
SS   *Le Soulier de satin* (pp. 647–933) in *Théâtre*, Vol. II.
Th.   *Théâtre.* Vols. I–II. Paris: Gallimard-Pléiade, 1956.

Preface

With psychotherapists like Rollo May reversing orthodox Freudian dogma by arguing that the basic cause of man's psychic disorders is not sex but death, with the increasing awareness of violence and aggression around and within us, Claudel and his drama of death seem suddenly quite contemporary. And yet, the first centenary of his birth passed almost unnoticed in the United States in 1968, and he is not much better known here today than during his years as the French Ambassador in Washington (1927–33). At that time, his star had not yet risen even in his own country, and Agnes Meyer felt that France would be the last country to know and appreciate him, since he was too "Biblical in thought and language" and "too tempestuous" for the "petty, polished classicists" (CCC, VI, 167–170). But his ascendancy has been continuous in France since World War II, thanks largely to the theatrical genius of Jean-Louis Barrault. It is doubly ironic that this most planetary of poets and dramatists since Shakespeare, who was one of his early influences, should be the least known of France's major writers here in the country of his second longest diplomatic service and whose language he knew the best after his own.

It would be absurd to claim that the prevalence of the theme of death is the prime reason for American neglect of Claudel's dramas. The difficulty of his dithyrambic lyricism, the baroque richness of his mysticism present initial obstacles to popularity even in French and cause him to suffer considerable loss in translation. As he noted of Marivaux, "the French language obeys only those who do it violence" (J, I, 575). Violent by nature, he sometimes lets sound overshadow substance. Still, it may not be far-fetched to theorize that a secondary explanation for American neglect of this aggressive Paul Bunyan of French letters ("with swipes of his censer he's devastating our literature," once bemoaned the classicist André Gide) may be his constant concern with death and destiny, with metaphysical mystery. For there is growing agreement that the idea of death is now more taboo and repressed than sex ever was in Victorian times.[1]

It is, in any case, the basic theme in Claudel and would seem to be a proper thread to pursue through the maze of his heroes' motivations to an authentic appreciation of Claudel's viewpoint. To achieve this, I find it more valuable to concentrate on his four major plays, since even they are not well appreciated in English-speaking circles, and, until they are, I see little advantage in a more comprehensive but superficial survey. My approach is essentially literary, as I have tried to give only those biographical facts that might help elucidate certain aspects of the plays. Little or no previous knowledge of Claudel is presumed, and yet an attempt is made to treat the four plays rather comprehensively and from a new perspective. Whence the abundant notes for those who may wish to pursue a particular idea.

Although the original inspiration for and work on this book date back to 1963–64 and the University of Colorado, it has been thoroughly updated and rewritten to include valuable recent works, especially Claudel's *Journal*. Copious quotations are offered because so little of Claudel is available in English, and no prose analysis or paraphrase can give an adequate idea of the quality of his unique literary style, which he claimed was based on the natural rhythms of breathing and speaking. Except when otherwise indicated, all translations are my own. No claims are made for their luster; they are offered only as reliable approximations.

Many friends helped me in writing and preparing this book. I am particularly grateful to Wallace Fowlie for his perceptive and genial direction of the original manuscript, to colleagues like

---

[1] See Milton McC. Gatch, *Death: Meaning and Mortality in Christian Thought and Contemporary Culture* (New York: The Seabury Press, 1969), pp. 2–18; or Josef Pieper, *Death and Immortality* (New York: Herder & Herder, 1969), p. 132, n. 13.

Fr. Timothy Fry for much advice and support in the revision and to Mme Renée Claudel-Nantet and M. Pierre Claudel for use of their archives and other courtesies. A modest grant from the Kansas City Regional Council of Higher Education and St. Benedict's College enabled me to consult the unpublished *Journal* in the Claudel archives in Paris for a month and to attend the centenary colloquium at Loches in July 1968. My chief debt of appreciation, however, is to Claudel himself for so many memorable lines and characters, for his provocative interrogation of mortality, for his constant quest of hope and immortality.

Atchison, Kansas
July 2, 1970

Claudel's Immortal Heroes:
A Choice of Deaths

I

Perspectives: Life, Love, Death

Death haunts great hearts. The sense of death gives each moment its ineffable price.[1]

All carnal possession is incomplete in its span and duration. . . . What capture, of an empire or of a woman's body in unpitying arms, is comparable to this seizure of God by our soul, like lime seizing sand, and what death (death, our very precious patrimony) finally allows us such a perfect holocaust . . . ? (*OP*, p. 199)

Life, love, death. These three realities compose the basic triad of the human condition and consequently of literature. Unless he is a fraud or superficial, no poet can long extoll life or exalt love without confronting death. Walt Whitman discovered this incompleteness in his early poems and added such masterpieces on death as "Out of the Cradle Endlessly Rocking" and "When Lilacs Last in the Door-Yard Bloom'd" to the third and fourth editions of *Leaves of Grass*. For the poet's task is not only to create but also to eternalize, to raise out of the void and chaos and by his art to confer a kind of eternity on his vision of existence. As a creator and seer, the poet lives more consciously than the rest of us and is less capable of ignoring death or of lightly treating life and love. He perceives the air of mystery that shrouds each member of the triad and seeks to explore and elucidate some of it in terms of human emotion. Of the three, death usually seems the most remote and mysterious, looming as a constant threat to the life-love pair, which are intimately intertwined by their inherent desire to continue forever. All true love wills itself eternal, stronger than death, and every true lover seeks to save the beloved from extinction.

Still, willing is not fulfilling, and death remains an inevitable menace of varying proportions and shifting imminence, tinting life and love with many hues, enriching or impoverishing them according to the vision of each person. Eros and thanatos are interwoven in complex ways, as poets have always known and some psychotherapists are now reminding us: "In both, we are taken over by an event; we cannot stand outside either love or death—and, if we try to, we destroy whatever value the experience can have." [2] It is not surprising, then, that the theme of death recurs throughout the whole period of Western literature, whether in classical tragedy, medieval and romantic poetry and drama, or even the modern novel. Since neither Eurydice, Lazarus, nor Jesus has left posterity any revelations of their experiences beyond the tomb, imaginative writing about death has tended either to bewail its suddenness, terrors, and inevitability or to focus on the best way to deal with the scourge: Is it better to go gentle into that dark night, or to rage and storm against the absurd thing with heroic passion?

From Aeschylus to T. S. Eliot, writers have probed the many facets of mortality in a constant quest for understanding man and the universe. In French literature alone, an immense and erratic scale could be plotted from the heroic, hopeful, violent deaths sought out by Roland, Olivier, and Turpin on the one hand and the realistic gallows so shunned by François Villon on the other, down to the clinical descriptions of dying offered by Flaubert and Zola. Between the medieval and naturalist epics come the courtly exaltation of love over death, d'Aubigné's baroque verses singing of massacres and martyrs, Corneille's stoic scorn of death, Racine's fatal females, and the romantic death wish cultivated by Musset, Nerval, Vigny, and others. In contemporary literature, the subjective attitude of the hero toward his own death plays an increasingly large role, resulting in "an immense variety of stances, from Julien Sorel's death to the slow and gradual enfeebling of Beckett's Malone," as Frederick J. Hoffman points out. "At the one extreme, the hero forces the issue of his death and dramatizes the occasion. . . . At the other extreme, the self diminishes to the point of annihilation." [3] In between, but closer to Sorel than to Malone, is the calm humanist stance of Saint-Exupéry, the Dostoievskian obsessions of Bernanos' saints and sinners, and the meaningless deaths in Camus and Sartre.

In modern English literature, the concern with death appears more in poetry than in drama: we think immediately of Gray's "Elegy in a Country Churchyard," Young's *Night Thoughts*, Keats, Shelley, Byron, Tennyson, Whitman, Lowell ("Quaker Graveyard"), Emily Dickinson, T. S. Eliot ("Hollow Men") and Wilfred Owen. By contrast, post-Renaissance French treatment of the death theme has been decidedly more dramatic than lyric, falling into two broad categories. In the first, the death obsession provokes a dramatic expression and some degree of exorcism, as in Ionesco's *Le Roi se meurt*, Cocteau's *Orphée*, Camus' *Caligula*, or Claudel's *Tête d'Or*. In the second category, the death concept is utilized for histrionic effects, either simply to impose a satisfying conclusion (Voltaire's *Zaïre*, Cocteau's *Les Enfants terribles*, Sartre's *Les Mains sales*), or as one of several sources of deep emotion and dramatic tension (*Chatterton*, *Hernani*, *Lorenzaccio*, *L'Otage*, *Les Mouches*, *La Reine morte*). Here there is little obsession and less exorcism; death is less a mystery than a problem and is faced more obliquely than directly. Most of Shakespeare's tragedies, for all their corpses, violence and intensity, would seem to belong to this group, with perhaps only *Hamlet* fitting the first category.

Few indeed, in any case, are the deaths of tragic dimension in today's literature of any genre. Malraux has been one of the last to try to invest death with meaning. His heroes seek to vanquish it through action, by dangerous deeds—not as a diversionary escape but as a hunt, by stalking death in a voluntary affirmation of human strength, dominating it by scorn and defiance. Perken (*The Royal Way*) and Hong (*The Conquerors*) typify this attitude by their desire to die "as high as possible," that is, significantly. For Malraux, death is tragic because it renders irremediable what preceded it, transforming life into destiny.[4] Nevertheless, his heroes see in their deaths a triumph over fatality and mediocrity, since they do not accept an empty and passive death but choose it by an intense, conscious act. They make of it their own logical, necessary seal of eternity, stamped on their human combat.[5]

But the French writer whose mythopoeic imagination has been the most deeply kindled and perturbed by the mystery of death is undoubtedly Paul Claudel. He dramatizes more acutely than anyone else both a metaphysical *angst* and a supernatural hope in the face of death as his attitude evolves from the first extreme to the last. While Malraux's view remains fixed in a semitragic stance and Hemingway's heroes find in death little more than a catalyzing agent for intensifying their comradeship, Claudel's characters exemplify a host of attitudes, ranging from pagan to Christian, both clear and ambiguous, in the course of their creator's evolution towards a positive Christian attitude of acceptance and joy.

With his frequently perverse genius, Claudel encountered and dramatized death before life and love, so that the triad in his case might be schematized as an inverted pyramid. The results of this precocious contact never ceased to color his conquest of life and love, for the theme of death runs like a constant but evolving current through his two dozen dramas, from the surviving fragment of *Une Mort prématurée* (1888) to *Jeanne d'Arc au bûcher* (1934). It leads from the labyrinth of despair and suicide apparent in the first play ("Die, life! That's the dirge I chant over myself," *Th.*, I, 25) through devious passages and uncertain conflicts up to the triumphant last cry of Joan in flames: "Joy is the strongest! Love is the strongest! God is the strongest!" (*Th.*, II, 1226). This preoccupation with death for half a century is, indeed, central and axial to a proper understanding of the better-known Claudelian themes such as faith, love, vocation, grace, suffering, exile, prison, joy, space, and time, all of which are in large measure responses and reactions to the mystery of death. They cannot be fully appreciated apart from this, the primary source of Claudel's dramatic tension. The resonance of these many ramifications enables him to confront death frequently from within, not just as an obstacle, and to evoke more significant reactions and deeper pathos than any other modern author.[6]

Because of death, life and love and passion are seen as insufficient of themselves and are inevitably colored by a quest for infinity, a yearning to eternalize them. Hence the tendency to a voluptuous religious transposition, as in the passage of *Art poétique* that his best American friend, Agnes Meyer, considered "an etherealized sexual spasm" and that made her hair stand on end (*CCC*, VI, 198). Not that Claudel found anything reprehensible in sex or finite love as such to make him yearn for a more idealistic version. Rather, the fear and fascination of death and the beyond, a constant yearning for a more enduring and perfect form of life and love propelled him towards deeper concerns, religious and eschatological. An experience of radical homelessness made him desperately aware of the death in every now. Hence, "it is a great misfortune to have given one's heart to another" (*J*, I, 307). Claudel finds in human love only the symbolics of laceration, a sign of contradiction. He sees love as a mystery not of participation in the union of Christ and humanity spoken of by St. Paul but rather of participation in separation—in the separation of the soul from its principle and its origin. Whence the theme of frustrated marriage in his later plays.[7]

What is perhaps unique about his case is not only the degree to which death permeates and directs his drama, under countless guises, but also the fact that it seems to have been the original and primary stimulus for his creative efforts. It is almost as if each character he created were engendered in a visceral struggle with mortality in order to incarnate and dramatize all the voices of his inner dialogue on the subject. He wrote in 1895: "But I must bring once more to where men dwell this countenance lifted since infancy . . . towards Death."[8] He once confessed to Francis Jammes that "my dramas have never been for me anything but more or less complicated devices for working out my interior conversation."[9] Thus all his contradictory tendencies tussle and dialogue throughout his plays. He pointed this out to Marcel Schwob in 1900 about *L'Échange* (1894), which is centered on love, money, and death and is thoroughly American in inspiration: "In short, I am all the characters: the actress, the deserted wife, the young savage, and the calculating merchant."[10] Later, clarifying the meaning of his historical trilogy (*L'Otage, Le Pain dur, Le Père humilié*), he spoke of "the bitter debate of my mature years" and evoked "this whole group of men and women at the center of my life who desperately interrogate one another on nothing else but God."[11]

The image of a monolithic, dogmatic patriarch of faith and

orthodoxy so often associated with him in the past half century is thus a misleading view of this restive titan, who in 1917 confided: "Poetry is for me . . . the means of this progressive campaign of evangelization of all the regions of my intelligence and of all the provinces of my soul, which I have been trying to pursue since the day I was converted, in spite of a rebellious, capricious, pagan, and barbarian nature." [12] This constant struggle is so evident in some of his dramas, and so violent is the conflict in them between revolt or submission in the face of death, that it is still debated whether they are pagan or Christian. Only a superficial understanding of Claudel, perhaps limited to a couple of his later plays and some of his religious poems, could allow such an otherwise astute critic as Jacques Guicharnaud to find Claudel's theater to be without "doubt or anguish, but of a rather Corneillian agony and effort" only.[13] Few attitudes are further from Claudel's anguished interrogation, like that of a recalcitrant Job, of the problem of evil [14] than Corneille's stoic voluntarism and scorn of death and suffering for the sake of heroic honor and grandeur of soul.

On almost every other page of his *Journal*, begun in 1904, is some entry to attest to his endless fascination with death, judgment, the hereafter: quotations from the Bible and the liturgy, from patristic writings (especially those of Sts. Augustine and Gregory), from Michelangelo and Chesterton, reflections on Newman's "Dream of Gerontius," a photo of the death mask of Keats, epitaphs, last words, accounts of the funeral of Emperor Kouang Hsii in Peking in 1909, of the heroic death of a French doctor in Tientsin, and even of the assassination of Louis d'Orléans in 1407. Of all these entries on deaths and funerals, perhaps the most curious is the one on St. Cassian, "martyred by his students with their iron styles" (*J*, I, 68). In 1920 he entered his own epitaph, "Here repose the remains and the seed of Paul Claudel." In 1923 he was deeply touched by the emotion and solicitude that the false rumor of his death (in the Tokyo earthquake) awoke in France and Europe. It is significant that his obsession diminishes shortly after this, with the completion of his greatest play, *Le Soulier de satin*, in which he finally checkmates his demons in a towering vision that culminates in Christian humility and renunciation.

It is hardly surprising, then, that the first dramas of Claudel are full of the cries of carnal creatures who refuse to die. Although a few of the characters, like Cébès and Mesa, experience more of an acute mental anguish at the thought of death, most of them are prey to "the profound visceral protest [la réclamation de l'entraille profonde]" (OP, p. 14), such as Tête d'Or, Ysé, Amalric, Pierre de Craon, Mara, Camillo, and Rodrigue. Both the mental anguish and the visceral protest have deep existential roots in the playwright's psyche, and his diverse characters reflect his efforts to project and exorcise, or at least comprehend, death's demons. These are confronted face to face, in various dramatic situations—almost as rehearsals for his own death. It is as if he were surveying the kinds of death possible and striving to choose one and integrate it into his life. D. H. Lawrence put it this way in "Ship of Death": "Oh build your ship of death, oh build it in time/ and build it lovingly, and put it between the hands of your soul." [15]

The idea of a choice of deaths evokes immediately the memory of certain heroes whose manner of dying mirrored perfectly their style of life: Molière, Saint-Exupéry, Amelia Earhart, Lawrence Tibbett, Socrates, Dag Hammarskjöld, Benedict of Nursia, and even those great or near-great writers who suffered tragic auto accidents—Albert Camus, Roger Nimier, Nathaniel West, T. E. Lawrence. For we choose our death each time we willingly expose ourselves to it, risk it, engage in any adventure or career. In the course of a varied career, we may have elected multiple deaths of uneven value before our choice is made final. Except for conscious effort, persevering awareness, and some luck, human hazard militates against the likelihood of that finality's being the apogee of the series. Still, insofar as the self must choose what it is and what it will do by way of assuming a position with respect to its death, it can be said that a person chooses his death. The choice is a means of self-definition, closely linked to the psychological problem of willing the persistence of self-identity in time. [16]

Malraux is reported to have claimed that the problem that underlies all he writes is how to make man conscious that he can establish his greatness, without religion, on the nothingness that crushes him. [17] This is remarkably similar to Martin Heidegger's ontology of death, wherein man is "exhorted to prove his autonomous freedom by 'choosing' death in advance, 'anticipating' it." [18]

This radical appropriation of the final act for oneself holds a great appeal for human pride and can provide a sense of satisfaction and superiority over death for those convinced of the void of the hereafter. On the surface, the choices made by some of Claudel's heroes appear to be similar to this "freedom in relation to death." At bottom, however, they are profoundly different, for in varying degrees they all experience a radical homelessness that will not let them accept the void of oblivion and personal extinction. The difference between a hero of Malraux's and one of Claudel's in this respect is akin to the distinction often made in French between *espoir* and *espérance*. Both mean hope, but the latter has a transmortal connotation.

Minds with a strong symbolic bent like Claudel's tend to interpret man in the light of an affective inner experience of origins and destination, of the conflict between totality and liberty. This experience or test is often an encounter, sometimes even a duel, with God.[19] The existential origins of Claudel's fear of death precede his duel with God, however, and in a sense direct it. They go back to 1881, when he watched his paternal grandfather, a doctor, dying hour by hour of a stomach cancer. This created a profound terror in the adolescent, and the thought of death would not leave him (*OPR*, p. 1009; *MI*, p. 14). More of an external shock, but equally fixed in his memory, was his view of the national obsequies and burial of Victor Hugo in 1885. Even in old age he remembered the ceremony as a "crapulous, repugnant, Mardi Gras parade" that deeply shocked him (*MI*, p. 20). That he could stand for three hours on a ladder to watch it, after having seen the funeral of Léon Gambetta three years earlier,[20] indicates the degree of his fascination with death.

The sense of helplessness and ignorance which the sight of death evoked in him was deepened into despair by the raucous, loveless atmosphere of his home and by the deterministic universe of ideas which he encountered in the lycée Louis-le-Grand: "I believed that everything was governed by 'laws,' and that this world was a hard chain of effects and causes that science would succeed in perfectly untangling the day after tomorrow. It seemed to me all very sad and depressing" (*OPR*, p. 1009). "And then the fear of death, the memory of death, a feeling of a wholly forsaken child

who has no guide and knows not which way to turn" (*MI*, p. 21).
He was also affected by the nearby cemetery and the liturgy of
All Souls' Day (*OPR*, p. 1006). Thus life in the family, in the
country, in school, and in Paris all conspired to engender dejection
and despair in a youth whose maternal uncle and namesake had
taken his own life.[21]

The young Claudel underwent diverse artistic influences in various degrees as well: Aeschylus, Plato, Job, Shakespeare, Wagner,
and many others, especially Rimbaud. One strong early influence,
consistently overlooked by commentators, was Baudelaire, whose
fascination with death naturally accentuated Claudel's morbid
anxiety for a time. In 1949 he confessed that "for some years my
daily bread was Baudelaire, Leconte de Lisle, and Flaubert [partic-
ularly the poetic novel *Salammbô*, with its vertigo of destruction
and sensual style]—admirations that I am far from having now"
(*MI*, p. 21). Much earlier, he had praised Baudelaire as "the most
alive and precious" (*OPR*, p. 17) of French poets and concluded
his appreciation by citing one of his favorite Baudelairian couplets,
which could well have been Tête d'Or's motto:

> Minutes, giddy mortal, are veinstones—
> Not to be released without extracting their gold.
>
> [Les minutes, mortel folâtre, sont des gangues
> Qu'il ne faut pas lâcher sans en extraire l'or.] [22]

Much of Baudelaire's sepulchral imagery and atmosphere are
discernible in *Tête d'Or*, especially in the first version. The most
significant similarities center on the third and fourth "Spleen"
poems, which are brought to mind by the mournful opening
monologue of Cébès and the gloom that hangs over most of *Tête
d'Or*. The poet's theme of the earth as a vast prison, escape-proof,
is echoed in much of the play, especially in the utter pessimism
of Eumère and the fifth guard.

Multiple echoes of not only the "Spleen" cycle but also of such
poems as "Le Crépuscule du soir," "A une Passante," "Les
Aveugles," "De profundis clamavi," "Une Charogne," and countless others can be discerned in *Tête d'Or*. These evocations are
most apparent in the horrors that surround a death without hope:

solitude, ennui, separation, gloom, corruption, oblivion. Even in the first version, however, it is evident that these sources have been dramatically transformed and transfigured or surpassed by an attempt to analyze and resolve the mystery of death on a more significant level than the physical. Encouraged by Baudelaire's example in *Oeuvres posthumes*, which Claudel read in 1889, as well as by his own spiritual struggle between 1886 and 1890, the dramatist found funereal metaphors less and less adequate in expressing his feelings and convictions about death. He turned increasingly toward religious symbolism as a more satisfactory technique for grappling with his metaphysical problems. Two facts point this up. The second version of *Tête d'Or* omits the three feminine personifications of death, which are so typically Baudelairian, and tones down much of the cruder realism of the earlier version. Secondly, the echoes of Baudelaire in both versions are limited almost wholly to posing and depicting the problem in a realistic manner; they do not extend to its symbolical resolution. These overtones occur principally in characters who are spiritually dead and hopeless, or in the early struggles of Simon and Cébès against despair—a bit more perhaps in Cébès, who is closer in temperament to Baudelaire. The one influence that lasts throughout the play is the wide range and disconcerting mixture of styles, from the very macabre to the most noble, as in "Spleen IV," although this stylistic device may owe as much to Shakespeare as to *Les Fleurs du mal* (MI, p. 33).

In 1927 Claudel said that the three most important plays of his career were *Tête d'Or, Partage de midi,* and *Le Soulier de satin.*[23] However, he also considered *L'Annonce faite à Marie* as "one of the summits" of his work, not only because of its wide diffusion and popularity but because its many facets made it more representative of his polyvalence than most of his other dramas (MI, p. 241). Since the shadows of death hover so closely over all its characters, it must be included in this study. These four dramas contain the essence of Claudel's approach to the mystery of death. Studying them in depth from this angle offers a better perspective for the evolution of the theme than would an exhaustive analysis of all the allusions to death in his less important plays.

A word about method. Each play is approached differently because of the great disparity of the works themselves. *Tête d'Or* is so thoroughly permeated with pessimism and death, so arcane and often bordering on the incomprehensible, that only the most complete and detailed analysis of imagery, atmosphere, sources, and characters can do justice to it. The "Canticle of Mesa" and the final love duet, on the other hand, so highlight and summarize the death theme in *Partage de midi* that concentrating on a careful analysis and explication of its final act seems both necessary and sufficient to clarify that drama. In order to go beyond the obvious Christian values of *L'Annonce*, three moments of especially poignant confrontation with death have been chosen to study the use of death as a dramatic technique to advance the plot and to develop characterization there. Finally, a brief comment on the trilogy and then a consideration of the Christianized conqueror Rodrigue in *Le Soulier* will disclose the apogee of this thematic evolution, in a hope-filled, interplanetary vision of immortality, embracing and surpassing the whole firmament.

II

Tête d'Or: *Light in the Valley of Death*

> The idea of this book is this: in the privation of happiness, desire alone subsists. Tragic situation! I experience an immense need for happiness, and I find no way to satisfy it amid things visible. Is this from refusal or lack? A mystery which demands to be explored with torch and sword. The unity of the work is there; the first part is the conception of desire, the second the leap, the third the consecration (*CPC*, I, 140).

In this letter to Albert Mockel, written within a year of his first important and probably most mysterious play, the dramatist himself offers a generic and rather enigmatic explanation of his youthful masterpiece. Most commentators have emphasized the second half of that idea, analyzing every aspect and implication of this desire, identifying it with Tête d'Or himself and with the essence of Claudel's dramaturgy. In the process, however, the first part of the idea—the privation of happiness—has been strangely neglected or else reduced to a mere acknowledgement of his irritation with the hidebound tradition at the Louis-le-Grand lycée and at the spiritual confinement he felt in the "prison of materialism" of the times. Indeed, the poet himself has not been reticent about the spiritual crisis of his adolescence, which he compared to that of Rimbaud (*OPR*, pp. 1009, 1012; *MI*, pp. 50–53), for it led to what he always considered the most important event of his life—the ineffable revelation of God on Christmas, 1886, in the Cathedral of Notre Dame and his return to the Church four years later. Still, the suspicion arises that his privation of happiness has roots in a deeper subsoil yet—in an emotional encounter with death. In the words of Jacques

12

Madaule on the occasion of the first performance of the tragedy in 1959, Claudel "learned one thing, a thing which forever discolored the world for him, and that great reality was death." [1] Agreeing with Gabriel Marcel in finding existential anguish at the root of the play, Madaule called it "the poem of death."

Already in the earlier *Fragment d'un drame* there is a preoccupation with death, which Marie bequeaths as a dowry to her fiancé, Henri, as she cries:

> But one thing is better than all: to sleep
> The sleep of blood and death!
>
> [Mais il y a une chose meilleure que tout: c'est de dormir
> Dans le sommeil du sang et de la mort!] (*Th.*, I, 25)

After a momentary submission to these blandishments, however, Henri experiences a sudden revulsion and with a deft volte-face leaves Marie to mourn alone in the night.

These themes of melancholy, separation, and death, which are sounded so clearly in that fragmentary adolescent drama, "the first awakening of what I call my intellectual puberty" (*MI*, p. 30), attain a precocious maturity in the fully orchestrated but baffling tragedy of *Tête d'Or*, written in 1889 when Claudel was twenty-one. Here, death seems to reign supreme in each of the three parts, dominating every situation and character. The *liebestod* opens with a lugubrious burial scene as a young wanderer, Simon Agnel, having returned weary to his native soil, dispassionately and even disgustedly inters his female companion, whom he could not save from death. Aided in this unhappy task by Cébès, a doleful youth who has stumbled on the gravedigging, Simon recognizes in him a weak and gloomy complement to his own forceful personality. Out of pity he offers Cébès his undying friendship, in a brotherly blood pact.

In the second part, Cébès lies dying in a palace while King David and his retinue wait in despair for news of the collapse of the Empire before a superior invasion force. However, an upstart genius named Simon Agnel, henceforth called Tête d'Or because of his awesome golden locks, recruits a motley volunteer army and wins an incredible victory to save the country. Savior of his nation, he is unable, however, to save his alter ego, Cébès, who dies cradled in his friend's arms. The horrified hero then avenges himself on death by killing the old King and seizing the supreme power, exiling the mysterious, beautiful Princess and marshalling all his military might for a conquest of the world.

Finally, the third part finds the restive hero enlarging his empire up to its continental limits, under the obsession that he is thereby pushing back the frontiers of death and bringing new life to his nation. But in the final battle high in the Caucasus, he is mortally wounded, although the example of his courage inspires his cowardly followers to halt their flight and return to rout the enemy. In lieu of a deathbed, the dying King is placed on a huge rocky rampart, asserted by legend to have been the site of Prometheus' undoing by Zeus's eagle. In a long lyrical agony, he resists death until the end, refusing the consolation that submission and acceptance would bring. The persuasive charms of Grace, in the person of the exiled Princess, does not avail to save him. The Princess, crucified by a deserter on a nearby tree, is unpinioned by the dying warrior. She then joins him in a compelling threnody and in death.

Such is the brief synopsis of this drama, which has almost as many interpretations as commentators, ranging from the Freudian views of actor Alain Cuny and the Jungian inspiration of Jean-Claude Morisot to the mystical-liturgical ones of Father André Blanchet. A questionnaire distributed to members of the audience at the Barrault production in 1959 elicited a variety of opinions even as to the subject of the play: the desire of possession, the will to power, the duality of dream and action, the conflict of pride and sincerity.[2] While it is characteristic of works of genius to provoke a multiple response, it is rather surprising in this case to find the omnipresent motif of death so widely neglected, even in relation to other problems.

The basic text for our study of *Tête d'Or* is the second or 1894 version, with references to important variants in the 1889 version. The 1894 version is generally conceded to be the less chaotic text, more nearly perfect from a literary point of view.[3] Claudel himself was soon ashamed of the first version,[4] which Jacques Petit suggests may have been modified in order to attenuate a certain anarchist aspect in it (*CPC*, I, 157).[5] But Claudel also wanted to diminish some of the bold images and "the language of frightfully poor taste, resembling gibberish and nonsense," which he probably imbibed from Shakespeare in his youthful and indiscriminate infatuation for the bard (*MI*, pp. 33, 35). Curiously, however, his father, Louis Claudel, found the first version superior on the whole to the second (*CPC*, I, 123).

A comparison of the more noteworthy variants is enlightening. The complete omission of Eumère, a kind of male Cassandra in the first version, lightens the air of doom that oppresses the palace in part two. Only an adolescent attitude of anarchism or Satanism could have prompted such pessimistic ranting as this by Eumère:

> May Death come very soon!/ . . . . /
> . . . I rejoice that the twilight is coming for every-
> one!/ . . . . /
> Remember your dreadful life, and . . . give in to pure
> despair! (*A*, p. 59)

Equally important is the calmer, more hopeful death of Cébès in the second version, including an amazing flash of hope in Tête d'Or's self-sufficient soul:

> . . . . This hope warms us like coffee!
> O divine geranium! O clot of sun! It throbs, it bleeds like
> a lump of meat!
>
> [. . . . Cet espoir nous réchauffe comme le café!
> O divin géranium! ô caillot de soleil! il palpite! il saigne
> comme une loque de viande!] (*B*, p. 225)

Cébès is an almost utter prey of ambiguous sadness and pessimism in the first version:

> Consider me doomed, and let that expand your heart!
> Imagine that we are
> Like two lovers who, only a moment before Never, kiss
> good-by
> Forever, when the bride already has her wedding gown!

[Songe que je suis funèbre, et que cela augmente ton coeur! Songe que nous sommes
Comme deux amants qui, un seul moment avant jamais, se débaisent
Pour jamais, quand la femme déjà a la robe de noces!]
(A, p. 87)

Who will tell of how many deaths before this one, of how many heartaches, this life is made!
A man goes alone to bed. . . .
. . . And our very death happens far away from us!

[Qui dira de combien de morts avant celle-ci, angoisses du coeur, est faite cette vie!
Un homme se couche seul. . . .
. . . Et notre mort même se passe loin de nous!] (A, p. 88)

Death is strangling me with her soft, sinewy hands.

[La Mort m'étrangle avec ses douces mains nerveuses.]
(A, p. 89)

Blacker and blacker! everything swirls and goes out!
Oh! I'm sinking! My heart dies!

[Noir, de plus en plus noir! tout tourbillonne et s'éteint!
Ah! je sombre! Mon coeur meurt!] (A, p. 90)

Much of this suffering and despair gives way in the second version to a certain joyful hope:

O Tête d'Or, all pain has passed! The net is broken and I am free! I am the plant that has been snatched from the earth!
This is the joy which is in the final hour and I am that joy itself and the secret that can no longer be told.

[O Tête d'Or, toute peine est passée! Le rets est rompu et je suis libre! Je suis l'herbe qui a été arrachée de la terre!
C'est la joie qui est dans la dernière heure, et je suis cette joie même et le secret qui ne peut plus être dit.] (B, p. 226)

Hints of a hereafter abound in this revised version of the death of Cébès: the almost literal introduction of the psalmist's cry, "The snare is broken and we are free" (Ps. 123), the allusion to the paschal sacrifice and *Agnus Dei* symbol in Tête d'Or's exclamation, "O sacrifice that I bear in my arms like a sheep whose feet are bound!" (p. 226), and especially Cébès' more optimistic last words, referring to the morning freshness and cockcrows.

Furthermore, the omission of certain images, some of them quite Baudelairian in their realism, tends to soften the second version:

> See, we are children to Death!/ . . . . /
> Slowly, slowly one dies! The sick person
> Stares and can no longer wake up, so much does the
> cinerary darkness descend on him!
> Old recollections
> Stir in the dazed memory. A deathly weariness.

> [Vois, nous sommes enfants à la Mort!/ . . . . /
> Lentement, lentement on meurt! Le malade
> Regarde et ne peut plus se réveiller, tant le choie le soir
> cinéraire!
> D'anciens souvenirs
> Soufflent dans la mémoire hébétée. Une paresse de mort.]
> (A, p. 36)

Both the idea of death as irremediable yet restive sleep and its evocation by means of sibilants and long, open vowels are reminiscent of *Les Fleurs du mal*.[6] One possibly unfortunate omission from the second version is the personification of death as a very aged woman: "Her hair is white like cotton, and the spider webs of many centuries have blurred her face" (A, pp. 38–39). This, too, suggests a probable pastiche of Baudelaire, who had a penchant for such portraits of death, as in "Danse macabre."[7] Omissions of this sort and the softening of the early macabre imagery indicate that after his conversion Claudel found most of this superficial in comparison with the biblical, patristic, and liturgical treatment of death according to its nature and significance. His adolescent admiration for Baudelaire diminished greatly, at any rate, and it is plausible to attribute this in part to his realization of the inadequacy of such decadent figures of speech.

Another notable omission is the hero's pre-Sartrian, pre-Samuel-Beckett evocation of fetal viscosity:

> O this tiresome world! Man, like a fetus in its mucus,
> Wallows in his imbecility.

> [O ce monde ennuyeux! l'homme, comme un foetus parmi les glaires,
> Se repaît de son imbécillité.] (A, p. 104)

> What difference is there between a man and a mole who are dead,
> When the putrefying sun begins to ripen them in the belly?

> [Quelle différence y a-t-il entre un homme et une taupe qui sont morts,
> Quand le soleil de la putréfaction commence à les mûrir par le ventre?] (A, p. 113)

Finally, it is worth noting the omission, at the end of part two, of the long Aeschylean-type chorus in the guise of the two groups of weeping women who come to mourn and bury Cébès (A, pp. 114–116) before Eumère's cynical conclusion that life is only a "pellicle of air around nothing" and that men "booze at the sign of the Tomb or of winged Love" (A, p. 118).

A comparison of certain other passages that have been altered rather than omitted in the second version reveals again the tendency to tone down some of the earlier pessimism and realism:

A	B
the wild wind, like a whore	the wind, like a mad woman
[le vent fou, comme une catin] (p. 40)	[le vent, comme une femme folle] (p. 179)
And girls . . . whose meager heap of bones . . ./ Ooze a cadaveric liquid.	And women whom cancer attacks like punk on a beech tree.

[Et des jeunes filles . . . dont le maigre tas d'ossements . . ./ Chuinent une liqueur cadavérique.] (p. 41)

[Et des femmes où le cancer s'est mis comme l'amadou sur un hêtre.] (p. 180)

A poor vulgar ass, a dull ignorance, a wisdom stuffed with hay.

A man of chimeras.
No, I have been, rather, a man of desire!

[Un pauvre âne vulgaire, une ignorance appesantie, une sagesse bourrée de foin.] (p. 148)

[Un homme de chimères.
Non, mais j'ai été un homme de désir!] (p. 283)

Other contrasts and comparisons of consequence in the two versions will be noted later, but the preceding ones suffice to show the shift to a more controlled, coherent, even optimistic tone.

IMAGERY OF DEATH

The preceding quotations have already pointed up the evocative power of Claudel's imagery, which was mainly responsible for Maurice Maeterlinck's astonishment in his letter of December 21, 1890: "Are you the resurrected Count of Lautréamont? And is Tête d'Or the tragedy of Maldoror? . . . You have given me so many hammer knocks on the head! and I am still as stunned as a diver attacked by a shark, and your wonderful images are coming out of my ears, mouth, and nose!" (CPC, I, 137). Indeed, it is this imagery that first evokes the atmosphere of death and places the reader under its pall. Of the half-dozen important images concerning death already quoted, the most vivid ones are three striking personifications of death—(1) as an ashy sandman lulling the sick, like children, to endless slumber (A, p. 36); (2) as an aged woman whose haggard face is blurred by centuries of spider webs (A, pp. 38–39); and (3) as a strangler with soft, sinewy hands (A, p. 89). Death's slowness and a hypnotic suggestion of heavy sleep are underlined by the long nasal vowels and the sibilants.

Allegorical personifications of death, however, are minimal in the second version. With the omission of the three above, and discounting four minor clichés, only one remains in B—the hallucinatory evocation by old King David of how "Death-Agony, plumed, with copper cheeks, like a colossus, shakes our scaffold! . . . like a blazing haystack, brandishing the flail, gripping in (his) teeth a sword broad as an oar!" (B, p. 208). This surrealistic imagery so convinces one of the guards that he leaps up to defy the monster, hallucinating in the same key: "Hack me, slice me into bits, and my severed head will jump up and bite!/ . . . like Ajax spouting the thunderbolt and seawater from nose and mouth . . ." (B, p. 208). The opening lines of Baudelaire's "Duellum" come to mind: "Two warriors rushed on one another; their arms/ Splattered the air with sparks and blood." [8] In their barely coherent raving, the two appear more demented than King Lear, for this dramatic encounter marks the apogee of the nation's awareness of its impending doom.

This powerful *prosopopée* is immediately followed by the King's evocation of rotting corpses ("like starved animals, we'll rot among the nettles and the scabs") in a cameo-like reduction of Baudelaire's noisome "Une Charogne." These grisly, violent evocations, along with the following one, show that Baudelaire's influence, though reduced, is not entirely lacking in the second version. With these two exceptions, however, the imagery of death in this version concerns the act of dying and its attendant agonies. Some twenty such images are evoked, three-fourths of them visual and the rest mainly tactile, with a few overlapping, as in the deserter's grisly realism—reminiscent of both Villon's "Epitaphe" and Baudelaire's "Un Voyage à Cythère"—after he has nailed the Princess to the tree:

> Stay there, and when night falls the wolves will come,
> And setting upon you they will tear you apart and yank off
> your legs,
> And the crows will pluck out your eyes.
>
> [Reste là et quand viendra la nuit les loups arriveront,
> Et se dressant contre toi ils te dépèceront et ils t'ar-
> racheront les jambes,
> Et les corbeaux t'extirperont les yeux.] (B, p. 265)

Although to compare the act of dying to a handful of sand slipping through the fingers (B, p. 177) is rather banal, and to liken curling up in the death-sleep to re-entering the maternal mold (B, p. 176) is hardly more inventive, Claudel has rather vividly renewed the ancient image of the bark of Charon in the messenger's depiction of the massacre of the enemy: "les tas de mourants/ Bourbiller comme les poissons [var. "comme des crevettes" A, p. 74] au fond d'un bateau! [the heaps of dying people/ piling up like fish in the bottom of a boat!]" (B, p. 214).[9] Less vivid are two other watery images, both of Tête d'Or's death: "Infernal Neptune is covering me!" (B, p. 286) and "like gold sinking beneath the water" (B, p. 287). These are paralleled by two images of wind blowing out his life, like a dandelion and like the soul's flame (pp. 285, 287). But dying is not always evoked in such elementary natural images. There is the startling comparison of an enemy soldier probing for the chink in the hero's armor to a cook opening a crab at knife-point (B, p. 276). This cool external appraisal of the warrior's humiliation is counterbalanced by the insider's fiery version, relived in delirium:

> —Oh! ah! sparks and fire, battle!
> And the warrior bellowing, like a tower, from his wheeling
> charger, with horny hands! Oh! ah!
> Charge! Plunge on, and on!
> —Swirl of red! Hole, mouth, glory mug, indefensible gate-
> way! O you, Powerful ones!
> Let them cut off my hands and feet and I will stretch out
> to you the stumps, and will walk toward you on my bones!
> (B, p. 281)

This agony evokes the symbol of a sacrificial ceremony—possibly Mosaic, for the hero calls himself "the most powerful bull" moments later. As the captains, "standing stupidly around him, like animals around a water trough," watch their delirious chief rip off his bandages and re-enact the fatal battle, the standard-bearer exclaims:

> What blood he squirts! How the mare flays the air with
> its tail! What tigerish
> Ferocity fires his bones! How he roars! How he
> Twists, covering the altar with his blood, which flows
> down the furrows.
> And the soil all around drinks it in. (B, p. 281)

Later, in a lucid interval, Tête d'Or experiences himself as a sacrificial libation: "The vintage is utterly pressed, and my wounds no
longer yield anything but water" (B, p. 293). This image is elaborated in his ecstatic apostrophe to the sun:

> Like vintagers towards their vats
> Leaving the pressing-house by every door like a torrent,
> My blood surges from every wound to meet you in
> triumph!

> [Comme les gens de la vendange au-devant des cuves
> Sortent de la maison du pressoir par toutes les portes
> comme un torrent,
> Mon sang par toutes ses plaies va à ta rencontre en
> triomphe!] (B, pp. 295–296)

In contrast to the rather pallid deaths of the others, that of
Tête d'Or, as befits his colorful name and violent personality, is
thus characterized by heat and light, imaged forth by the vivid golds
and reds evoked by fire, sun, spurting blood, raw wounds, and
running wine. Small wonder, then, that in this kaleidoscopic vision
of exploding glory he appears to the Princess as someone drunk and
blind (B, p. 294). However, the divine intoxication of the dying
hero is exactly the contrary of the hopeless death of the common
man, who, "drowned in night and misery, stretched out all alone
in his filth, . . . will look aloft,/ Like the drunk lying in the ditch
whose wild eyes gaze at the bleak February setting sun" (B, p.
199). For, bathed in the splendor of the setting sun and thinking in
his delirious ecstasy that he is embracing a pantheistic savior and
that he will be absorbed into the glory of the awful orb, Tête d'Or
has come to accept death without despair, even making a kind of
self-offering. However, if he momentarily sensed that "an odor of
violets excites my soul to surrender" (B, p. 295), this fragrance
could only have derived from the Princess' self-immolation and
sanctity: "Oh! Let me be like the cut flower which smells stronger
and like the mowed grass!" (B, p. 293). Thus her experience is
reminiscent of Cébès' dying evocation, "I am the plant that has
been plucked from the earth!" (B, p. 226). But in Tête d'Or's
mind, her efforts to bring him consolation and hope place her in

rivalry with the sun, and he chooses the sun, rejecting the odor of sanctity despite its appeal.

Except for Tête d'Or's sudden and joyful surrender to the sun, most of the images emphasize the solitary character of dying, as well as the slowness of the process, which at times appears almost as a life-long decomposition. Cébès is the one who conjures up the most anguished image of this solitude, when he exclaims:

> Alone I die!
> For I know not who I am myself, and I flee and vanish
> like a lost spring!/ . . . . /
> More alone than the child killed by his mother and buried
> under the dunghill with
> The broken plates and dead cats in the earth full of big
> pink worms! (B, pp. 222–223)

SEPULCHRAL ATMOSPHERE

Images, however, for all their evocative power, are often superficial and disparate, even distracting, unless they flow from a deeper current. In Tête d'Or the images of death usually grow out of, and epitomize, the general moral and physical atmosphere and the personalities of the characters. Thus, Cébès' horror at dying alone is all the more psychologically real and gripping because of his personal involvement in the damp and chilly burial at the beginning. From the atmosphere of the grave-scene to the desolation of the Caucasus, strewn with skulls and bones and resounding with "a Gorgonian lamentation" (B, p. 287) at the agony of Tête d'Or, a sense of doom is all-pervasive. Death, both physical and moral, seems to hover over and slowly float down upon the whole nation, enveloping all life in an infinite but invisible smog and isolating everyone in varying degrees of loneliness. Although no one feels its horror as much as Cébès, even the Princess cringes at the thought of having to "go forth alone like a widow driven cruelly from her home" (B, p. 206), and Tête d'Or thrice laments the solitude into which Cébès' death will plunge him.

Heightening the sense of solitude and of impending death is the gloom of the night, characterized principally as long and dark.

Cébès and old King David suffer the most from this, the former sighing, "How long the night is, O God!" (B, p. 196) and the latter asking, "Will this atrocious night never end? . . . the blackness is suffocating us like a blanket" (B, p. 190). The first watchman concurs: "The night is black and there is no hope" (B, p. 194). However, when Cébès exclaims, "O mystery of the night!" (B, p. 197) and "O when will the sun return!" (B, p. 199), he is already becoming aware, albeit vaguely, that the presence or absence of physical light is symbolic of something deeper, of a state of soul:

> Why was I born? For I am dying and behold, I no longer exist.
> But darkness overtook me so that I slept in it and awoke in it. And I saw nothing; and I was deaf and heard no noise.
> Here I am like a man buried alive, and I am enclosed as in an oven! (B, p. 219)

Here again Baudelaire comes to mind, especially the first stanza of "Spleen IV." Cébès' spiritual anguish then erupts in a fourfold cry for light. But to this plea for enlightenment, Tête d'Or can offer little more than the equivocal comment, "The night is vast and deep, and the sun disappears in it,/ And silence exists where there is no voice or word" (B, p. 222).

Indeed, nearly the whole drama is bathed in the blackness of a seemingly interminable night, progressing as it does from the dismal dusk, followed by nightfall, in the countryside scene of Part I, to the midnight interior of the palace, lit by only one little glow, in Part II, and culminating in the sunset and apparent eclipse of mankind's hopes at the end of Part III. As already implied, this constant use of night as a theme serves a dual function. It renders more palpable the threat and terror of death, but it also symbolizes a mental and spiritual state of torpor or ignorance.

It is highly significant, then, that night should overtake Simon and Cébès as they leave the grave site, ambling over the hillside and discussing the meaning of their existence and encounter: "Standing in space we have on each hand the darkness,/ The melancholy of the earth" (B, p. 179). This darkness reflects their own ignorance of the meaning of life and death. Feeling like a dethroned king with his head in a sack, because he can find no clear answers to these mysteries, Cébès cries out:

> I would like to find happiness!
> But I am like a man underground in a place where one hears nothing.
> Who will open the door? And who will come to where I am, bearing the yellow flame in his hand? (*B*, p. 180)

Revealing both deep empathy and unlimited self-confidence, his friend Simon declares emphatically and much more optimistically than in the first version: "I am myself in this deep place! I will rise and smash in the doorway and I shall appear before men" (*B*, p. 181). This awareness of the darkness in which his soul dwelt was apparently possible, then, only after the death and burial of the false spouse, whose seductive charms had lulled and obscured the desire for truth and a higher happiness. For Cébès, however, the problem is more spiritual, centering on an ennui and malaise caused by the absence of happiness. He seeks salvation passively, like a contemplative, looking for a trustworthy latter-day Lucifer to bear him the light that will clarify these obscurities of life and death. Simon, on the other hand, sees it more as a physical quest or conquest of the earth and extolls his prowess and vigor: "Juice of life! Strength and acquisition! Ah! all strength and sap!" (*B*, p. 181). Supremely self-confident, he is quite certain that the mere desire to dominate will assure him the successful leadership of his generation. "Who needs a path? I know where I am going. Follow me!" (p. 181). Almost certain, anyway, for a lurking doubt will haunt him sporadically: "But I am full of trouble myself" (*B*, p. 182).

The darkness of night, then, like the loneliness imposed by bereavement, is not purely negative in its symbolic association with physical and spiritual death.[10] Rather, it can also be a beneficent condition for self-discovery, self-knowledge, and reassessment of values: "We are both only children by night in the midst of this enormous universe," says Simon. "But there is a strength in me, and I take pity on you!" (*B*, p. 185). In the anguish of this inner darkness, heightened by the heaviness of the night, and after plumbing their weakness and nothingness in the face of the universe, they make a marvelous discovery. The key to their problem, as to their nature, surely resides in their mutual dependence. And so they conclude a fraternal pact, sealed in blood, a kind of mutual-aid pact against death: "O Death! O Night, here are two guilty persons who have found themselves!" (p. 185). And when Cébès feels something running on his head, Simon explains:

> It is my blood; thus man, although he has no breasts, can shed his milk!/ . . . . /
> Receive my blood on yourself! Oh, I will strike my heart so that my blood may gush forth, as when with a firm hand you plunge the spigot into the tun!
> It's my blood! That's how we greet each other, you and I, who through the shadows bear hot blood in our veins!
> Like two relatives who, on the other side of death, recognize each other in the eternal night without seeing,
> And fall into one another's arms awash with tears! (p. 186)

Thus in this nocturnal stillness that figures forth the black silence of the grave, as if in a kind of oneiric vestibule, they recognize themselves and embrace as blood-brothers in a private rite that solemnizes Simon's earlier defiance of death: "I will not die but live! I don't want to die but to live!" (B, p. 178).

As Cébès departs, a few stars appear in a rift in the clouds. This symbol of hope, like a door opening slightly on their inky isolation chamber, helps confirm Simon's resolve to let in some light on moribund mankind:

> And I too will do my work, and crawling underneath I will make the huge rock budge!
> And with one heave I will shoulder it, like a butcher who shoulders half a beef on his back! (B, p. 187)

However, the enormity of the task overwhelms him and, in the vibrant soliloquy that closes Part I, as he lies stretched face forward on the ground, he cries out before he loses consciousness:

> O Night! Mother!
> Crush me or stop up my eyes with earth!
> Mother, why did you slit the skin of my eyelids across the
> middle! Mother, I am alone! Mother, why do you force me
> to live?
> I would rather that tomorrow in the East the steamy globe
> not turn red! O Night, to me you seem very good!
> I cannot! Look on me, your child!
> And you, O Earth, behold, I stretch out on your bosom!
> Maternal Night! Earth! Earth! (B, p. 187)

This convergence, this commingling of the themes of death, mother, and earth in that of the night, is crucial. The phenomenon calls for a parenthetical elaboration, given the divergent views of several critics. In a detailed psychoanalysis, Jean-Claude Morisot finds the themes all indissolubly linked in the poetic vision and signifying a triple refusal. Because Simon buries the woman face down, deeper than the grain in the silo (B, p. 176), and tramples on the grave until it is indistinguishable, it seems that woman, earth, and death present an interchangeable nature to Simon's imagination, which is constantly recomposing this synthesis—whether considering woman as spouse, temptress, or mother—while his will just as constantly rejects it in globo. His rejection of the three faces of Eve stems from her inevitable allurements to sleep, forgetfulness, abandon, and death. His rejection of home or of any native ground in favor of limitless roving stems from a fear of suffocation in stability and hence from his intolerance of creeping death. Like Rimbaud, he rejects home and women, for he is not a family-circle type but the man of the crossroads, in quest of a new and unbounded life.[11]

It is important to note, however, that his weeping soliloquy delivered while sprawled on Mother Earth is not an utter rejection of the fourfold equation of night, woman, earth, death. Rather, as in other sporadic moments of doubt, he is strongly tempted to succumb to these enticements, hesitating to undertake his superhuman vocation. He begs to be spared the destiny proffered him, feeling his utter loneliness and incompetence. To the extent that any interpretation overlooks that fact, it is inadequate. For as at Gethsemane, this hesitation of the hero and his momentary surrender are essential to revealing his humanity, to enlisting any sympathy for him. Essential also for mounting any dramatic tension.

More penetrating insights are offered in the biographical-liturgical approaches of André Blanchet and André Vachon, who detect in Simon's trance in the first version (A, pp. 42–48) in the presence of Cébès and the peasant, Claudel's first confidential hint about the illumination of 1886 in Notre Dame. When he rises from the ground, he exclaims, "A great thing has happened to me!" (A, p. 45). Someone has spoken to him; he feels chosen for an exceptional destiny.[12] This text was suppressed in the second version, perhaps out of modesty or because of its seeming obscurity. And yet, the more one studies it, the more do Simon's soliloquy and indeed his whole heliotropic orientation, as well as the structure of the drama, unfold their wealth of meaning in this interplay of night-day, dark-light, death-life.

Calling him "Eagle of the night," Cébès makes a very suggestive remark after the first ecstatic seizure:

> An old nurse has recognized you, and clamping her teeth
> on your ear, like a calf's,
> She has held you back to whisper secrets to you.
> You, if some illustrious law
> Truly shines for your eyes, if
> Some order and nonhuman will . . . (A, p. 44)

The image of the old nurse for his forsaken Church would be a natural one for the young Claudel, but more important is the reference to his revelation as something that shines, for Simon does indeed find himself suddenly illumined:

> Is it dark? For me this field is lit
> With a light brighter than the full moon./ . . . . /
> A glory has been bestowed on me; harsh, an enemy of the
> tears of women and kids, it is not weak! (A, p. 46)

Furthermore, in this first version the blood-pact contains a reference to "the tree of the crucifix" (A, p. 47), and just before the soliloquy only one star—a clear reference to Christmas—beckons to him through the rift in the clouds: "Is that my bright star burning on its immortal pyre,/ Between Jupiter and Pluto?/ . . . Shall I attain thee? Who will give me the strength?" (A, p. 48). Here follows the soliloquy, which in this version was the culmination of four moments of hesitation, of temptations to turn aside from the call.

Why the repeated emphasis on the element of light in this trance and on the sun throughout the drama? Because of Rimbaud's often acknowledged influence, it has become a commonplace to call Claudel another "son of the sun" (fils du soleil) [13] and to attribute this predominance of sun and light in Tête d'Or, and perhaps even the title, to the almost hypnotic effect exercised on the Champenois youth by his first contact with the dazzling Illuminations of the obscure Charleville poet in June 1886. Indeed, there is considerable basis for this attribution. The second poem in the May 13, 1886, issue of La Vogue, entitled "Enfance," opens with the gripping image, "This idol, with dark eyes and yellow hair, without parents or palace . . ." In the next number, May 29, appeared "Vagabonds," with its greatly controverted phrase, "fils du soleil." [14] Light and a certain shimmering sheen are evoked in this fashion throughout Les Illuminations, heightening the suggestivity of the title. A final curious fact is perhaps worth noting. Sandwiched between the issues (numbers 5, 6, 8, 9) containing Les Illuminations, number seven of La Vogue (June 7–14, 1886) presented snatches of earlier Rimbaud poetry, including two items entitled "Tête de faune" and "Age d'or." [15]

In 1949, the playwright named "Après le déluge" and "Enfance" as having been a veritable revelation for him (MI, p. 28). Indeed, the latter poem's "Long do I watch the melancholy golden wash of sunset" could well be a source for the golden death scene of Tête d'Or. An even clearer link with Rimbaud's sun and light imagery is apparent in the transposition of "I have embraced the summer dawn" from the opening verse of "Aube" into the dying hero's embracing of the golden sunset. Similarly, the death of Cébès is not without parallel in Rimbaud. "Délires II" in Une Saison en Enfer, which Claudel read in the autumn of 1886, has this arresting conclusion, which evokes the circumstances surrounding Cébès' death: "Happiness! Its tooth, sweet at death, warned me at cockcrow—*ad matutinum,* at the *Christus venit*—in the darkest cities."

It would be a mistake, however, to credit this sun symbolism in Claudel solely to Rimbaud.[16] There was also the supernatural inspiration, rooted in his mysterious Christmas experience in Notre Dame. Although he never clearly and publicly expatiated on the event before 1913,[17] his earlier works are not without allusions to it, and *Tête d'Or* in particular reflects the rebellious recipient's reaction to this grace, which so dazzled him that it took four years for him to absorb its meaning and accept its practical implications by a humble return to the Church and the sacraments. In his old age, Claudel himself stated the matter in the clearest terms:

> *Tête d'Or* is a little the result of that bedazzlement and at the same time of that struggle. At the time when I wrote *Tête d'Or,* in 1889, I had not yet made my definitive capitulation into the hands of the Church, and *Tête d'Or* represents a little the sort of fury with which I defended myself against the Faith that was calling me and which is symbolized by the Princess. (*MI,* p. 51)

It is highly likely, then, that the drama of Claudel's illumination and slow conversion is reflected in Tête d'Or's gradual emergence from the darkness of ignorance and of the menace of death to his vocation and discovery of his true nature as a sun child. Without a single Catholic friend to consult, too ignorant and prejudiced to seek reconciliation, the youth gradually discovered the divine truths for himself by frequent private visits to Notre Dame, by poring over the liturgical texts, especially those for Christmas, Easter, and the Office of the Dead, and even by haunting the Bibliothèque nationale, where he devoured the Church Fathers in Migne's *Patrologia.*[18] What did he find? Among other ideas, constant reference to the Son of God as the true sun of justice and righteousness, for the ancient feast of the nativity of Christ was instituted to counteract the creeping solar pantheism rampant in the Roman Empire in the second and third centuries. Almost simultaneously there sprang up a dual celebration of Christ's birth on the day of the winter solstice. In the Eastern section of the Empire, where the solstice had long been mistakenly observed on January 6, the Alexandrian Church instituted, towards the end of the third century, the Christian solar feast of the Epiphany, in opposition to the pagan celebrations of Aeon. In Rome the increasing syncretism of sun worship evident in the vast and splendid temple built to Sol on the Campus Agrippae by Aurelian for the celebration of Natalis Invicti on December 25 and the spread of Mithras worship in the Roman army caused the Church of Rome to institute Christmas to honor the birth of the true Light and to push pagans like Constantine beyond the visible symbol to the invisible reality. All relevant fourth-century texts show that, like the Epiphany, "the nativity feast of December 25 was always regarded as a Christian solar feast and that men saw in it the Church's answer to the sun cults of the fading Graeco-Roman world." [19]

Little wonder, then, that the pre-Christian Claudel, imbued with the solar symbolism he had just discovered in Rimbaud, should see in his Christmas illumination by the Son of God a revelation "as of light and milk" [20] of the divinity symbolized by the daystar. Like Constantine at the Milvian bridge, he found his infatuation for Helios crowned and completed by the theophany of the God-Man at Bethlehem. His bedazzlement must have been confirmed at each reading and pondering of the liturgical texts, such as the antiphons, "The Savior of the world shall arise like the sun and descend into the Virgin's womb" and "When heaven's sun has arisen, you shall see the King of Kings coming forth from his Father." Indeed, it was during the singing of the latter antiphon and the Magnificat canticle framed by it that Claudel, standing near the entrance to the Cathedral choir, was struck by the dominant event of his life, which he termed "an ineffable revelation" and "a single flash of lightning" (OPR, p. 1010).

The whole Christmas liturgy is resplendent with similar evocations of the divine light. In the Mass for midnight occur these passages: "You have made this sacred night shine with the brightness of the true light," "a new dawn of glory," "the light of your glory has flooded the eyes of our mind anew in the mystery of the Word made flesh," and "Light of light." Similar gems abound in the second and third Christmas Masses: "This day will be the dawning of light upon earth," "we are drenched in the new light of the Word become Man," "a Son, who is the radiance of his Father's splendour." [21]

This liturgical light mysticism is even more predominant in the most ancient of all Christian feasts, that of Easter. In the famous article on his conversion, Claudel told how profoundly stirred he was by "the reading of the Office of the Dead, of that of Christmas, the spectacle of the days of Holy Week, the sublime chant of the Exultet, beside which the most intoxicated accents of Sophocles or of Pindar appeared insipid to me . . ." (OPR, pp. 1013). Indeed, the whole Paschal liturgy radiates and glows with the new light of the risen Redeemer, epitomized in the Easter-vigil blessing of the new fire and the Paschal candle, with the joyous evocations of the exuberant Exultet: "In the radiance of this glorious light . . . universal darkness is dispelled." "Such is my joy that night itself is light." Although the reference here is to a universal enlightenment, it is still a very plausible source for the personal illumination of Simon Agnel (alias Paul Claudel) quoted already (A, p. 46).

To conclude this lengthy parenthetical investigation of the light theme, let us note finally the third of five Easter homilies by St. Maximus, a fifth-century bishop of Turin, for it may help us understand the theme of sleep in Part II. This sermon was very possibly read by the poet during this period—for it occurs in the breviary on Easter Monday (which is still a holiday in France)—along with the Gospel account of the Emmaüs adventure (Luke XXIV, 13–35). This was a pivotal chronicle for Claudel because it was the first scriptural passage he read as he opened at random that Christmas night a Bible given his sister by a German Protestant friend. In fact, the Emmaüs story oriented his extensive appreciation of the Scriptures in the direction of the allegorical rather than the literal sense.[22] In that Easter sermon St. Maximus speaks of Tartarus being opened by means of Christ's Resurrection and of the dead rising up like new shoots germinated from an invigorated earth.[23] Now, this image of Tartarus, the unlighted cavern in which the wicked dead grope ceaselessly and hopelessly about for some ray of light or exit, an image frequent in Greek literature and used in the Mass of the Dead, is as basic to the moral climate of Part II as it was to the psychological state of Cébès and Simon in Part I.

There, as we have already seen, the two youths, realizing that they were floundering in a black pit of metaphysical ignorance, but burning to escape, made a mutual-aid pact, with Simon swearing that he would burst open the door of the prison, shoulder aside the huge rock, and bring Cébès and mankind the yellow fire of freedom and hope. In Part II, the night theme is less an irritant to evoke a distressed awareness of man's fate than an atmosphere to enhance the state of torpor and moral lethargy or despair of the moribund monarchy. Hence the complacent somnolence of the palace guard at midnight and the general resignation to destruction in the face of the barbarian invasion: "Listen to these watchmen watch!/ One whistles, another snores, and another cries out, so hard does he sleep!" (B, pp. 189–190). The inept King David, on the other hand, abandoned by the dishonest prime minister and even by his domestics, is unable to sleep: "O Sleep, kill me with your arrows of lead!/ But I can't sleep and would keep opening my eyes in the void . . . / But the darkness suffocates us like a blanket" (B, p. 190). Because of his decrepitude and despair, he is as helpless as his guards to cope with the Tartarean darkness, with its "Horror and deadly Lunacy." So he wanders without hope "in the trenches of death." The darkness of Gethsemane and three sleepy Apostles immediately come to mind when the King wakes up the guards and reproaches them thus: "Could you not watch and wait?/ But, like fat valets, they sleep!" These "watchmen" have not the slightest inclination to watch and wait, however, for they flippantly tell the King to extinguish the light and join them in their chthonian antechamber (B, p. 193).

That more is at stake than merely a night's sleep is clear from the intervention of the third guard: "It's tedium. It's the wind, it's the exhalation of the void that is in us./ We spoke and our words were only a noise . . . / But in truth we are dead" (B, p. 193). In short, physical death will be but the logical consequence of a moribund moral state, of which the whole nation is guilty, according to this lucid guard, because of its easy acquiescence in sin and ignorance, symbolized by their somnolent complacency:

> We have made supplication and that has been in vain.
> Our sin is on us and our ignorance is invincible.
> Why were we born? Now we may as well die. What
> should we do and why should we do it?/ . . . . /

> This parish dreams, and as a people which, like a nation of chickens,
> Perched on the walls of the embankments watches the disappearance of a sun which will no longer rise on the other side. (B, p. 194)

Thus internal decay and rejection of lofty ideals precede destruction from without. It is indeed amazing how frequently loss of life is evoked in terms of the extinction of light. We think of Othello's command, "Put out the light, and then put out the light!" when the fourth guard, who still maintains a flicker of hope, exclaims: "See, they are going to extinguish/ Like a lamp that infects the air and is snuffed out with a wet rag" (B, p. 194). Without even a condemned prisoner's slim hope of saving himself at the expense of his fellow convicts, the others, "these people who drivel on in the shadows of the bedroom" (B, p. 197), can only curse one another. After exchanging venomous words with the King himself, the angry fifth guard, like the legendary drowning victim seeing his whole past life in a flash, execrates his teachers, his parents, and himself:

> Accursed be you in your race, and in your office, and in the contrivance of your inert power, temporal King!
> Accursed be my masters! . . .
> For they took me when I was only a child and gave me earth to eat.
> Accursed be my father and my mother with him! May they be accursed in their food, in their ignorance, and in the example they gave me!/ . . . . /
> I will curse myself!
> Myself, because I am vile, lost, dishonored,
> Abased below all beings and cowardly beyond all measure. (B, p. 195)

Since misery loves company, he would persuade all to submit to Tartarean despair:

> I tell you that you are taken and that you cannot be delivered.

> And the slab is sealed upon you; it is sealed and cemented
> and attached with iron claws.
> We are in the deep pit . . . (B, p. 199)

This scene of a nation given over to sleep and despair, then, is in no wise a counterpart of the slumbering guards in *Macbeth*, nor does it spring from the relatively superficial psychological opposition one can make between "necrophilous and biophilous" consciences,[24] although this is not absent. Rather, for those who are familiar with the playwright's early pessimism, it stems from the personal sadness of his youth and the metaphysical hopelessness promulgated by his elders. The former was typified by the gloom he encountered at Villeneuve and in Zola's *La Joie de vivre* (1884); the existential anguish at a destiny of despair derived mainly from the monist and mechanistic scientism of the time, under the aegis of Renan, Taine, and Berthelot. The fifth guard's unmitigated curses against his elders find manifold sarcastic echoes in later writings of Claudel. Thus, in his 1952 commentary on the Apocalypse, he could still describe how

around us and from one horizon to the other was this vision of death, where everything lost meaning and interest, headed stupidly toward annulment, ourselves interiorly gnawed by an inexorable enemy. Reader, if you don't understand what I mean, I urge you to read a novel of Émile Zola's which is prettily entitled, *La Joie de vivre*.[25]

In the guard's condemnation of his masters is apparent a dramatic transposition of the young poet's first rejection of "the choir of pessimists," "this voice of complacency in despair, of communion with the night" which he found in Taine and especially in "the languid belching of the slimiest of batrachians, Ernest Renan." The reproach leveled at him and "this swampy concert" is that of going a step beyond Buddha in focusing men's attention on something "softer than nothingness, which is doubt," and he accused Renan of sprawling in it with delight.[26]

These recriminations have repelled many readers, who ascribe them to the recalcitrance and irascibility of a belligerent bourgeois without Christian charity and critical understanding. No doubt the brashness is disturbing to many sensibilities. On the other hand, the fulminations at the dreary leadership of the 1880's are more understandable if we remember his wild enthusiasm for Rimbaud, whose own denunciation of an ineluctable mechanism was anything but restrained. Secondly, it must be kept in mind that Claudel's personal suffering in that "prison of materialism" drove him to such despair that he once nearly committed suicide himself: "I rehearsed the final act." [27] Moreover, for most of his life Claudel was confronted with the ravages of materialism and especially of Renan's *La Vie de Jésus*, in the moral and then mental deterioration of his older sister, Camille, whom he had so admired and feared in his youth.[28] Little wonder, then, that such an ardent apostle ("not a hothouse flower"), released quasi-miraculously from "a cemetery dug by lemures," should occasionally deliver himself of an impatient broadside against those who had dug the pit of doubt and "sealed the slab" on his generation:

> And just as you withdrew Joseph from the cistern and Jeremias from the deep pit,
> So have you saved me from death. . . .
> You have put the horror of death in my heart, my soul has no tolerance for death!
> Pedants, epicurians, masters of the novitiate of Hell, practitioners of the Introduction to Nothingness,/ . . . . /
> Your methods and your demonstrations and your discipline,
> Nothing reconciles me, I am alive in your abominable night, I lift my hands amid despair, I raise my hands in the trance and transport of wild and heedless hope! (*OP*, p. 254)

This recalls the poignant chant in the Mass of the Dead, "May Tartarus not swallow them up, may they not fall into darkness." [29] For evoked here, almost twenty years after *Tête d'Or*, is the very atmosphere of moral depression that obtained in old King David's land, then its violent rejection by "the new man" (whether Tête d'Or or Claudel), whose desire for a greater happiness transcended "the privation of happiness" in his exploration of this dark mystery with fire and sword. It is precisely the horror of death that provokes this violent reaction against all that smacks of demise: necrophilous preference of law to life, of the mechanical to the functional, of force to love, of having to being, of sadness to joy, of things to people.[30] And the measure of the violence must be judged by the extent of the horror, which is remarkably similar to Baudelaire's in "De profundis clamavi," where he seeks pity "From the bottom of the dark pit in which my soul has fallen./ It is a dreary universe with a leaden horizon,/ Where horror and blasphemy swim in the night." [31]

The newly enlightened dramatist must have received a wealth of suggestion, then, during those four years of hesitancy and self-instruction in Notre Dame, while composing *Tête d'Or*, each time he heard the "Great O" Magnificat antiphons, especially the ones for December 20 and 21:

O Key of David, and Scepter of the house of Israel . . . : come and bring forth from his prison-house the captive that sits in darkness and in the shadow of death.

O Dawn of the East, brightness of the light eternal, and Sun of Justice, come and enlighten them that sit in darkness and in the shadow of death.

"To enlighten those who sit in darkness and in the shadow of death." There is the essential key to this symbolist drama and to its hero's incredible attempt to stamp out death, or at least to root out complacency in its darkness. For there is a death worse than physical decomposition, and that is the demise of desire. Such, too, is the essential role of the mysterious Princess, whom the author termed "exceedingly important" (*MI*, p. 51).

III

Tête d'Or: *Fiery Tiger in the Night*

KING DAVID

Least important among the major characters in *Tête d'Or*, but by no means to be overlooked, is the aged King. He is chiefly tormented not by fear for his own life but by horror at the impending destruction of his dynasty and his race: "O nation! O city! O my poor country, destroyed, devastated, swept like a sheep-fold!" (B, p. 190). This is a typically Israelitic conception of death, for the Jews, unconcerned with personal immortality and not given to distinguishing between soul and body, worried more about the temporal future of their people, since for them, a person continued to exist in his children.[1] There was a sense of belonging to an imperishable structure, because the past and future of the entire tribe were seen as present in the destiny of each of its members.[2] Similarly, it is to this notion of tribal continuity as supreme value that the old King appeals in the face of the insurgent Tête d'Or, just before being slain by the latter:

> Respect what is mine. Respect the possession of the father of the family.
> This kingdom was created by my fathers, and I reign over it according to the order of succession./ . . . . /
> Do not take what is mine; do not despoil my daughter. For where shall there be blessing among men,
> If you trample underfoot the sacred heritage law? (B, p. 241)

38

For him, destiny was terrestrial heritage, little more. So the King must die, to make room for "the new man" and higher aspirations:

> Miserly old man who wants to keep what he can't use!
> O latesome King . . . .
> You are the man of the present, but now it is already past.
>
> (B, p. 241)

For decades he had been a conscientious and satisfactory ruler, "solitary, a seeker of Wisdom"; but lacking desire or longing for higher values, "fixing his arid eyes on duty," he proved inadequate to the new generation and to the ultimate questions of man. He is bogged down in the mire of materialism, although he had been a clever helmsman, adept at following the course of the stars (B, p. 209). Wherefore he is duly hoist on Absalom's poniard—or perhaps it is Hamlet's.

Is this "a classical Oedipal act," the impulsive murder of a symbolic father, as Alain Cuny insists? [3] Yes, but the paternity severed and rejected with the dagger thrust is, above all, the spiritual parentage of the masters of the 1880s—Renan foremost, of course.

THE PRINCESS

The Princess, David's daughter, first appears on the midnight scene just after her father's vitriolic altercation with the sleeping guards. She braves the motley male assembly because she is afraid to stay alone after the flight of the servants. She sits down near the dying Cébès to try to console him, despite his obtuse loyalty to his absent brother, Tête d'Or. A short time later, unwilling but in filial obedience, she changes garments, and even personalities, to stage a play within the play, or rather to radiate a role that mystifies her as much as it does the gaping soldiers and many critics. The extensive stage directions reveal the great significance that the author attached to this scene:

The Princess returns, vested in a red dress and a gold cope which covers her from head to foot. On her head is a kind of miter and a long, thick black braid comes down over the shoulder on her breast. She ad-

vances, eyes closed, in extremely slow, measured steps and stops between the light and shade. (B, p. 200)

Her first words in this trance-like state describe her new role: "She
who has closed her eyes and is going to awake from a long sleep"
(B, p. 200). As she stands silent and with eyes closed before the
amazed assembly, the fourth guard, who is the youngest and hence
less impervious to light and hope than his drowsy and despairing
companions, utters the very revealing remark:

> Here is another sun in this room, looking on us with its
> radiant face!
> Who is she who, covered with such a vestment, hides her
> hands under a garment of gold?
> Who is this who, in human shape,
> Clothed in a too copious cloak, is standing between the
> lamp and night? (B, p. 200)

This brief speech, which had been entrusted to Cébès in the first
version, contains an important key to her nature: into the midst of
these men sitting in the shadows of the valley of death has come
another sun, a kind of "light of revelation to the gentiles." The
biblical language and the maiden's aurorean appearance readily
evoke the personification of divine Wisdom.

It is well-known how deeply influenced Claudel was by Proverbs
VIII, the second passage he read that Christmas night when he
first opened a Bible:

> This whole magnificent personification of *Proverbs* had greatly struck
> me, and all the figures of women in my subsequent work are more or
> less related to this discovery. There are hardly any feminine characters
> in my whole work where there isn't some trait of Wisdom.
> For me, woman always represents four things: the human soul, the
> Church, the Holy Virgin, or sacred Wisdom. (MI, p. 51)

Which category best fits the Princess? Each has had its critical
champion. Claudel himself stated in the letter to Albert Mockel
cited at the beginning of Chapter II: "The Princess is suavity,

woman, wisdom, piety" (*CPC*, I, 140). Blanchet adds "anima" and "muse" [4] and S. Fumet "grace." [5] Hence it is wiser, given the author's interpretation and remembering that this drama was born in the very womb of symbolism and of figurative exegesis stemming from the Emmaüs incident, to see a multiple inspiration and symbolism in the Princess as well as in Tête d'Or. She is by turns, sometimes simultaneously, in a sort of telescopic interpenetration of symbols, the eternal woman, Wisdom, grace, piety, Mary, the Church.[6] This view was early fostered by his discovery, in the epistle for December 8, of the liturgical application to Mary of some of the attributes of Wisdom: "I was not long in recognizing that this radiant figure evokes the traits of the Mother of God, as well as those of the Church and of created wisdom." [7] His genius has synthesized these many aspects in the role of the Princess— without robbing her of her very human qualities of fear of solitude and suffering, of pity, love, and anger—in order to set her as a living symbol against the elements of darkness and despair and death. The stage direction that has her stop midway between the light and the shadows is laden with meaning, as is her kinship with King David.

In substantiation of this theory of multiple symbolic interpenetration, it is sufficient to observe the consummate mastery with which the young playwright has interwoven in this scene not only the two levels of realistic and symbolic perception but also some finely nuanced symbols in the Princess' evolution from a blind, silent dependent to a lucid sibyl.

The playlet is framed in two periods of solemn silence and of her filial attention to the King. The silence underlines the symbolic value of this trance-like state, while her hesitant obedience evokes the flesh-and-blood reality of this "poor girl, concerned about her nails and her face" (*B*, 207). And the symbols? Besides the early evocation of Wisdom already noted, with its analogies, there is the maiden dancing, asleep, amid the lilies of the valley (*B*, p. 201), reminiscent of the bride in the Song of Solomon. The third guard's liturgical salutation, in Latin, "You are our joy and delight," evokes Mary. More suggestive of the exiled woman of the Apocalypse, who is the symbol of the Church, is the Princess' prophetic self-appraisal after the nightingale's song:

The bird sings in summer and keeps quiet in winter, but I
sing in the harsh and bitter air, and when everything freezes
I rise madly towards the deserted sky!
    For my voice is that of love and the heat of my heart is like
that of youth. (B, p. 203)

This symbol becomes quite evident when she adds: "Every woman
is but a mother. I am she who raises and nourishes . . ." (B, p.
204). But as she continues speaking, she seems to assume the role
of Wisdom:

    I see clear through you, to the bottom. Nothing is ob-
literated by the fraudulent shadows./ . . . . /
    I could call each of you
    By his name and tell him to get up.

Wisdom's clairvoyance leads to reproaches, not without justification:

    You have rejected me here, but now I will accuse you and
you will hear me.
    I will accuse you with a sharp and piercing voice, which
will go through your heart like a sword,
    And I will be harder and keener than a nagging wife is to
her husband! (B, p. 204)

Should these female sentiments be ascribed to grace, woman, the
Church, Mary? Perhaps to all, insofar as they are addressed as
warnings to the spiritually dead. The men fail to see in the Princess
anything more than an empty woman, despite her invitation to
follow the Muse and to seek after Wisdom:

    I do not always stay in the grotto by the springs and in the
deserted ravines among the oaks,
    But I stand at the crossroads, and even in the cities
    I stand at the markets and at the exits of dances, saying:
    "Who wants to exchange handfuls of blackberries for
handfuls of gold, and to weigh
    Unending love with the weight of his heart of flesh?"
                                              (B, p. 205)

In the face of their rejection, she can only pronounce the death sentence:

> Several times, in like darkness, I have warned you gravely;
> you have rebuffed me:
> Here, in this glimmer of light,
> Now that you are counted for death, I appear,
> Not to repair the rupture but to certify it!/ . . . . /
> It is fitting that you should taste death. (B, p. 205)

Can this be the role of Wisdom, to mete out justice and death? Indeed it is, according to Chapter One of Proverbs, which is the source of this passage. Or better, Wisdom's role at the end is simply to verify and attest the condition of men's souls, to reveal whether they are written in the book of life or death. The fourth guard had recognized this eschatological aspect when he addressed her earlier: "O Notary of the dying! Behold, you approach us with the register and the book" (B, p. 203). So Wisdom is the touchstone of life and death: "For he who finds me finds life, and wins favor from the Lord; but he who misses me harms himself; all who hate me love death" (Prov. VIII, 36). To hardened hearts she is a reproach, but the permeable can still be healed: "You must believe me, Cébès, and love me" (B, p. 206).

Before finishing her role-playing, the Princess evokes simultaneously both Wisdom and the Church as the exiled woman of Revelation:

> Oh! How late it is! And I must leave this house,
> Alone like a widow harshly driven from her home!
> You will be sorry for me in the last hour.
> But I leave you, and this dwelling, and may spiders make
> their webs here! (B, p. 206)

But after returning from the symbolism of the playlet to reality and suffering, she still retains the clairvoyance to foretell, "Soon, I shall lie fully extended on the ground, my hands open" (B, p. 207). Not only is the symbolism multiple here, but there is constant interchange, interpenetration of symbol and reality, between the Princess and Wisdom in all her analogical guises.

The second appearance of the Princess occurs after Tête d'Or has assassinated her father and assumed the crown. Here, in the pedagogue's weeping reference to her radiant beauty and to a mysterious healing power she has on her birthday, there is only the slightest hint of a preternatural value (B, p. 253). Rather, her intensely human qualities stand out in this confrontation with her father's murderer—her aching sorrow and utter contempt for the traitors. Even more representatively feminine is her undaunted devotion to the dead. She alone, like Antigone in the midst of a male assembly, stands for fidelity to the deceased, as did the women with their funeral chant over Cébès in the early version, for woman represents the soul of pity and compassion bent in recollection over death. Only the Princess has the piety and re- spect to kneel before the dead: "Sire! O sacred corpse, let me touch you and be not indignant, for they are the hands of your daughter" (B, p. 255). Only she has the courage to remove and bury the corpse. With her departure into exile, there disappears from the kingdom all sweetness, compassion, and pity for fallen man.[8] Only in his own death agony will the conquering hero come to realize this.

Having encountered spiritual death and the corpse of her be- loved father, the Princess is morally strengthened to face the ultimate disasters of Part III. The desolation and dangers she en- counters in exile again evoke the woman of the Apocalypse, as the minimum protection offered by the army officers also evokes her. This impression, that she symbolizes the Church persecuted, in- creases when she warns the deserter, who is about to crucify her, that "these hands . . . can bring a better food than bread,/ Al- though I can make bread too" (B, p. 263). Her human weakness is evident in her efforts to dissuade her psychotic executioner with her pleadings and threats, as are her high courage and royal dignity in refusing to whimper before him. Instead, she spits in his face and insults him: "I despise you, imbecile, you crass brute!" (B, p. 264). And after he has left her alone, she says proudly, "I will not complain./ I will die standing,/ As it becomes those of my race so well" (B, p. 265). The most amazing evocation of all, how- ever, is that of the Christ image, of the Savior ruling from the throne of the tree, inspired perhaps by the Holy Week hymn Vexilla Regis. "I am bound to the stake! but my royal soul/ is not diminished, and thus,/ This bond is as honorable as a throne" (B, p. 264). Is it also possible that the author, who was reading Bossuet at the time, had come across his famous definition of the Church as Jesus Christ extended in space and time? Years later he would make this perceptive comment on the Vulgate text "clamabat ut parturiens et cruciabatur ut pareret [And she being with child cried, travailing in birth, and in torment to be delivered]" (Apoc. XII, 2):

(Note the word *cruciabatur* where the idea of the cross enters in.) No difficulty if it is a question solely of the Church and of that mystical body of Christ which she brings forth down through the ages in effort and in sorrow.[9]

How well is this symbolism maintained in the fourth appearance of the Princess, in her threnody with the expiring Tête d'Or who had exiled her? At first the human and realistic aspects of her suffering predominate, but her symbolic value increases throughout the final scene, without however submerging or destroying the very human qualities. The symbolism here is rather subtle, never becoming as full-blown as in the playlet earlier.

When she first regains consciousness and perceives the usurper almost dead nearby, she experiences some compassion for him but maintains her royal rights in reminding him that his death is well deserved, "because I was the one who was to rule and not you" (B, p. 290). Forgiveness, however, is implicit in her compassionate attention to him after he has unpinioned her from the tree. Tête d'Or is so moved by her display of courage and compassion in the face of death that he sees womanhood in a wholly different light and exalts these new-found feminine values:

> There is the courage of the wounded, the support of the infirm,
> The company of the dying. She managed to bring me here with those bleeding and dislocated hands.
> By this same sweet courage with which you dragged me here, by this naïve patience,
> Woman in her housework is the image of fervent resignation, she teaches good will;

> As, formerly, servant of the home, she became servant of
> God! (B, p. 292)

In fact, he even goes so far as to acknowledge the legitimacy of
her regal claim: "Thy face is beautiful and by itself alone shows
sovereignty./ Rightly do you hate me" (B, p. 292). This humble
recognition of her personal and symbolic worth and of his previous
injustice towards her is undoubtedly prompted by her noble and
selfless courage and charity on the threshold of death. Such recognition on his part would be quite impossible in lesser circumstances
than their dual deaths.

If the heroic attitude of the dying Princess has produced this
unexpected about-face on his part, his sudden sympathetic and
generous disposition in turn totally dissolves her former animosity:
it not only elicits the absolution of her "I do not hate you" (B,
p. 293) but provokes a startling outpouring of gratitude and tenderness for the persecutor who had perpetrated so many abominations
on her.

> O Tête d'Or!
> I am glad that you killed my father!
> Oh, but I'm happy! It is you
> Who took my throne from me, who caused me
> To wear out my feet on all the roads, in confusion and in
> poverty, scorned, contradicted, outraged, and to arrive here
> dying! (B, p. 293)

No doubt there is a psychological basis for such an emotional revolution, explicable not only by subconscious admiration for his in-
defatigable pursuit of a superior happiness, but also by the imperative attraction of a reciprocal generosity in their human loneliness
on the brink of death. It would be beyond our scope to delve
further into the complicated workings of this motivation.[10] Suffice it to note in passing that Tête d'Or had never shown hatred
for her person but rather for her position and had unconsciously
befriended her before going into his last battle, giving her bread,
water, and his cloak, thus softening her rancor. Claudel had also
just found a literary model, no doubt his psychological source too,
in Dostoyevsky, whom he called the inventor of the polymorphic

character, the discoverer of spontaneous mutation (*MI*, p. 37).

However, this human aspect of the Princess is subsidiary though fundamental to the symbolical and mystical values of her role in this scene. For here she reaches the apogee, in religious symbolism, of the woman in exile as a figure of the Church suffering and of the Mystical Body, of one teaching by example that suffering is the royal road to eternal happiness. "What could be more subtle and more ingenious? What better path to perfection?" asks Acer in *Conversations dans le Loir-et-Cher*. "For life has interrupted its work on whoever does not suffer" (*OPR*, p. 766). Certainly it is primarily in this sense, mystical and redemptive rather than masochistic, that one must understand her love for her persecutor, a love that springs from *Caritas* more than from *Eros*.[11]

> I would have liked for it to have been you too
> Who had nailed me to that tree,
> And I would have closed my eyes to feel it better.
> And in loving you I would have died in silence.
> Dearest! my most precious possession!
> See, this affliction that you caused me was not useless. I
> am truly dying like you! (*B*, p. 293)

Beyond the psychological insight that human love, at least in its more idealized expressions, tends to eternalize itself by desiring to die with and like the beloved rather than endure separation, there hovers the mystic's gladness at having been accounted worthy to share in the Savior's sufferings, as well as her gratitude towards the mediator of these spiritual favors. The source of this joy, found in and through suffering, lies in its redemptive quality:

> Oh! may I be like the cut flower that smells stronger and
> like the mown grass!
> Oh! I am happy to think that there is not one of so many
> sufferings that is not thine,
> And that now I can give back to you like a perfume, O my
> master! (*B*, 293)

This union of souls at the peak of an altruistic and identical immolation suggests a kind of mystical espousal, like that of Sts.

Cecilia and Valerian. The Princess already had a presentiment of
this higher calling and of the redemptive value of her suffering just
after being crucified: "O hands! I had thought that I would bring
you both to my spouse,/ So that he might free you from the
nuptial bonds./ But these nails suit you better" (B, p. 265). Her
purpose now is to lead and entice this hero's soul beyond the
satisfaction of his personal achievement to the happiness of communion by means of an oblative death, full of hope.

The King is, indeed, much attracted to her in these last moments, recognizing her supernatural charm:

> O Grace with the transfixed hands!
> Soft as the sinking sun!
> Happy he who can take rapture under the arms and kiss it
> on its very soft cheek!
> I am charmed at the sight of you, Benediction! (B, p. 293)

Her supernatural charm is seen in her efforts to save him from
desolation and despair (B, pp. 294–295) and attains apparent success, for his dying decision is to have her crowned to succeed him,
be her reign briefer than the splendor of a falling star.

Her coronation by the soldiers sparkles with delicate symbolism.
It evokes not so much the Marian prophecy of the Magnificat ("All
generations shall call me blessed") as the apotheosis of Wisdom,
Woman, and the Church. "It is I, woman, clothed with this
sumptuous mantle!" (B, p. 300). There is celestial significance in
her donning the long white garment called *l'Aube* (meaning both
Alb and dawn), in her exchanging "the footgear of exile" for "the
imperial sandal with straps of gold" (B, p. 299), and in the appearance of "the moon like a curved finger with its pointed nail"
(B, p. 301).[12] Such is the fulfillment of the prophecy and the
realization of the symbolism contained in the palace playlet. Humanity at the end accepts this true woman, image of Grace, Wisdom, and the Church, and rather than bury her royal remains in
the dirt of oblivion, as had been the fate of the false woman, the
commander orders, "Lay the Queen out in her royal apparel on a
shield! We will carry you back with us" (B, p. 301).

Although the Princess recognizes her redemptive role, "like the
tree they crucify so it will fructify," even in the midst of her corona-

tion pomp she is realistically aware of the tenuous nature of her earthly reign: "O ashes! . . ./ Why call me Queen, unless it be queen of things past/ Or of leaves in the instant they swim in the dusty air?" (B, p. 300). The richness of the Princess' character lies in the fact that she is coherent and attractive on the human level as well as the symbolic and that the symbolism is suggestive, not obligatory.[13]

CÉBÈS

As for Cébès and Simon Agnel, a greater polarity of personality is scarcely conceivable.[14] Both burn to escape from the black pit of their metaphysical ignorance concerning death and believe they have discovered the secret of their nature and the key to their problem in their mutual dependence, in their brotherly blood pact. In the one is found great physical strength and courage, self-confidence, and an overriding will to power—all characteristic of the active, masculine mentality. Cébès, on the other hand, typifies the receptive, feminine principle, tending towards contemplation, consolation, suffering, and sympathy. Each one is incomplete and needs the other for fulfillment.

This is especially true of Cébès, who appears veritably obsessed by a fear of solitude. Simon is just the opposite, rarely feeling alone, for always accompanying him is "the voice of my own word" (B, p. 178). The difference is not insignificant, for the weaker obtains a kind of insider's acquaintance with death, a growing connatural and existential knowledge of mortality, whereas the stronger will be limited to the less perceptive apprehension of an outsider.

What is the basis of Cébès' loneliness and perturbation? It is evidently imbedded in his lack of identity. From the very outset, in his opening monologue, appears the theme of an existence in search of an essence: "What am I? What am I doing? What do I expect?/ And I reply: I do not know! . . . 'Who I am'?" (B, pp. 171–172). This is a frequent secondary theme but less apparent in the other major characters, although all in varying degrees are searching for their deeper identity. This quest for the unknown self is primordial in Claudel, as Charles Du Bos observed in his comments on the opening argument of Art poétique.[15] Now, it is precisely his existential suffering and insatiable curiosity about the why and the wherefore of death and about his own place in the scheme of mortality that impede Cébès in his search for his full identity. Until he can come to grips with the mystery of death and know where he stands in relation to it, how can he ever attain a satisfactory self-image or self-definition? Such is the gist of this long complaint that first irks, then intrigues his companion:

> There are people whose eyes
> Melt like slit medlars that let their pips ooze out.
> And women whom cancer attacks like punk on a beech tree.
> And new-born monstrosities, men with a calf's snout!
> And children abused and killed by their fathers.
> And oldsters whose children count the days one by one.
> All ills have an eye on us: the ulcer and the abscess, epilepsy and head twitching, and in the end come gout and gravel to prevent pissing.
> Consumption kindles its fire; the shameful parts grow moldy like grapes; and the belly
> Bursts and empties out its entrails and excrement!
>   (B, p. 180)

These realistic fantasies of mortality, impinging on him from all sides as they had impinged on Claudel,[16] propel Cébès closer to Simon in his search for a valid explanation. The latter exudes such mysterious confidence after his lengthy contact with "that tree of knowledge" (B, p. 183) that Cébès attains a certain degree of identity and self-discovery through his new relationship: "O Father, Father! for am I not your child here/ By reason of all I lack, I beseech you!" (B, pp. 184–185). And a moment later, indeed, he arrives at this provisory self-definition: "I am he who beseeches you, young elder!" (B, p. 185).

More than one critic has seen in Cébès the other face of the adolescent soul of Claudel, "that feminine part of himself, of which Claudel spoke so often, later."[17] Even stronger is Fumet's opinion that the person most fully Claudel in this drama is Cébès and not Simon-Tête d'Or.[18] The most notorious demurral of Cébès' symbolic aspect is Cuny's Freudian hypothesis and homosexual imputations,[19] too tenuous and unfounded to be taken seriously. The evidence points rather to the view that Claudel has here fragmented his own rich personality into its two main tendencies, active and passive; or better, perhaps, Cébès and Simon personify the two poles of personality, the determinant and determinable elements that everyone has and that Claudel later developed in his parable of animus and anima.[20] The author himself has applied this to his two youthful heroes (MI, p. 31) and also accepted Jean Amrouche's distinction, in a slightly different context, that "instruction is the food of animus, and delectation would be the sustenance of anima" (MI, p. 49). If Cébès can call himself Simon's image (B, p. 184), it is in the sense that their temperaments and spirits, though divergent, dovetail and complement one another, being linked, like rational and intuitive powers, in their common effort to subdue death. This is the deepest and most satisfying interpretation of their blood pact and of their fraternal threnody in Part II when Cébès is dying.

Consider their reunion upon the return of Simon—now Tête d'Or—after his surprise victory over the invaders. The hero relates how he succeeded "since I saw and I knew," attributing his triumph over that form of death to his rational faculties: "The eye and reason say at the same time: it has to be!" Not so Cébès: "And I see not and know not!" (B, p. 217). He is knowing in one thing only, in how to give himself (B, p. 218). His state corresponds to the description of anima as "a longing, a breaking away of desire from the self towards an object or a person." [21] Cébès' problem, however, is to choose the right beneficiary for the gift of himself, since "nothing imperfect can suffice me, for I am not sufficient to myself." His is a quest of an absolute, in other words: "I am looking for the one who is perfectly just and true,/ So that he can be perfectly good and I can love him the same way" (B, p. 218). Nothing weak, nothing mortal will suffice.

This explains why he rejected nature (epitomized in the nightingale's pure song) as a possible response to his inner need ("But you are only a voice and not a word" B, p. 197) and also declined the Princess' consolation, preferring to remain loyal to his oath of adoption: "Woman, you will not console me, and I'll have no part with you. But I am waiting for my older brother to return" (B, p.

197). Thus his adamant allegiance to Tête d'Or, with all his rational and virile appeal, impeded his recognition and acceptance of a higher wisdom, although he had a partial insight at the close of the playlet: "And what must be done, Grace-vision, to be healed?" (B, p. 206). In the first version he was clearly guilty of resistance, as the Princess declared over his corpse: "At present, from the womb of his death he no longer knows me./ But if he had loved me, he would not have died" (A, p. 110). Here, he is at least partially exculpated from this false fidelity, for he is hesitant to be abandoned by her—in contrast to the guards, who had tried to escape her. Hence a hint of hope remains even as the apparition wanes; an invitation lingers on even as the spell evaporates with the Princess' mysterious prognosis: "Towards the Spouse goes he who loves,/ And the door opens with no one in sight" (B, p. 207).

In his fraternal colloquy with Tête d'Or, a kind of intuition ("a thing more ancient than I . . . indignant towards my reason and towards my weak senses" B, p. 218) at times not only leads him to distrust nature and society ("I see the sun rising and setting,/ And in nature I find no joy. And as for men, they are like me" B, p. 218), but it even prompts him to doubt his strong friend's power to save him from death: "You've returned, Victorious,/ Resembling for everyone the return of happy days, and me alone you do not save!" (B, 219). His unquenchable thirst (cf. B, pp. 188, 196) is but a symbol of his insatiable desire. He yearns not so much to evade the inevitable ("It's not suffering I fear, and cramp, and the horrible effort to vomit,/ When bile and blood fill my mouth . . ." B, p. 219) as to understand its purpose ("give me light! for I want to see!" B, p. 220) and hopes the hero can assuage this metaphysical thirst.

> But give me some water to drink, for thirst consumes me, so that I may die in peace!
> O brother! I've put my confidence in you, you won't shake me off? (B, p. 220)

But this fierce desire for the ultimate, for light on what lies beyond sense and reason, is what his big brother is least able to satisfy, as he confesses in tears, "I know nothing!" although moments earlier he felt that a supreme and perfect being existed (B, p. 218).

Cross-examined by Cébès, however, who will not take tears for an answer, he is gradually badgered to go beyond "the silence and breath proffered by the black open mouth" to the cruel commands, "Then go to the common pit!" and "Don't hope to subsist, being dead,/ For will man see without his eyes?" (B, pp. 221–222). In this nadir of doubt and despair, Cébès discovers that even the fraternal presence and affection of the greatest of men, though helpful, is inadequate to allay the solitude of death. The brotherly bond provides no companionship in the beyond because it is an insufficient foil to his lack of identity:

> I am dying alone!
> For I do not know who I am myself, and I flee and escape
> like a lost spring!
> So why do you say that you love me? Why lie?
> For who can love me,
> Since I don't exist when I no longer subsist? (B, p. 222)

Neither human strength, nor reason, nor affection, he now discovers, can suppress this fundamental solitude, for they do not suffice to reveal his inner essence, his deeper self, vis-à-vis death. Little wonder that he falls into a momentary frenzy, mistaking his friend for an executioner and trying to escape.

Beyond reason and the senses, however, something ineffable kindles in him, after the pain and frenzy are past—a secret flame, "a gentle forget-me-not of fire which shines sadly on us with a faithful light!" (B, p. 225). Completely detached from earthly ties ("For I no longer cling to anything and am like a branch cut off" B, p. 225), and consequently freed from the bondage of mortality ("The net is broken and I am free" B, p. 226), Cébès finds in an intuitive hope that secret self he had so long sought: "Here is the joy of the final hour, and I am that very joy and the secret that cannot be told" (B, p. 226). Such is the highest potential of the anima,[22] but more than that it is apparently not given to human lips to utter:

O Tête d'Or, as you gave yourself to me,
So do I give myself to you,
And as you have not given me your secret,
So shall I not give you mine.
I am weightless, and I am like something that cannot be held.

(B, p. 227)

He has become subject to a higher center of gravity and, like the apparition of Wisdom at the end of the Princess' playet (B, p. 207), seems to fade out of this life in a lyric enchantment just as night fades into early dawn, the symbol of rebirth: "And the morning . . . is reborning!/ I scent the freshness of the wind. Open the window!" (B, p. 227). With these last words, Cébès' secret self takes wing, heeding the Princess' recent invitation. On this calm note of peace and in the daybreak of hope, death gently dissolves the blood pact made in darkness by these adopted brothers, who had first met in the twilight burial of their mutual but false love.[23]

Cébès' death, however, does not put an end to his influence. His corpse, which is not removed until the end of the act, remains as a constant reminder to Tête d'Or either to join him or to avenge him by seizing the supreme power and conquering the world. Even deeper, though, is his spiritual, intermediary role between the false woman and the true one on the hero's behalf. The burial of the former, with the rejection of her death-dealing wiles and sensual allurements, was a necessary condition for their fraternal, platonic friendship. The "feminine" values of altruism, sacrifice, contemplation, and intuition which Cébès represents are, after all, spiritual and stand midway between the carnal and the supernatural values symbolized respectively by the two women. His friendship for Cébès preserves Tête d'Or from the paralysis of masculine pride and enables him on his Caucasian deathbed to transfer this esteem and affection for a natural anima to the supernatural grace represented by the Princess. He had, indeed, called both of them "servant of God" (B, pp. 186, 192). Thus Cébès' mediatorial action perdures until the death of his companion and counterpart.[24]

Guillemin has suggested that Barrès' definition of his own 1887 book, Sous l'oeil des barbares, as the story of a soul with its two elements, feminine and male, would fit *Tête d'Or*, with Simon and Cébès.[25] This interpretation of their reciprocal attraction seems to be borne out by the ambiguity over the gender of Cébès: "Neither woman nor man" and by the protean aspect of their relationship:

> Shall I call you child or brother? For I was more attentive to you
> Than a father would have been to a pale visage. And my heart was yoked to yours by a stronger and sweeter bond
> Than is an elder brother to his brother, when he plays and talks gently with him in the evening and helps him undo his shoes. (B, p. 226)

True, in the first version Tête d'Or, in a paroxysm of grief, spoke of their "broken nuptials" (A, p. 87) and reassured his dying "spouse" that "never did arms hold such a sister!" (A, p. 88). However, these expressions are not literally erotic but rather metaphors to heighten the intimacy of their spiritual bond. The contexts leave little doubt: "O indissoluble knot, our two innocences embrace, our two souls face to face/ Look at each other in laughter!" and "Contemplate yourself in me!" (A, p. 86); "O all the tenderness that there is in me, I hold you in my hands!" (B, p. 226). And Tête d'Or's final farewell to his departed alter ego etherealizes all their high aspirations: "I was for him like Athens for Argos! . . ./ —O soul, adieu! enter before us into the splendor of Noon!" (B, pp. 232–233). The homosexual imputation, then, derives from an inability to recognize a metaphor or to distinguish between a symbolist tragedy and slice-of-life realism, or to see anything in friendship but a disguised expression of incest.[26]

TÊTE D'OR

Just as Cébès was a Claudel who would like to choose hope and to abandon himself to a greater power, so Tête d'Or too is Claudel, "but an obstinate Claudel. Closed in on his powerful ego, he insists he is self-sufficient. Full of his compacted and impatient genius, he sees what he can 'give' but refuses to 'receive'—even from God." [27] In fact, the note that Romain Rolland entered in his diary March 3, 1889, about Claudel could be very accurately applied to this wild hero, who was then in gestation:

very incoherent . . . with a violent personality and a passionate sensitivity; . . . there exist, in his eyes, only Nature, Instinct, Sensation, Love, Passion, Desire, Fire, Life . . .[28]

Fumet, on the other hand, offers a brilliant, if exaggerated, insight when he claims that Camille Claudel was the principal inspiration for this gladiator. The evidence cited seems rather slight: the long locks, "the perfidious smile of a girl" on the corner of his mouth (B, p. 215), the brash nihilism.[29] The inspiration for this character was surely composite, however—derived partly from Rimbaud, partly from Claudel's own personality, and in part too from that gifted sister he had admired and feared and whom he still remembered so well in his old age as being "hot-headed, indomitable, full of a consuming fire . . . of a frightening violence, with a furious genius for raillery." [30]

These, and perhaps other sources, have of course been thoroughly transposed in the creation of this commanding character, whose dominant trait of masculinity, both physical and moral, has been sufficiently traced by now. It is this dominance of the animus, with its tendency to pride and self-sufficiency, that limits his knowledge of death to that of an outsider, without empathy. His reaction in the face of death is invariably one of horror and revulsion. The note of relief is apparent in his laconic "all right" on learning that his parents are dead (B, p. 173). Obvious, too, is his haste to dissociate himself completely from his dead mistress by the secret and barbarous burial, face down, as well as by immediately disclaiming responsibility for her death: "I did not make her die" (B, p. 172).

This does not require the inference drawn by some critics,[31] however, that Simon Agnel was a neurotic misogynist who symbolically rejected all women in his ritual disposal of his mistress. There is no doubt at all that he had loved her alive. What he hates and rejects is not his mistress but death and corpses, and that is why he curses his native soil for robbing him of her: "Accursed be this land!" (B, p. 174). This theory is substantiated by his

abrupt revulsion from the corpse of Cébès as soon as he realized
that the dear friend he held was dead. Shivering with fright, he
throws aside the still warm body, crying "Horror!" and then: "In
truth it matters little to me that he is dead./ Why should we
lament? Why should we be moved by anything?/ What man of
sense would lend himself to this buffoonery?" (B, p. 228). Having
been first attracted by his mistress' promise of life, he is repelled
when he comes to realize that woman's brief beauty is fleeting
and not worth the candle because it impeded his quest of destiny:

> You see, this taste
> For this being with the face of a child
> Is strange; I think their gaiety is not real.
> They swell up when they are old and become like hens.
> But if she leaves this way, like a handful of sand escaping
> between the fingers . . . (B, p. 177)

His obliteration of all signs of her grave and refusal of any sympathy or tenderness for the departed do not proclaim feelings of
guilt but the desire to bury death itself. Unlike Cébès, he has
no connatural acquaintance with it. Therefore, he cannot appreciate even the possibility of any relationship between life and
death, or between the living and the dead. They are for him diametrical opposites. Death is an external enemy and must be everywhere repulsed, without compassion for its victims and without
comprehension of its nature.

If Cébès could be characterized as an existence in search of its
essence or soul, Simon can to some extent be considered an essence
in search of an existence, in search of an ardent and unbounded
destiny to be confirmed by the whole world: "What have I sought
but, turning my vile eyes hence,/ From the midst of all men the
testimony of myself?" However, it is not mankind but mortality
that first defines his existence: "And it is from here that, girding
its feet, it has come to seek me out" (B, p. 174).

Although Simon is a more complex character than Cébès, having more inner tension than his young friend, who is almost wholly
other-oriented, it may be said in general that he already possesses
a strong self-image or consciousness of his essence. His need is not

so much to discover his own identity as to reveal and impose it
on the world, thereby enlarging and consolidating his existence.
His self-confidence reflects that of his poetic creator:

> I live! Let the rain and time come! Insensitive,
> Bearing my destiny and knowing my delay,
> I walked with a laugh under the horrible country
> Of the stars which a road of milk traverses.[32]

The contrast with Cébès is immediately obvious, and the polarity
of their personalities is best seen in the divergence of their attitudes towards solitude. The younger, as we have seen, feared it;
Simon welcomed it.

The reason is not far to seek. In the one, solitude evoked an
empty inner ache resulting in loneliness. In Simon's case, solitude
was the necessary condition for his self-awareness, so that, like the
poet, he could hear "his corolla cover crack,/ Dismayed, like a
tree in rut, with happiness! [craquer sa robe de corolle,/ Effaré,
comme un arbre en rut, avec bonheur!]" (Th., I, 1156). Thus it
was only while walking alone at night, dimly aware that he would
be abandoned the next day by his mistress' death, that he was free
to discover his deeper self: "I felt this life in me, this thing/ Un-
married, unborn,/ The function which is inside myself" (B, p.
177). How different from the Sartrian solitude that deflates and
crumples and reduces the ego to its minimal consciousness of existence so that it can construct its own essence from scratch! Simon's
essence is not a construct but a donnée seeking expression in a
more extended existence. Self-awareness, impossible without solitude as a nurturing soil, is of course the catalyst in this quest.

The frequency with which he seeks out solitude is thus not surprising: "And I had to gain solitude to nourish darkly this griev-
ance, which I felt swelling up in me" (B, p. 182). While others sated
their souls in familial and social existences, he sought a disciplined
existence apart: "There is no place to receive me; I will not enter
the homes of others. . . . But I will sit on a rock and be rich
enough./ I am my own table and my bed" (B, p. 178). His unsated desire for self-realization propels him far from the beaten
path: "What need is there of a route? I know where I am going."

His intention is to serve mankind the better: "and I will appear before men" (B, p. 181). Without this solitary asceticism and pruning, his vigorous essence might well be sapped of the proud destiny it is called to fulfill:

> May I not lose my soul! This essential sap, this interior
> humidity of myself, this effervescence
> Of which the subject is this person that I am, may I not
> lose it in a vain tuft of grass and flowers! May I grow in my
> unity! May I remain unique and upright! (B, p. 183)

Indeed, it is this need of solitude that inhibits his friendship for Cébès until he can recognize and accept him as not "another" but as his other self, thanks to their mutual quest and perfectly complementary characters. Thus, the only time Simon experiences loneliness is when Cébès dies, for he feels that a goodly part of himself has been removed. Only then, after initiation into death by his better half as it were, can the state of outer solitude vibrate a chord of loneliness within him. This momentary resonance, rendered possible by that partial emptiness in his formerly self-sufficient soul, brings with it the chance for an insider's view of mortality: "He is dead and I am alone./ Am I stone? It seems to me the leaves of the trees are canvas, or iron/ . . . . / Yes, and like an unfeeling trunk of coral,/ I could see my limbs fall off./ Why live? To live or to be dead is all the same to me" (B, p. 228). But the resonance quickly fades as he mutes the chord of mourning and reverts to his former mentality, where being alone is not an inner dread but an external challenge:

> Alone! Against them all! I shall shatter the very snout of
> bestiality with a mailed fist!
> I shall speak before this assembly of skunks and weasels!
> Either I shall die, or I'll establish my own empire! (B, p. 229)

Thus he prefers to hew out his destiny and confront death with the sword instead of the torch: "Sword! Sword!/ Pledge, real hope, you who/ Have vanquished once already,/ I'll lift you like a torch, sign of the immortal victory that I grasp!" (B, p. 246). Or rather, he blindly confuses the two instruments, gratuitously attributing metaphysical power to his physical prowess and proudly identifying the two in his own person: "But I am the fire and the sword! . . . and I'll reunite everything male around me" (B, p. 240). This confusion of means, resulting from his unmitigated hybris, produces his tragic downfall.

Tête d'Or seems compelled to face death constantly, on all fronts, at home and abroad. This is not a psychological obsession with him but a lifelong ontological contest of increasing intensity, an incessant struggle on more uneven terms than those of Jacob with his angel. For this adversary is a demon and invisible to the end; what arms could even a Hercules muster? Still, Tête d'Or is at first successful in repulsing the monster's external threats abroad by his physical feats and courageous leadership, but he is completely defenseless on the home front, on the hearth, where he is interiorly wounded and defeated by the death of the two people he had loved. Each defeat has the twofold result of strengthening both his defense and his offense, as it were. On the one hand, his shell of solitude is hardened; on the other, each death increases his reliance on the sword alone, on physical valor and defiance, to extend the kingdom of the new man against the encroachments of death, even though he has a strong inkling that this type of valor must also end in the ignominy of mortality: "Oh world! Oh myself and my very shameful destiny!/ May I become iron and like a plank of wood!" (B, p. 224). This is especially so after the death of Cébès, his other self, his hearth god and feminine principle, who could have been counted on not only to applaud or listen patiently but also to temper his volatile hybris with the spiritual fire or light of the contemplative's wisdom. But once Cébès is dead, this lesson is lost and the hero's tragic fate all but sealed.

Analyzing the psychological implications of this pursuit of solitude, Morisot discovers a double purpose in it: to be dispossessed of self and to be one's own mother. He sees this as a drama of time, a search for a pure, eternal present. "Man's participation in a mother-absence is what implants him in his mortal condition," he writes. This of course is what Tête d'Or, like Rimbaud's "son of the sun," is too proud to accept, pursuing instead "a passion of innocence, a flight beyond the human." [33]

Solitude, sought so compulsively, begins to take on the image of a kind of antiradiation zone or shell to shield him from the contamination of the temporal and the mortal while he extends and intensifies his existence. Is not this the deeper significance of his efforts to identify with the tree, an effort to root his existence in some stronger soil than the mortal condition? "For, before I was born, and after we have passed on,/ It is there, and the measure of its time is not the same" (B, p. 182).

This protective zone of solitude was meant to inhibit all exchange, which he felt could only diminish his unity of soul and limit his existence. Compared to this basic integrity and fidelity, however mistaken, physical death was of small moment for Tête d'Or, especially since Cébès' demise. "It is indifferent to me whether I live or die" (B, p. 228). Bodily death is now only an inconsequential symbol of that decay within, which is the supreme evil for him. Indeed, in answer to the Princess' prediction that his blood will gush forth like a spring, he seems to accept and desire death in glory as the apotheosis of his destiny:

> Joyfully! Joyfully do I accept the augury! May it be so! May it be so! I desire that day!
> May I go forth and submerge the world! May the vein of my heart be pierced! May my blood leap like a lion, may it spurt forth like a subterranean spring under the drill shaft!
> (B, p. 255)

This explains his recklessness in rushing headlong, unarmed and unmounted, into the jaws of death instead of fleeing with his panicked army: "Then he threw his sword to the ground and, getting off his horse, removed its bit./ And all alone he advanced towards the enemy army . . ." (B, p. 275). Flight would have been compromise, the exchange of his heroic nature for that of a common coward. But this solitude even in death shields his soul from such contamination, while a warrior's death fulfills his destiny, consecrates his existence at the peak of its intensity. So his action is not a suicide induced by frustrated ambitions but a fulfillment of his desire to face death at its worst, that the example of this desire might deliver his followers from their fear of death and from their soul-sapping acquiescence to it. His action produces the same challenge and triumph for his routed troops as did the heart of Bruce of Scotland when it was hurled into the midst of the enemy:

> Three times we charged into that crowd, and finally, bend-
> ing beneath our despair, they dissipated like a flock./ . . . . /
> And we found the King on the ground
> Like a sack of gold flung away by robbers,
> Dead, deprived of life.
> And here we are returning, bringing this booty back with
> us. (B, p. 276)

Tête d'Or's need to insulate the integrity and supposed inno-cence of his essence from contamination with the common con-dition of mortals even while redeeming them explains in large part his insistence on dying alone even after being rescued. There is also a natural scorn for their desertion: "Throw them my clothes! Throw them my remains! For, as they rejected me, I strip myself of them, and the effects of the dead King fall to them" (B, p. 284). But it is mainly because he feels their tears and sympathy would only dilute his heart's integrity that he alienates them and sends them away:

> So that men will not trouble me; for I do not want to go
> down into the earth.
> That will do. Do not bewail me; impose no pompous mark
> of grief on my army.
> Leave without looking back.
> The affair is between me and oblivion. (B, p. 285)

He recognized this solitary death as foreordained, "For this is the place marked out for me to die in. . . . I will die alone!" (B, p. 284). There is a curious, almost humble manifestation of his persistent pride in the wish to die naked and alone, stripped of all human panoply ("As on the day when the maternal dwelling brought forth a male! Strip me!") and wrapped "in a cloth like bread!" (B, p. 279). The purpose appears to be pantheistic—a freer communion with nature, an easier absorption into the universe: "Here I lie to rot, to lose my countenance like a veil,/ Munching on the moon with knots of worms!" (B, p. 285). It is the final attestation of his innate innocence.

This proud insistence on preserving his essence uncontaminated by mortality makes him reject even the spiritual succor and consolation offered by the Princess: "For my part, I want none of you./ Let me die in solitude!" Despite the great admiration and attraction he suddenly developed for her in his final agony, his masculine pride resists the temptation to yield to her entreaties of belief and hope: "You can't undo this hard soul with your woman's nails" (B, p. 295). Thus he is faithful to the end to the prediction he had made in seizing the kingship:

> Yes, and eternity can take on a voice and grieve, it will not shake my royal heart.
> For what can the very chaos of the night of creation do
> Against him whose soul, in the perfection of darkness, in the very horror of silence, remains firm,
> And who fears not suffering and death? (B, p. 248)

This unbending rigidity and pride provide the glory and the key of this tragedy.

His pride is not so indomitable, however, nor his soul so smug as this proclivity to solitude might indicate. If his character were so univocal, it would be a caricature. Tête d'Or is not a strident, garish Gilgamesh. Rather, he has many moments of genuine doubt and hesitancy as to his nature and calling, as seen already in his soliloquy at the end of Part I and in three earlier moments of doubt (B, pp. 182, 185, 186). His first words on returning to the palace after his victory also indicate a surprising uncertainty, as he asks, "Who am I?" (B, p. 216). And in the very ecstasy of his successful seizure of the throne and his self-coronation, as the throng kneels to salute His Highness, he is shaken by profound misgivings:

> Me, King! Ah!/ What say you?/ Who am I? What have I said? What have I done?/ . . . Alas! I myself am weak! . . . I am but a Beggar! I cannot! Come, now!/ If someone out there knows any other way that leads,/ Let him say so and I will live in the grass like a bull. (B, p. 249)

Similar momentary doubts about the validity of his Promethean vision of himself and of ultimate reality had plagued him, of course, beside his friend's deathbed even as now plague him on his own. To Cébès, he admitted a quasi-belief in a Supreme Being: "You put a finger on an old wound in me too!—He exists" (B, p. 218); but then he begged, "Don't interrogate me" (B, p. 220), before finally explaining, "I'll tell you what I know, even though I don't know" (B, p. 221).

But the diametrical difference between the two adoptive brothers is evident even in these shared doubts. Cébès was a "nobody" in need of external help and light to define and identify his essence. The drama of his existence was the gradual discovery of his essence, of his secret self. His was a need, a potency to be filled. Tête d'Or, on the other hand, was a "somebody," highly conscious of his superior essence and of the need to fulfill it in a splendid existence that will communicate the innocence and superiority of his pure essence to all who need filling—to all mankind. His drama is the gradual revelation of his secret self to the world: "At the end, you who are there, will you not recognize who I am?" (B, p. 244). His enterprise is to give the universe back to man, to take up in the poem of his own destiny the destiny of all things, to reach an eternal present, in the words of Morisot. "His drama is that this will to innocence cannot be realized outside a hope that surpasses it." [34] The occasional doubts that beset him in the face of this staggering destiny are but brief blots on his brilliant career, almost an external eclipse, whereas Cébès' dark quandaries belong to his yet undiscovered, undefined essence. And that is why solitude is for the one a problem and for the other a promise.

There is, however, a deeper ambivalence apparent in the hero's character in the curious symbolic mixture of Christ and Prometheus. The fraternal adoption scene opens as Simon evokes the image of the Crucified in promising "I will lift up my arms and hold them extended!" (B, p. 181) and closes on the fulfillment of the promise: "And you, now,/ Here you are like a servant who, before leaving,/ Embraces the tree of the cross./ But this crucified thing with its granite jaw draws towards heaven its chain of brambles/ And a green finch chirps on the battered shoulder" (B, p. 186). Because of the symbolism of the tree, this is clearly an answer to Cébès' evocation of the first Adam in his query, "Have you learned nothing under this tree of knowledge?" (B, p. 183). Simon's decision to undertake the role of redeemer is therefore a fully conscious one as he tells Cébès: "Stay, and let me serve as an altar for you./ Approach and rest your head on my side. . . . Receive my blood on you!" (B, p. 186), and his friend recognizes the sacramental symbol: "And behold I have tasted of your blood, like the first wine that leaves the wine-press!" (B, p. 187). After seizing the throne, Tête d'Or proclaims publicly his messianic aspirations, applying to himself some Isaias-like titles for Emmanuel: "King, Father, Stem of Justice, Seat of Prudence!" (B, p. 251).

The extent to which this messianic aspiration derives from a Promethean impulse of pride has already been seen in his obsession to escape mortal contamination, or rather to decontaminate mortality by transforming becoming into being, aspiring to pure act. Indeed, to the degree that Tête d'Or soils his soul in bloodletting and conquest, the Christ image fades into that of Prometheus. The redeemer image is superseded by that of the enchained rebel in Part III, which opens with an evocation of the Titan: "It is here that the ancient fire Thief was attached,/ When the eagle, like a lightning bolt,/ Clutching him, would pull the liver out of his body" (B, p. 258). Like Prometheus, Tête d'Or rejects defiantly any imposed destiny and exhibits an iron will to be of and for himself.

But the two symbols seem to alternate in the ambivalence of his agony: the divesting of the bleeding corpse, the surgeon's probing of his wounds, the sponge, the winding sheet, and on the other hand the hero's resistance, recrimination, mythic evocations (Mars, Cybele, Isis, Neptune, Gorgonian lamentations, etc.) and despair—"My hope wrenched from my jaws! everything lost!" (B, p. 280). The two images tend to merge, however, in the hero's temporary feeling of darkness and abandonment, in his self-despoliation for the sake of mankind, and in his fidelity to his destiny. Thus it is possible, though by no means mandatory, to see in this merger of symbols the interpenetration of type and antitype, to interpret the pagan myth of Rimbaud's "son of the sun" as a type or foreshadowing of that hero-victim who, on a humbler but more historical hill, brought men a spiritual redemption, a

truer deification, by offering His life to His Father. Such is the
subtle symbolism of Tête d'Or as he commends his soul to his
solar god, makes over his life, essence and existence, to its source:
"O Father,/ Come! O Smile, spread over me!" (B, p. 295). Although he claims to reject the Church in the person of the Princess, his thirst for the infinite takes him beyond the despair of
"death is nothing" and "darkness! darkness" (B, pp. 293, 294) to
a baptism of desire by which death is finally accepted and his essence bequeathed to the care of his deity, where his destiny will
be fulfilled in an existence without end:

> My blood through all its wounds goes to meet you in
> triumph!
> I am dying. Who will relate
> That, dying, my arms outstretched, I held the sun on my
> breast like a wheel?
> O prince clothed in glory,
> Bosom to bosom, you blend with my earthly blood! Drink
> in the slave!
> O lion, you cover me! O eagle, you have me in your grasp!
> (B, p. 296)

Any other interpretation misses the delicate yet abundant symbolism of the play—especially that unmistakable coda of "O Sun!
O Father! O Smile" in an almost harmonic reply to the "O Night!
Mother! Earth! Earth!" of the soliloquy at the end of Part I. By
this symbolism of light, death is not only lyrically charmed out of
its dark terrors, but a personal and metaphysical victory over death
is suggested in moderately transparent symbols, in part derived
from Rimbaud but largely of biblico-liturgical inspiration. This
view is reinforced by the recurrent symbol of the tree, which frames
the hero's enterprise in the Christian cycle of the Promethean fall
of Adam (the tree of knowledge: B, pp. 182–183) and the redemptive victory over death of the second Adam (the tree of life, the
Cross). It is true, of course, that only the Princess, "like the tree
they crucify so that it may bear fruit" (B, p. 300), is actually crucified, but Tête d'Or and she are so closely associated in their sacrificial agony and dying that they are joined symbolically in our
imagination in this Calvary theme. Thus the loss of Paradise is

rectified in the Paschal mystery, Promethean pride rectified and redeemed by the Princess' pardon, the shattered psyche restored by the reintegration of animus and anima.

Such, too, is the persistent explanation offered by Claudel himself, who maintained in 1949 that "this blind, wild force, this instinctive force frequent among all youths, finds something stronger than it in the Princess' presence; it is obliged to submit to her, more or less gnashing its teeth" (MI, p. 51). He pointed out, too, how the conclusion of Tête d'Or resembles that of Rimbaud's Une Saison en enfer ("And in the morning, armed with an ardent patience, we shall enter the splendid cities"), remarking: "Only, this ardent patience is the Princess, is woman, who teaches him it" (MI, p. 52). If Tête d'Or was not explicitly Christian, "perhaps he was so implicitly," said Claudel, and he went on to show the biblical roots of his young hero's quest and to compare the latter's fulfillment to Job's:

And the Almighty, in the end, intervenes and puts Himself so to speak, like the sun, between Job's arms and says to him: "I come not to resolve but to fulfill," as the Gospel says, that is to say that I come to substitute possession for analytical and dialectical responses. (MI, pp. 54–55)

Although the drama is psychologically valid on the human plane, although it is accessible to fuller understanding on the level of myth and symbol, its profoundest meaning lies in the figurative interpretation of the natural and pagan elements in terms of Christian symbolism of light and grace.

Jacques Rivière, one of the first to perceive this symbolism, wrote to Claudel in 1907: "I was first seduced by that bottomless anguish of Cébès . . . by the frightful restlessness of all Tête d'Or. Only later did the explanatory, luminous, triumphant aspect appear to me. . . . At that moment I had a glimmer of hope. . . ." [35] On the other hand, many readers and critics see only its pagan roots. Du Bos, for instance, called it "the only non-Christian work of Claudel's," [36] while Guillemin is convinced that "what he wrote between Christmas, 1886, and Christmas, 1890, bears few traces of that faith which dwells in him" and finds its preservation from "all Catholic contagion" exceeded only by that of the black and frenetic *La Ville*.[37] In an otherwise astute recent study of the play, Marie-Madeleine Fragonard maintains that a "pagan imagination, a disordered spirituality" reigns in full power in *Tête d'Or*, "submerging the few really Christian symbols" in a more coherent mythic design.[38]

The variety of critical response to a work of such rich texture is not surprising, of course; it certifies the tensile strength of its multilayered fabric to elicit and support a wealth of interpretations. The commonest mistake is to fail to see them all together, or to insist on isolating one source, symbol, myth, or meaning to the detriment of the whole. To overemphasize the pagan aspect of *Tête d'Or* is to miss the pattern and purpose of the images and symbols. Interpenetration of several levels, simultaneity of multiple symbols—there is the key to this symbolist drama. Blanchet noted this very well:

> What can be disconcerting here is to see the enormous human indictment and the whole modern revolt borrow the voice of Job, and the Nietzschian will to power open onto God. Claudel rejects nothing. He assumes everything and, through the Cross, gives everything its fulfillment. Tête d'Or is Job justified and Prometheus saved.[39]

The ambivalence in *Tête d'Or* is masterfully controlled and delicately resolved in the highest symbolism. A typical example, to close on, is the supporting theme of the abyss. Already evoked visually by the opening scene at the grave, the growing darkness, and the metaphysical and moral plight of the two youths, it is finally mentioned explicitly by the first guard during the night watch in the palace scene:

> O night! O opening!
> O open door through which comes the wind!
> We had come here and stretched out flat on your threshold.
> But the abyss remained speechless, and man does not penetrate its routes. (B, p. 194)

Here, the abyss is equated with the impenetrable blackness and silence of death.

In his delirious agony, Tête d'Or sees even the sun being swallowed up in the void of the nameless abyss, along with all hope: "It's sinking! It's sinking! It's going down! It's plunging towards the lower abyss!/ It's not the Sun, it's the flaming citadel of our hope!" Moments later, he seems to undergo a personal experience of falling to the bottom of the abyss during a faint: "Death has thrown me back. . . . I had been lying there for centuries of matter. . . . A low, inert, cramped sleep. A detestable oblivion. There, the soul subsists all alone./ I touched the bottom and now I am rising like a diver" (B, pp. 282, 283). This marks, if not a clear turning point in his view of death, at least a subtle symbol of rebirth, of resurrection, as he even hints after his long denunciation of the very idea: "And yet,/ I could say that I am leaving the theater unsated. I am dying and I am alive!" (B, p. 285). Finally, in his last moment, the wisp of hope flames up, and the abyss is no longer a black void to be dreaded but the very source of light, to be loved and embraced. And the door to it is death.

IV

Partage de midi:
The Transformation of Tristan

It is not a drama, it is more than a drama. I seem to be attending an admirable Requiem Mass. The Canticle of Mesa is worthy of Dante, worthy of the Bible. I have always dreamed of dying like your Mesa. But how could you, possessing its meaning and embrace, repudiate such a death? [1]

Such was the enthusiastic reaction of a contemporary author and friend, André Suarès, to a first reading of *Partage de midi* (*Break of Noon*) on, appropriately, All Souls' Day, November 2, 1906. Five days later André Gide wrote in a similar vein: "I experience on certain pages of your drama that trembling of Moses before the burning bush; that secret enthusiasm." [2]

Between them, these two eminent critics early hailed, without however defining, the twin themes of love and death that permeate this whole play, so autobiographical that for over forty years it was known only to the privileged few through two private editions totaling only 250 copies. Suarès was prompted to advise the author to keep it from Mme Claudel. Thirty months later the younger and more ardent Jacques Rivière wrote how profound a responsive chord these two themes had struck in him: "Basically, what I find so seductive in your dramas, especially in *Partage de midi*, is this ethic of fulfillment, of destruction," adding, "My love has brought to full light my instinctive need of perishing." [3]

Little wonder, then, that Claudel decided on a considerable re-

70

vision before allowing Jean-Louis Barrault to produce, in 1948, this literary exorcism of a personal spiritual crisis. The reasons he gave Barrault are easily understandable:

The play has taken on an enormous importance for me. Scarcely a day has passed that I haven't meditated on it. Its performance will have an importance that I shall venture to call "historic." . . . It is a question of my whole life, the meaning of which I was led to try to comprehend. It is a question of much more than literature. (OC, XI, 315)

His primary concern was to prune away the overblown lyricism which he felt smothered the characters and was unsuitable to the rigors of passion.

In 1905, when I composed the first version . . . I strove only to vent my feelings in the language that was then mine. In 1948, . . . the time had come to see if the anecdote could lay claim to the dignity of a parable. . . . (OC, XI, 323)

There is no doubt that he succeeded in rendering his second and third versions less rhapsodic and more visual and dramatic, but the first version is preferable for study and analysis because of its lyrical and psychological superiority.[4] "Each word," wrote François Mauriac of the original, so long accessible only quasi-clandestinely, "seemed irreplaceable to us then." [5] Jacques Madaule, too, felt that the first version is unsurpassable both as a psychological document and in its purely lyric beauty.[6] For all its lyricism, however, this first version has little of the arcane, recondite, and mythical qualities of the original Tête d'Or, and precisely because it is "a kind of unconscious explosion of my inner feelings" (MI, p. 188), it will always loom as a most important landmark of Claudel's spiritual and artistic evolution. Finally, there is the splendid original Canticle of Mesa, which has spellbound so many readers since Suarès and is a kind of lyric sunburst whose rays illuminate the whole drama and radiate far beyond it. From its unifying center we shall attempt to explore the treatment and significance of the theme of death. But first, the context, to provide the setting for the canticle.

Like Tête d'Or, Partage has deep existential roots in the private

life of the author, in a liaison dating from his long return voyage
to his consular post in China in 1900, dejected by the knowledge
that his desire to renounce diplomacy and literature in favor of a
monastic vocation at Ligugé had been rejected, yet pharisaicly in-
flated by a consciousness of his spiritual superiority over most people. In this state of forlorn pride, he was dazzled and enthralled
by a captivating, mischievous married woman, a Polish blonde
named Rosalie, who became both his inspiration and his torture—
especially after she left him in August 1904, bearing their unborn
child, and then evaded the pursuing poet in Belgium eight months
later.[7] His diary contains almost no allusions to this heartache, but
much of his poetry and drama resonate with it,[8] and Mesa and
Ysé are vibrant, authentic incarnations of Paul and Rosalie. The
highlights of this affair are relived in the first two acts, while the
third produces an unexperienced but half-desired climax. Unlike
Tête d'Or, therefore, this play does not attack the problem of death
directly but obliquely, through its relationship with love.

The first act, which occurs in midday brightness on a China-
bound vessel in the Indian Ocean, finds all four characters at the
peak of life, as the title symbolically suggests, resolute on greater
fulfillment and success in the second half of their lives. Ysé, beautiful but unstable and unfulfilled despite a couple of children and
ten years of married life with De Ciz ("the male insect, puny in
appearance but sexually well-endowed around the resplendent
female" OC, XI, 318), easily dominates not only her husband but
the sensuous, nonbelieving adventurer Amalric and the lonely,
religious, but egotistical Mesa.[9] "By her voice, look, hand, and that
long stride of a goddess when necessary," reminisced Claudel, "she
took charge of the chessboard, the human pawns no longer func-
tioning but by her" (OC, XI, 324). De Ciz and Amalric are principally interested in accumulating wealth, whereas the unfilled
aspirations of Ysé and Mesa are more vague, but they quickly come
to feel an odd mutual attraction, a sentiment of belonging to each
other and of having been fated to meet. For the first time in his
life, the self-centered Mesa becomes genuinely interested in another;
for the first time in her life, Ysé is perturbed by a man's religious
depth and reserve, which she cannot fathom. She is attracted by
this mystery which does not open to her; he, restrained by it,

hesitates to betray God for her: "He gives me no rest!/ I have
fled to this extremity of the earth!" (A, p. 1005). Suddenly she
realizes and confesses, "I am the one you would have loved" (A,
p. 1007), and remembering her marriage and the danger of infidelity, she becomes the stronger of the two. Foreseeing dire conse-
quences if the growing infatuation continues, she takes the initia-
tive in forswearing any adulterous love, forcing him to repeat it
three times:

> Playing is out of the question with you. I do not wish to
> give myself completely.
> And I do not want to die, for I am young
> And death is not beautiful. What seems beautiful to me is
> life; how life has gone to my head on this ship!
> That is why everything must be over between us.
> All is said, Mesa. Everything is over between us. Let's agree
> that we won't love one another.
> Say that you won't love me. Ysé, I won't love you.
>
> (A, p. 1009)

Thus in the very calm of noon lurk danger and death, as Suarès
grasped so well: "That is the best stroke of your *Partage*: at the
hour of noon, which is considered shadowless, the Shadow of God
is everywhere: He is the hero of the tragedy." [10]
All four players seem more or less aware of this by the end of Act
One, when the soft and rosy sunset on the chameleon sea, "which
is like a peacock, and like Lakshmi, who is blue in the middle of
a green prism!" (A, p. 1015), evokes not so much paradisaical stability as endless becoming, the "impossibility of stopping in any
place" as Mesa says (A, p. 1016). All realize that they have passed
a certain line, a mysterious demarcation in life symbolized by their
passing Suez, and Amalric's half-jovial, half-earnest banter ("We'll
never return, hurrah! But we'll all be dead next year, hurrah!" A,
p. 1013) evokes the fate that will weigh more and more on Ysé
and Mesa.
With the end of Act One, noon has passed into dusk, symbol of
the imminent moral decline of the four Europeans and of the
sudden death awaiting three of them. In fact, the rest of the drama
is unravelled in an encircling, sunless gloom which parallels

their spiritual descent to the very gates of hell. This climate of mortality had been suggested at the very beginning by the startling image—so much in contrast with the peaceful closing ones (A, p. 1005)—of the Indian Ocean seen as a groveling heifer branded and sacrificed by Baal's plunging knife, in the guise of the sun's piercing rays (A, p. 988). This image of sacrifice and mortality is taken up again and completed by Amalric at sunset: "You should have come to see our steer killed./ It's being skinned now. It's beautiful to behold" (A, p. 1009). The mythopoeic sun-earth-night-woman-death imagery of *Tête d'Or* is here refocused in the following sequence of oppositions, formulated by Watanabé thus:

$$\frac{\text{Sun}}{\text{Sea}} - \frac{\text{Baal}}{\text{Cow}} - \frac{\text{Lover}}{\text{Beloved}} - \frac{\text{Executioner}}{\text{Sacrifice}} - \frac{\text{Male}}{\text{Female}} - \frac{\text{God}}{\text{Soul}}^{11}$$

All but the last member of the equation are explicit, but as Suarès noted above it is the implicit awareness of this ultimate opposition that gives such poignancy and tragic depth to Mesa's odyssey from the solar passion of a religious vocation to a searing erotic passion.

Act Two, set in a Chinese cemetery, suggests death as a constant presence and possibility. In this lugubrious trysting place, chosen perhaps both in quaint defiance of death and in some queer hope of conferring eternity on their forbidden love, occurs Mesa's great lyrical seduction of Ysé's heart, more rapturous than the Tristan-Isolde love duet because freer and unphiltered. This central theme is framed by two interviews with De Ciz. The first provides further motivation and sympathy for Ysé's subsequent infidelity by showing her sincere but unsuccessful efforts to restrain her husband from abandoning her temporarily and to make him understand her frailty and need of protection in her great moral crisis. The second interview consists in his subtle assignment by Mesa to a rendezvous with death, at Ysé's behest, reminiscent of David's treachery towards Uriah in order to acquire Bath-sheba: Mesa cleverly tricks De Ciz into begging for an extended and dangerous mission in the interior.

Act Three takes place in a besieged pagoda in a port city in southern China. After a year of impetuous and imperfect liaison, Ysé has abandoned Mesa to find a more tranquil existence with

Amalric, opting for sensuous fulfillment and domestic tranquillity over unsatisfying romance with a man whose nostalgia for God impeded her total possession of him, even though she was carrying his child.

> How then can he reproach me? For he did not give him-
> self, and I withdrew.
> I too wanted to live and see the earth's sun again and relive
> A normal life and escape that love which was death!
> That is what has happened, and I accept everything.
>
> (A, pp. 1043–44)

And indeed she does, preferring to remain and die with Amalric when the Chinese revolutionaries reattack during the night, rather than to escape with Mesa, who arrives suddenly with a safe-conduct pass for two. To his heart-rending appeal, she responds only with a dazed silence. Mesa, in a struggle with Amalric, is left crippled and unconscious on the floor. Ysé, still dazed, flees with Amalric and the pass to safety, leaving Mesa to reap the benefits of the time bomb Amalric had rigged to avoid being captured alive by the revolutionaries. Such are the circumstances when Mesa awakens in the dark room, lit only by the moon and countless stars, realizes his plight, and takes stock of his destiny in his famous canticle.

An analysis of the canticle reveals that it is highly structured, for although Claudel believed in inspiration and claimed his role was merely to keep his spirit free and attentive for it, he also held that art involved strict, logical composition (OC, XI, 323, 324). The seventy-nine verses, unrhymed and varying greatly in length, are organized into six principal divisions, as follows: I. Monologue: Mesa admires the nocturnal sky (lines 1–10); II. Dialogue with the stars (11–19); III. Interrogation of Christ (20–37); IV. Dawning of understanding (38–50); V. Chastened comprehension of love (51–63); VI. Acceptance of death (64–79). It is clear at a glance that there is no artificial symmetry or symbolism in the number of lines, an artifice that would have weakened the lyrical unfolding of an *état d'âme*. On the other hand, there is both a progressive movement from the material universe to the inner, spiritual world and a center on which the whole pivots or hinges, namely, part three. Finer structural details may be seen in an analysis of the six parts.

I. 1.   Here I am, lying in state!
        And on all sides, right and left, I see the forest of
        torches that surround me.
        Not lighted tapers, but powerful stars, like tall dazzling
        virgins
        Before the face of God, such as one sees in holy paint-
        ings of self-effacing Mary.
   5.   And here am I, man, intelligence,
        Lying on earth, ready to die, as on a solemn catafalque,
        At the bottom of the universe and in the very midst of
        this starry bubble and of the swarm and cult.
        I see the immense clergy of the Night with her Bishops
        and her Patriarchs.
        And I have above me the north star and beside me the
        moon, and the Equator of teeming animals of the vast ex-
        panse
  10.   Called the Milky Way, similar to a strong cincture! [12]

Part I is subdivided into two complementary sections, both moving upwards from earth to the sky. It opens simply enough, with Mesa's recovery of consciousness and an intuition of his plight, stated in terms of liturgy and light, evoking a chapel ablaze with candles around a catafalque or coffin. This image sets the tone for the principal imagery and metaphors of parts I and II. The adjective *ardente* suggests both the ardor of the death agony and the heat and light that will be produced by the explosion of Amalric's bomb, although it is not clear how Mesa would have learned of the bomb. His consciousness, beginning to take stock of the situation, then extends beyond his presence in the dark chamber (suggestive of a tomb) to apprehend the countless stars, seen first as a maze of flaming trees all round him and then individually. Next comes the interpretation of the fiery sky. The negative reference to lighted candles is a brilliant device to link the terminal requiem imagery of lines one and six (*chapelle ardente—catafalque solennel*), while skipping lightly over the banal "tapers" to develop the striking comparison to tall dazzling virgins, perhaps in the elongated

El Greco style. This continuity between man and nature, as well as the latter's value as symbol, is reminiscent of Baudelaire's famous sonnet, "Correspondances," with its evocation of a temple of living pillars and forests of symbols. The sonneteer, however, sees his two-layer world coalescing "in a deep and dark unison," whereas the dramatist and his hero move on to a third dimension, the supernatural. In his mind's eye, Mesa sees the starry virgins bent in adoration like the Virgin before God, Who is still hidden, however, from the sinful wayfarer. His vision, therefore, is dependent on his recollection of the painted imagination of others. This realization completes the movement or cycle by returning our attention to earth.

The second subdivision (5–10) repeats and elaborates the preceding. It begins with an enlarged consciousness of the self, seen as a microcosm of the universe because of the faculty of intelligence by which man can absorb immaterially all things into his being. Mesa the individual, moreover, now becomes a universalized particular, representative of all rational mortals on the threshold of death, that moment of intensified relationship between man and the beyond. The situation is analogous to Simon's in his weeping soliloquy but differing in Mesa's calm reaction and his upward orientation. Even with his feeling of reclining corpselike at the bottom of the universe, he is conscious of being surrounded by a cosmic and clerical throng (7–8). Because he experiences a certain Teilhardian solidarity with the universe, even while helpless in its dark depths, he is neither overwhelmed by solitude nor by a Pascalian fright at the silence of infinite space. In fact, the author believed that space was finite, circumscribed by God's infinity. After *Tête d'Or*, as has been pointed out, his work bears the stamp of his conversion not only to God but also to the notion of limit and measure.[13] This conviction of finitude he derived not only from his long meditation on the two Summas of St. Thomas Aquinas but perhaps even more from his admiration, begun in 1900, for the English poet and convert, Coventry Patmore.[14] Furthermore, his enthusiasm for Poe's *Eureka* and Alfred Russel Wallace's *Man's Place in the Universe* (1903) stemmed from the poetic and scientific confirmation he found there of this essential intuition.[15]

Claudel's feeling of solidarity with the universe is evidently also

Mesa's, as is suggested by the emphasis on the faculty of sight as the means of contact with the cosmos. Thus Mesa refers no less than five times in the first eight lines to the splendid function of this "portable sun" by which he enters into communion through understanding ("to understand is to commune") with the universe.[16] Through this visual power, we are simultaneously at the point of circumference which we see, where sight projects us, and at the center from which we see. External space, with all that it embraces, can therefore be possessed.[17]

Such is the philosophical basis of Mesa's review of the nocturnal universe. Its religious basis, to be developed in the next section, rests on the conviction that this communion with, and vision of, the cosmos may be crowned by the Beatific Vision. In the first part this idea is merely suggested through metaphors and comparisons —most subtly of all by the implied verticality resulting from Mesa's upward vision, which here culminates in tall virgins (3) and in a hierarchy (8) that would presumably be even taller because of their miters and crosiers. Thus is symbolized "the most important half, heaven, the third dimension, the vertical dimension." [18]

This whole cosmology was summed up with greater clarity three years later in his fifth ode, "La Maison fermée [The Closed House]":

> O catch, o miraculous draught! O million stars captured in the mesh of our net. . . .
> We have conquered the world and found Your Creation finite. . . .
> Thus the heavens have no more terror for us, knowing that as far as they stretch
> Your measure is not absent. Your goodness is not absent.
> And we contemplate Your stars in the sky
> Peacefully like sated sheep and grazing flocks. . . .
> (OP, p. 289)

The last two verses indicate the religious dimension of Mesa's optimism and an almost Franciscan fraternalism for all creatures, which is developed further in Part II as he enters into a kind of dialogue with the stars.

II. 11.   Hail, sisters! None of you, for all your shining,
         Supports a spirit, but alone in the center of every-
         thing, Earth
         Has germinated her man, and like a million white
         sheep
         You turn your heads towards her who is as the Pastor
         and Messiah of the worlds!
    15.   Hail, stars! Here I am alone. No priest surrounded by
         a reverent flock
         Will come to bring me Viaticum.
         But already the gates of Heaven
         Break open and the army of all the Saints, bearing
         torches in their hands,
         Advance to meet me, enveloping the terrible Lamb!

Like the first part, this one also has two subdivisions, marked by
the anaphoral invocations, "Hail, sisters!" (11) and "Hail, stars!"
(15), a rhetorical device used to substantiate or enrich his cosmo-
logical analogies as well as to strengthen the successive, wavelike
movements by which he has been propelled through his etherealized
sea to the extremity of his eccentric or centrifugal movement. This
by the end of Part I is the Milky Way (10). Consequently, this
dialogue begins on that far circumference and by a reflex movement flows back to earth, the point of departure and center of all
(12). Poulet compares this dual movement to inhaling and exhaling
and points out that for man to be born and to know (naître et con-
naître) involves not only a radial push outwards of all his force but
also the convergence on himself of the universe.[19] Thus it is no
archaic or recalcitrant belief in a Ptolemaic cosmography that lies
behind his vision of the mass of stars facing the earth like white
sheep around a shepherd. Rather, it is based on a kind of Teilhardian notion of evolution and cosmic convergence by which the
simplest unrational psyche is marvelously related to even the highest form of organized complexity—consciousness—through which
all creation tends towards an Omega point in or beyond a "noo-
sphere." [20] So this starry vision is a symbol of the material world
acknowledging its dependence and subservience to its spiritual
center. The double metonymy of line 14, which completes the

symbol while forming a terminal complement to "Earth" (12), also announces the more Catholic vision in the following section.

If the preceding subdivision opened on the far perimeter of the universe and transcribed a centripetal movement back towards the center of consciousness, the second section begins by further reducing that center to the point that is Mesa. This reduction is achieved through his sudden feeling of solitude, despite his harmony with the universe, at the prospect of dying alone without the viaticum (15–16) before he renders his final accounting to Christ the Judge. No sidereal presence can fill the void of such an absence, which does not, however, prevent all personal encounter between the soul and Christ—an encounter always possible in the intimacies of prayer. And so Mesa moves, in a visionary prayer, beyond the earlier astral periphery into the supernatural dimension of eschatological judgment, imagining the Lamb of the Apocalypse, accompanied by all of Heaven's host, rushing forth to meet him (17–19), not in welcoming acclaim, of course, but for the administration of eternal justice. Thus there is here a double movement, from center to circumference and back to center, complementing and consummating the earlier but lesser movements because God can be found at both extremities. Although the divine transcendence surpasses all human circumference and centrality, the presence of God is more intimate and certain within than without, in the center than on the horizon, for here a Divine Person has encountered man and established a kingdom, center of cosmic convergence.[21] Mesa had long experienced this presence within himself and its perturbations: "He lives, I live; he thinks and I weigh his thought in my heart. . . . I cannot free myself from him who made my heart" (A, p. 1005). And because of this long familiarity, he is emboldened to ask Christ directly for an explanation of his tragic situation, beginning with the bald "Why?" (20) which is the transition to Part III.

Before leaving Part II, however, let us note that the vision of Christ and His saints seeming to sweep down from heaven to the victim, rather than one of the latter being admitted before the throne of the Lamb, is somewhat curious, since in traditional eschatology this grandiose scene is reserved for the consummation of the world and the general judgment. There can be no doubt, however, that this transposition is deliberate on the part of Claudel, since by this time he was not only well acquainted with the scriptures but also with Cardinal Newman's impressive expository poem on death and particular judgment, "The Dream of Gerontius." [22] In a more orthodox fashion than Mesa, Gerontius is conducted, like the translucent soul of Count Orgaz in the El Greco painting, before the throne of Christ by an angel who explains the celestial state of things and how the arriving sinner will have only the briefest glimpse of his Judge until fully purified. Claudel, however, had two very good reasons for his poetic transposition. It serves to substantiate and complete his spiritual cosmology, symbolized in the double movement already noted. On the other hand, it is not a question of real death and judgment yet, but of a preparatory image, a prayerful rehearsal through an examination of conscience, with more than an ounce of misunderstanding, petulance, and fantasy, as we shall see.

III. 20.   Why?
            Why that woman all of a sudden on that boat?
            What did she come along to do with us? Did we
        need her? You alone!
            You alone in me all of a sudden at the birth of Life,
            You have been in me victory and visitation, number
        and astonishment, strength and wonder and sound!
    25.   And this other, did we believe in her? Or that hap-
        piness is in her arms?
            One day I contrived to be Yours and to give myself,
            And that was poor. But what I could,
            I have done, I have given myself,
            And You did not accept me, and so the other one
        took us.
    30.   And in a moment I am going to see You, and I am
        frightened
            And fearful in my Bone of bones!
            And You will interrogate me. And I too will inter-
        rogate You!
            Am I not a man? Why do you play God with me?
            No, God, no! Go ahead, I ask You nothing!

35. You are there and that is enough. Only be quiet,
     O God, so that your creature may understand! He
who has tasted your silence,
Needs no explanation.

This interrogation of Christ about the sense of Mesa's life and destiny has been thoroughly prepared in the course of his nocturnal monologue and the dialogue with the stars. Through his dual undulatory movement, he has attained the peak intensity of harmonic vibration with the exterior world: "We do not stop being born to the world, that is, our knowledge is the work of the circular blooming of our being, which is constantly in a state of vibration . . ." (MI, p. 195). In this state of vibrant awareness, he is most fit to understand himself and to establish contact with the Divine, which is not only transcendental but also immanent, on the level of personal encounter.[23]

With the insistent interrogation of Christ at the opening of this core of the canticle, the calm, expansive lyric tone of the two introductory parts gives way to a tortured dialectic, the simplicity of which contrasts strikingly with the rich imagery of light and liturgy in the preceding sections. The reality behind the symbols having been attained, they become superfluous; besides, in moments of intense emotion, flights of fancy are incongruous. So Mesa goes straight to the quick of his situation: the woman who caused his infidelity to Christ (21) and for whose sake he lies dying. How happy, alive, and full of grace he would still be, had she not suddenly overwhelmed him and displaced Christ in his heart! Even now, in this post-mortem, he cannot comprehend why his fall from grace occurred and remains astonished at the fact itself, so close had been his supposed intimacy with God, so close that he felt God was part of him: "us" (22). Proud as a Pharisee, Mesa tended to be self-sufficient, without need or concern for others. Ysé had helped him recognize this egoism earlier, on the boat:

Mesa: They bore me. I can't stand them.
Ysé: And what do they think of you?
Mesa: I don't know. I don't bother about them. I don't think of others.
Ysé: Mesa, Mesa!

> Mesa: Say, that's true! Do I think only of myself, then?
> Ysé: You're just finding that out? Now try to deny that
> women are good for something.
> You're concerned only with yourself, you're interested only
> in you. (A, p. 1011)

The lesson, however, did not sink in, and only later in this examination of conscience does he come to acknowledge his egoism as the cause of his present woe (49–50). Not that his self-centeredness was wholly innate. Rather, a natural timidity and a desire to excel ("O how I would have liked to see and appropriate everything,/ Not with the eyes or the senses only, but with the understanding of the spirit,/ And to know everything that I might be fully known" A, p. 1005) were reinforced—instead of purified and humanized—by his sudden conversion to God (23).[24] So thorough, in fact, was his experience of God that He became all in all for him (24).

This line (possibly inspired by I Chron. XXIX, 11) powerfully evokes both the grandeur of Mesa's earlier religious experience and his resultant egoism. Although a certain value, drawn from the Claudel-Mesa spiritual etiology, could perhaps be assigned to each of the seven substantives, what counts here is the general tone of a shout of victory, produced by what Gerald Antoine would call a "frenetic accumulation"[25] and Leo Spitzer a "chaotic enumeration."[26] The effect is to weave a hypnotic circle that spirals upwards from polysyllabic multiplicity to the synthesizing unicity of "sound," which both resumes the preceding six qualities (as Sunday does the weekdays[27]) and frames them in a kind of octave by complementing the subject, "You alone." By its enclosure on itself, however, this circle strongly implies the exclusion of other men. Mesa's was an effort to profit by the first and greatest commandment while neglecting the second one, of loving his neighbor as himself.

The movement of the opening lines of his self-examination, then, goes from the most recent event—his sin and death of soul —to that only comparable earlier event, his soul's birth in Christ. It is important to note that each event happened "all of a sudden" (21, 23), testifying not only to its lightning character but even more, perhaps, to Mesa's impulsive, immoderate nature. Thus had Ysé marked him during the voyage, and Mesa had agreed:

> He is quick to give advice.
> One of those fellows always ready to offer his life and who would give it to you,
> On condition they would be rid of you. A real extremist; crotchety, with no moderation. (A, p. 1010)

Hence, what he explicitly predicates of the effect of the first event on himself may be surmised to apply to some extent to his fall from grace, too. It is understandable, however, that he fails to formulate this effect in a crest line similar to line 24, for he is still probing the meaning of Ysé in his life. He can only question this rawer wound in his soul; about the older one, he can make definite statements.

The movement of lines 20–24 is echoed and elaborated in a lower key in the next five lines (25–29), thus continuing the repetitive process or wavelike motion already observed in the first two parts. Again, questions about the woman and statements about his prior life with God. The questions (as before, in lines 21–22) have a deprecatory ring, implying a negative answer. At the same time, Mesa tries to elude full responsibility by pretending to pin part of the blame on Christ: "Did we believe in her? Or that happiness is in her arms?" (25). And yet, even in the cemetery seduction scene he had known the contrary and told her so: "Ah, you are not happiness; you are what takes the place of happiness!" (A, pp. 1027–1028). Elaborating on his religious experience, he spells out his reaction to it in the form of his attempted monastic vocation (26–29). Rather than being a humble submission to, and exploration of, the possibility of serving in the Master's vineyard, however, it had been instead an attempted raid on God. That his apparent generosity with God contained a strong dose of egoism and negativism is clear from his shipboard account to Ysé of the experience:

> I have lived in so much solitude in the midst of men!
> I haven't found my place with them.
> I have nothing to give them and nothing to receive from them.
> I am of no use to anyone.
> And that is why I wanted to give Him back what I had.
>
> (A, p. 1006)

Little wonder he was turned away. As the author himself commented just before the *première* in 1948, "A complete sacrifice, not without ostentation, in which self-love finds all sorts of delicate compensations" (OC, XI, 305). The terms had been Mesa's, not God's (26), and he now humbly recognizes the fact (27). Still, he seems to persist in exculpating himself in part for his subsequent fall by attributing some of the guilt to God, both on the score of his rejection ("sent back naked" A, p. 1006) and because God too, through him, was in a sense ensnared by the woman (29).

The second section (30–37) of Part III is marked by a shift from this review of the past to anxious anticipation of the imminent moment of judgment, which chills him to his marrow (30–31). Like Newman's Gerontius, Mesa expects to receive at least a glimpse of his Judge at that moment, be it ever so different from and inferior to the beatific vision of the saints. Although less mature and less wise than Gerontius, Mesa envisages the judgment not as a revelation and decree of divine justice but as an inquest or interrogation in a divine court where, resting Job-like on his human dignity, he will be free to question the Almighty on a more or less equal basis (32–33). This childish petulance and momentary defiance in such a solemn moment reflect the impetuosity of his character (discerned at once by Ysé) and reveal a certain shallowness or immaturity, a definitely anthropomorphic tendency, in his spiritual life. This throws considerable light on the failure of his attempted vocation and the relative ease of his fall from grace.

Still, if he is momentarily childish, he is spiritually sound at bottom and quickly abandons his plaintiff stance. Modifying without entirely abandoning his tone of familiarity (34, 35), he quits demanding that God justify Himself to man and acknowledges that the Divine Nature is in itself sufficient justification for Divine Justice (35). He now begs only for understanding of the ways that surpass man's, seeking no longer a discursive explanation but sympathetic contact in silent prayer (36–37).

The transition to Part IV (38–50) is provided by a pause, as if to indicate a moment of recollection, and what follows may be construed as its fruit, as a developing prayer, for the tone is considerably more reverent and humble than hitherto. This is immediately apparent from the frequent use of the appellation "O God," first introduced in the fore-prayer (34, 36), and from the absence now of any further justifying questions. Following the normal movement of mental prayer, in the subdivision (38–44) Mesa confesses his sinful nothingness vis-à-vis the Almighty and expresses his sorrow, while in the next section (45–50) he petitions God for mercy.

> IV. 38.   Because I loved You
>   As one loves gold, beautiful to behold, or fruit, but then it is necessary to pounce on it!
>   40.   Glory refuses the curious, love refuses damp holocausts. O God, I execrate my pride!
>   Doubtless I did not love You aright, but for the increase of my knowledge and pleasure.
>   And I have found myself before You like someone who perceives that he is alone.
>   Well then! I have been reapprised of my nothingness, I have tasted anew of the matter I am made of.
>   I have sinned greatly.
>   45.   And now, save me, my God, because I've had enough!
>   Once more it's You and me! You are my God, and I know that You know everything.
>   And I kiss your fatherly hand, and here I am between your hands like a poor thing bleeding and crushed!
>   Like sugar-cane under the roller, like pulp under the press.
>   And because I was an egoist, you punish me this way
>   50.   Through the fearful love of another!

In this new, repentant attitude Mesa recognizes the distance that separates him from God and no longer presumes to use the "we" of familiar equality. Denouncing his earlier pride, he now sees that the nadir of loneliness consists in the absence of God's friendship. In that pit of solitude, he comes to realize that his intrinsic worth is zero, since he was created out of nothing. But this realization of his intrinsic worthlessness is not a new revelation. The double use of the unexpected prefix re- (43) [28] underscores the fact that he had previously experienced this state of utter deflation and humiliation. That would have been in the period of despair prior to his first turning to God. Its renewal now is the more culpable and embarrassing in proportion to the superiority of earlier graces and his more conscious infidelity to them. Consequently, it is only by a new acquaintance with, and acknowledgement of, his innate and acquired misery that he can descend again into that state of humility where pride is purged and where God will hearken to his cry. Out of that misery comes the unfaithful prodigal's lament (44). This hemistich closes the first subdivision, while summing up and emphasizing its theme.

The second subdivision (45–50), rather than merely elaborating, develops this theme of contrition into a plea for divine mercy, without which his humility would be for nought. His inner condition now corresponds to its physical counterpart, so that he is now a total sacrifice. The last two lines (49–50) are a résumé of this part and a transition to the following one, summing up his sin as egoism and acknowledging his suffering as just punishment, while announcing the analysis of the role of love in the economy of salvation.

V. 51.   Ah, I know now
            What love is! And I know what You endured on your
        cross, in your Heart,
            If you loved each of us
            Terribly, as I loved that woman, and the death rattle
        and the suffocating and the vise!
    55.   But I loved her, O my God, and she did that to me! I
        loved her and I am not afraid of You,
            And above love
            There is nothing, and not Yourself! You saw with
        what thirst, O God, and grinding of teeth,
            And dryness and horror and extraction
            I seized hold of her! And she did that to me!
    60.   Ah, You know all about it, You know, You,
            What betrayed love is! Ah, I have no fear of You!
            My crime is great and my love is greater, and your
        death alone, O Father,
            The death that you grant me, death alone can gauge
        them both!

Rather than being clearly subdivided like the preceding parts, this one is built on the polarity of Christ's love for man and of Mesa's love for Ysé. The continuation of his prayer consists in his effort to relate and harmonize these two loves as a means of rapprochement with Christ. The movement from one pole to the other of these two loves is along the axis of suffering, which is the test and gauge of love. The pivot on which this whole passage turns is of course the equivocal use of the term "love." No distinction is even implied between the dark passion and blind desire of eros on the one hand and the tranquil luminosity and altruism of agape on the other. Even less is any distinction implied between the relation of each to death, whether as undertaken or as imposed. What is implied is a certain identity between the two loves and the two deaths, regardless of earthly or heavenly origin, an identity based on the dual similarity of suffering. Apparently denied is the Christian notion that "love has two mansions, one in the spirit and the other in the viscera" and that "the one leads to God and the other to furious egotism or death in dark places where the *gens lucifuga* dwells." [29] Mesa stops there, however, and does not commit the next logical confusion, often found in the modern mystique of sex, the "conviction that delighting in the body is more than delighting in the body—possibly more than delighting in the person, too." Neither in passion nor on reflection would Mesa ever agree with any such theory of depersonalization, epitomizing eros in its most regressive direction, as in the statement, "Eventually, love itself is a form of piety that goes beyond persons." [30] Instead, in this dying meditation he conceives of love, by purification of egoism through suffering, as capable of re-forming the personality, reorienting it towards its highest potential, and reuniting the human person with another person.

Still, his tendency to identify all forms of love—regardless of origin, motive, or object—is philosophically fuzzy, even theologically inadmissible. The very ambivalence of the concept, however, yields a considerable poetic allure through its evocation of the infinite. It is even justified theologically to some degree by another ambivalence, namely, the implication (however slight) that perhaps Mesa's redemption will be effected not so much by the innate quality of his love or any intrinsic value in the quantity or quality of his suffering as by divine mercy. This would bring his reiterated absence of fear of God closer to hope than to his apparent presumption. The hint of this possibility, however, seems smothered by a return to the dominant idea of this part, the supremacy of love (62). Clearly this ambivalent outlook on love involves no effort nor even need to transform eros into agape.

A possible third ambivalence (emphasized in the later versions but barely implied in the original), devolving on the psychological effect rather than the nature of love, would be love's capacity (even in the lower forms of eros) to open the egoist's shell of self-love to outside influence, so that woman becomes an instrument of grace. Here, however, salvation is sought not in any growth in love, from a lower form to a higher, but in an attempted identification of adultery and charity, based on "a redoubtable play on words, tending to confuse those 'two simultaneous postulations' of which Baudelaire spoke." [31] But not on a pun alone. The resolution of this polarity is also attempted, and with better success, by Mesa's desire to graft his sufferings and death on Christ's in a union that would alone expiate his sin (63).

> VI. 64. Let's die, then, and leave this miserable body!
>   Let's leave, my soul, and with a single burst explode this detestable carcass!
>   Here it is, already half broken, dressed like meat on a hook, on the floor like a piece of bitten fruit.
>   Is this me? That broken hulk
>   Is the work of that woman; let her keep it for herself; as for me I am going elsewhere.
>   Already she had destroyed the world for me and nothing for me
> 70. Existed beyond her, and now she is destroying my very self.
>   And here she is, shortening the road for me.
>   Be a witness that I am not pleased with myself!
>   As you can see, that is no longer possible,
>   Nor for me to do without love, immediately, and not tomorrow, but always; you can see I need life itself, the source itself,
> 75. And the difference itself, and that I can no longer, I can no longer stand being deaf and dead!
>   You can see that I am good for nothing here and that I vex everybody
>   And that for all I am a scandal and a question.
>   Therefore take me back and hide me, Father, in your bosom! (A, pp. 1051–54)

In this expansive apogee, dealing with Mesa's acceptance of death, we once more find two subdivisions, the first (64–71) being a parenthesis in his prayer to Christ in which he addresses his soul momentarily. This in turn is composed of two sections: a desire to be freed of his broken body (64–66) and an attribution of destructiveness to Ysé. A strong negative, deprecatory tone towards his body pervades this aside to his soul. He is in a hurry to leave it behind, even to see it destroyed utterly. Such impetuosity is hardly surprising in the light of the two earlier lightning seductions of his heart (21, 23), and yet it reflects not so much an eagerness for death as—like the first two instances—a desire to join the one loved, a desire formulated at the end of the canticle. He bequeaths his remnants to the traitorous woman responsible for his condition, seeing her destructiveness as twofold (69–70). First she obliterated the world, insofar as she seemed for awhile to replace and subsume everything for him herself: "It is true, then, Mesa, that I alone exist and that you repudiate the world . . . ?" "Ysé, there is no longer anyone else in the world" (A, pp. 1029, 1031). And now she has lured him to his own death. In time, Ysé will admit to far worse.

Violence, cruelty, and destructiveness existed in *Tête d'Or*, but it is in *Partage* for the first time that "another" intervenes to determine the fate of the main character with a force akin to that of classical fatality. In this sense, *Partage* is at the opposite pole from *Tête d'Or*, for the action is no longer led by a male fascinated by a transcendent call to liberate humanity from its mortality but by a fascinating face, a promise of grace that cannot be kept—like Lechy Elbernon (*L'Échange*, 1901) and Lâla (*La Ville*, 1897). Indeed, the force and success of Ysé as a character, Claudel's first fully flesh-and-blood female, owes perhaps as much to his earlier experimentations with these somewhat shadowy temptresses as to his personal experience of illicit love. Even the pattern of Ysé's love and betrayal was prefigured by Lâla's shuffling from Lambert to Coeuvre, to whom she gives a son, then on to Avare and finally back to Coeuvre at the end. But Lâla exercises almost no hold on her partners, whereas Ysé, by her magnetic and erratic personality, is felt as more of a dramatic force than a symbol.[32]

Readdressing Christ, in purified tones (72–79), Mesa invokes

Him as witness that his egoism is definitively past. His former life had been a living death and deafness. Now he needs to escape from this trap of the self into the vivifying embrace of Him who is wholly "other." By now equating love with "the difference itself," he recognizes at last the impossibility of subsisting on the finite self. And so the canticle concludes with the plaintive prodigal's confession of ruin and worthlessness, a plea for readmission into the paternal mansion.

The spiraling movement of the canticle has thus brought Mesa—in spirit, at least—up from the dark pit of egotistic solitude through a sense of kinship with the cosmos and a contrite recognition of his betrayal of Christ to a desire for dissolution and union in spirit with Him.

GOD'S REPLY

At least ostensibly, it is not God but Ysé who answers Mesa's canticle and comes to him. In the light of her equally impulsive and much more vacillating nature, her sudden return is not beyond belief, although she cannot explain it herself: "There is no need for explanation. My heart. My heart with yours, so you can feel it" (B, p. 1147).[33] In the last version the return is also motivated by her desire to bring Mesa pardon and hope (B, pp. 1145–46) and to teach him his true name:

> Your true name. This true name of yours which I alone know.
> My soul which is your name, my soul which is your key, my soul which is your cause. This name of yours which is inseparable from me
> And which it will take force for you to snatch from me.
> (B, p. 1149)

In the original version, the only explanation seems to be her continuous daze, "in a state of hypnotic trance" (A, p. 1054), which lasted from Mesa's arrival in the doomed pagoda through her flight with Amalic and is dissipated only now as Mesa lightly places his hand on her head, a gesture that seems to restore her speech:

"Mesa, I am Ysé. It is I" (A, p. 1055). This magic talisman of the true name (emphasized in the above quotation from the final version) works its full charm on both lovers in this fourth use.[34] Each time it is pronounced almost by impulse, automatically, but not until this instance does it lead to true mutual comprehension of themselves and of their entwined destiny. Most of their death duet is devoted to exploring this mystery.

In this process towards ultimate recognition, the first step is verification of the reality of the enterprise. Ysé, released from her spell, brings wounded Mesa the reassurance that "the dreams are ended. Only the truth remains" (A, p. 1055). Persuaded—by her voice, long tresses, and bare arm draped across his knees—that he is not dreaming, Mesa tries to deepen their union into a spiritual dimension. Her very presence is evidence enough of her repentance for the earlier betrayal with Amalric, but only a spiritual union will provide the healing balm by which he can revoke his recent contempt and renunciation of her and reunite their hearts. Ysé, however, with her impetuous intuition, is already a step ahead of him in understanding their relationship:

> You don't fully know who I am, but now I see clearly who you are and what you think you are,
> Full of glory and light, a creature of God! And I see you love me,
> And that you are given to me, and I am with you in an ineffable tranquillity. (A, p. 1055)

The implication is that she has secretly intuited and now testifies to Mesa's recovery of grace in his prayer to Christ, for she clearly feels that her own salvation depends on her union with him. She is so deeply consoled thereby that, with a little effort, she manages to persuade him, too, that there is nothing more to fear: "no longer anything but love forever, no longer anything but eternity with you!" (A, p. 1055). Squatting at his feet, she acknowledges herself his spiritual inferior and dependent: "O my shining light, O my male sublime, you see me at your knees as one blind and yearning!" (A, p. 1056). It is a fine description of the two loves, of animus and anima, and will be elaborated by Mesa in the final lines of the play.

Mesa is understandably gratified at this total submission, soul and salvation, of his former fugitive. One suspects, in fact, that his fascination for her all along was not merely of a carnal nature but that he was even more captivated by her dark, unseizable soul. Had he not said, in the very storm of passion, "Here in my arms is the soul that has another sex, and I am your male" (A, p. 1031)? Its elusiveness, as well as his egoism, precluded the success of their liaison: "You were unable to uproot it, to take it, and I couldn't give it" (A, p. 1047). But now that her surrender is spiritual, the union of their inmost personalities is possible on an eternal basis and is compatible with his highest aspirations towards the God-head, to which he can carry her as his prey:

> I have vanquished you at last! The whole prey heavy on my heart, and not a limb stirring
> That does not yield to a stronger member, to the will of the ascending bird, of the vertical eagle!
> I feel the weight that yields to the wing, and I bear away with me this heavy body
> Which is my mother and sister and wife and origin! (A, p. 1056)

In his soul's surge towards God, he no longer mounts alone but undertakes to bear the dear burden of his earthly joy and anguish, who now, in the spiritual sphere of the "superflesh," has become the key and complement of his masculine principle (OC, XI, 327–328). The egoism of the solitary animus and the jealousy inherent in the anima are neutralized and sublimated in the high harmony of this victory:

> Here is consummated
> The victory of man over woman and the interpossession
> Of selfishness and jealousy.
> You say joy? But here is the joy that is above joy, like fire that becomes a flame and desire that becomes justice, and love that becomes acceptance. (A, pp. 1056–57)

Thus, after his prayer to Christ for an exclusive union with Him, Mesa comes to realize that heaven is a society. Ysé's return takes on the character of a token or pledge of Christ's forgiveness and friendship, not only by calming his fears and teaching him courage but above all by the prospect of a mystical espousal, an eternal union of souls, with her who had been the impossible, the forbidden one: "And our marriage/ Like the working of a star and like a being using his double heart!" (A, p. 1057). By this interiorization and spiritualization of their love, they reverse the disastrous dissipation of Tristan and Isolde, for they move from the torments of a guilty and unstable liaison to a union and joy of soul through purification and ascension.

This movement is not uninterrupted, however. Ysé has a relapse from rhapsody to reality as she recalls her crimes, begging Mesa to let her confess them. Without Mesa's forgiveness, how can she hope for God's? Forgiven by her paramour, though, she may legitimately presume that God's mercy will not be outdone. And so to clear her conscience, she begins with the most recent and culpable, at least in Mesa's eyes—the death of their child, for which she was evidently responsible. She prays to be delivered from her former pride, but her crimes come so vividly to mind in this Baudelairian vision of her husband's end that she begins to doubt the possibility of being saved:

> A miserable straw hut, a dead man
> With a frightful face, topped by a huge tuft of black hair!
> Twisted up by cholera in a stinking blanket. No more of
> the stale air I used to hate!
> And from the roof a drop of water keeps
> Falling right on the pupil of his gaping eye.
> And outside a rain such as I've never seen, a deluge, a
> forest as dark as an arum leaf.
> Each rope of rain as big as a lead pipe. (A, p. 1058)

She feels equally blameworthy for her two sons by De Ciz: "I think I deceived, abandoned, and assassinated them!" She does indeed seem to be ill-starred beyond comprehension: "I don't understand! I'm only an unfortunate woman! How did all this happen?" (A, p. 1059).

The answer, as Mesa realizes full well, is not in the stars but in the destructive quality of their illicit love: "Love brought it all about." Ysé has in fact conveniently forgotten how explicitly she knew and wished this destruction. It was inseparable from her lucid consent to adultery, as it is in some degree in every submission to this passion: all for love, and the world well lost. Thus, in the cemetery paroxysm, she was willing to let her whole family suffer extinction in order to heighten her "ineffable iniquity":

> So there are the past and the future together
> Renounced, and there is no more family or children or husband or friends. . . .
> But what we desire is not to create but to destroy, and oh!
> That there no longer be anything other than you and me
> . . . and our frenzy and tenderness, and the will to destroy you and to be no longer bothered
> Detestably by these clothes of flesh. . . . (A, p. 1030)

This will to destroy all in the ecstasy of passion extends even to a dissolution of self in the vapors of love, for this exclusive desire seeks a sensation of the absolute by trying to eternalize the instant and resolve the solid flesh and palpable time into the unlimited:

> Ah, it is not happiness I bring you but death, and mine with it.
> But what does it matter to me if I make you die,
> And myself and everything, provided that at that price which is you and me,
> When we are given, thrown about, yanked up, lacerated, consumed,
> I can feel your soul, for a moment which is all eternity, touching,
> Gripping mine like quicklime blistering and hissing through sand! (A, p. 1030)

This curious chemical simile is also a key Claudelian metaphor of the fundamental analogy between human and divine love, appearing earlier in *Art poétique* (OP, p. 199). Consequently, Ysé is probably not uttering a formal death wish so much as yearning and dreaming of infinite fulfillment. The notion of death serves her as the ultimate measure of erasing all concept of limitation. In the first phase, the lovers find the world dead, subjectively, through

their repudiation of it; the resultant exclusivity makes for a pro-
founder, more concentrated union between them. That is precisely
why she is willing for her husband to die. In the final stage, they may
even wish to escape from the boundaries of the body, but always
with a view to a more fervent union of soul.

Now, to the despondent and repentant Ysé, Mesa develops his
answer about love being responsible for everything, trying to bring
her peace and pardon by showing how their love, formerly illicit
and destructive, can become their means of redemption. In a teas-
ing tone, as an antidote to her momentary despair, he boldly inquires if they no longer define good by what promotes their love
and evil by what is opposed to it (A, p. 1059). Considered out of
context, the question borders on the blasphemous and has troubled
more than one critic.[35] In context, however, it is not a flaunting
of egoism but a spur to be faithful to the ultimate implications of
love, which at its zenith is so entwined with death: "Even death
does not cut cleaner" (A, p. 1059). Their earlier love was so pas-
sionately exclusive. as to be necessarily destructive in character,
both of their everyday world and of inner grace. Their new, purified
love, Mesa is pleading, while unable to recall the dead to life, can
restore their own souls to friendship with God if they now offer
their own deaths in as deliberate a penitential intention as they did
the others' in a passionate one. Having realized love's destructiveness, they must now realize its purifying possibilities by accepting
the destruction of their own bodies as a just payment on the debts
incurred by their illicit love. This solution—at which Mesa had just
arrived in his canticle and to which he now brings Ysé—is thus
seen for what it is: a poor, but acceptable, substitute for the innocence of those who have never deviated from the first commandment of loving God above all else. Repentance is not exalted above
fidelity but is a means of redeeming evil. We recognize here a primary Claudelian theme, the Augustinian "even sin serves": "But
even evil/Includes its own good which must not be lost" (A, p.
1059).

Consequently, the similar intensity of emotion and of destruction
must not lead to a confusion or identification of the two events,
for Mesa's reconciliation with, and aspiration towards, God show
that he distinguishes between the annihilation aspect of the ceme-

tery seduction and the purifying possibility of this reunion for death. Thus it is superficial to claim that the death of the husband, which frees Ysé, sanctifies her love for Mesa,[36] for Christian tradition prefers the purification of the passions to their suppression. It is not De Ciz's death that sanctifies their love but their repentance and submission to God. A more cogent exposé of apparent theological equivocation, especially in Act III, is made by Bernard Howells.[37] He sees it as combining the romantic myth of fatal passion with a Christian sense of responsibility for salvation and damnation, leading to a borderline theology of grace and liberty. While he is both more perceptive and less condemnatory than previous critics, and while he admits that "the fatalism is of a borderline variety," [38] he does not seem to descry sufficiently the lovers' repentance and submission to God, their embrace of death largely in retribution and as a just penalty for their crimes. Given Claudel's prior and prevailing orientation, we must qualify the statement that Mesa-Claudel "turned to religion as an excuse for his inability to give himself over unreservedly" to an adulterous liaison.[39] It would seem more accurate to say that this inability is not ultimately a neurotic negation but results from a superior passion—a preoccupation with the mystery of death and the question of eternity.

Good drama, of course, is concerned primarily with human emotions, not with theological or philosophical doctrines; if something gets slighted, it should not be the dramatic plausibility, the psychological truth. Fortunately, in the case of *Partage de midi*, despite some surface ambiguity, there is also a stratum of orthodoxy beneath its emotional structure. For in a sense Mesa is both priest and victim in this dramatic design of a fall and redemption, recalling the Paschal experience in terms of human love.[40] In fact, much of the ambiguity derives from Mallarmé's symbolist dream, like Wagner's, of a "total" art, one that would incorporate the resources of religion and liturgy. Although Claudel objected to much of what Mallarmé expounded in his 1895 article on "Catholicism," he was deeply impressed with his notion of substituting the Passion of man for men's passions. "It is a question of the only human drama," he wrote to Suarès in February, 1908, "that of the Fall and the Redemption, the Passion of man, as Mallarmé used to say." [41] Retaining Mallarmé's equivalence of violent love with re-

ligious sacrifice, Claudel sees Christ's Passion as exemplary of all
men's passion and sees it refracted anew in Mesa's experience of
love and death. Hence the apparent brazenness of his analogies.
Misleading and strong as they are, however, they remain more
allusions than identifications.

Having shown Ysé the way to peace and pardon after her momentary relapse from the transport of spiritual recognition, Mesa
now returns to the idea of their eternal union by proposing that
they marry one another on the spot. By their sinful complicity,
they had contracted certain sinful relationships (I Cor. VI, 16). By
marriage these can be purified and ennobled, their destiny and
attraction of soul fulfilled. And so they confer the sacrament, their
"Order," on each other, thus consummating Mesa's movement from
self-centeredness to alterity, via carnality and crime, in a redemptive reunion. Consequently, their marriage before the clergy of the
night, while suggesting to the unwary that Mesa's only penance "for
coveting his neighbor's wife is taking her for eternity," [42] is in fact
as superior to their earlier illicit love as agape is to eros, despite
the possibility of communication and movement from the lower
to the higher. Such a movement is indeed suggested in Mesa's
triple definition of their marital consent (parole), which includes
the confession (l'aveu) of past sin (while also suggesting the recognition of their interdependence, if we advert to the ancient feudal
ceremony between vassal and lord), the performance of a penance
(death, in this case), and the expectation of an eternal reward,
seen as the divine ratification of their union along the lines of a
religious community (notre Ordre, A, p. 1060).

The movement is a qualitative one, a purification and reorientation of soul, not a mere intensification. This brings them trust in
God, not ultimate defiance of creation and of its source, as in so
many love-deaths. In contrast to her earlier fear of death (A, p.
1023) and to her recent despairing desire to die with Amalric (A,
p. 1040), Ysé now surmounts fear and seeks to reassure Mesa.
When she declares that "woman, mother of man," is not astounded
at death, she seems to echo a famous Mallarmé line in "L'An-
goisse" which Claudel considered one of the finest verses in the
language: "You who about the void know more than do the
dead." [43] What fear remains in Mesa till the end is only the in-

evitable quivering of the flesh at the prospect of its dispersal: "The ignoble flesh quivers, but the spirit remains inextinguishable" (A, p. 1062).

As a pendant to Mesa's demonstration that love was responsible for everything (A, p. 1059), Ysé in turn sums up their past as the basis of their eternal union:

> And now all the past with its good and all its evil
> And repentance between the two like a cement is no more
> anything but a sort of base and a beginning and a single body
> With what is, what is at present forever.
> I was jealous, Mesa, and I saw you melancholy and knew
> That you were hiding part of yourself from me.
> But now I see all and am fully seen, and there is only love
> between us,
> Pristine and pure now, vivifying one another, in an inex-
> pressible
> Interpenetration, in the pleasure of the conjugal comple-
> ment, man and woman like two great spiritual animals.
>   (A, p. 1061)

This bold summary of their destiny, in line with Claudel's idea of a single Passion, repudiates any Calvinistic dichotomy between eros and agape. Implicit, instead, is the possibility of conciliation between human nature and grace, as between the animus and the anima.[44] For their "inexpressible interpenetration" embraces the whole person, rising to the higher faculties from the lower ones, which are never renounced, for in traditional Christian eschatology the body will be reunited with the soul at the end of time in a resurrection as glorious as Christ's. However, Ysé's exultation that now she will no longer have to worry about growing old and losing her beauty is closer to a naive carry-over of her earlier attitudes than an affirmation of hope in the resurrection. Still, it is not without its Christian significance in that she looks on death less as an agent to arrest her process of aging than as a catalyst to transform her earthly beauty into the eternal radiance of the spirit.

These moments between their "marriage" and the explosion of the bomb might be termed a frontier region of flux between time and eternity, sense and spirit. Ysé's role here is the greater, for she

is at once Beatrice (as she stands with her arms outstretched like
a cross) and Ophelia (with her eyes closed and her long tresses
undulating in the wind). She seems to advance towards the brink
by voluntarily relinquishing the faculty of sight and then that of
hearing, inviting Mesa to prepare to do the same after a last glance
at her visage. This image he can retain in the hereafter as a kind
of keepsake. As for the final sound she wants to hear from him,
it would serve as her means of self-knowledge (like a voiceprint,
perhaps) and of passage like a pure stream into the beyond, as well
as of eternal union with Mesa:

> Just give me the pitch, that I may
> Gush forth and be heard with my own golden sound for
> ears
> Starting, surging like a pure song and like a voice true to
> your voice, your eternal Ysé better than brass and drum!
> (A, p. 1063)

This implicit metaphor of water music has sustained some odd interpretations.[45] Surely her "own golden sound" is the magic name,
properly intoned by her true love, which will free her inmost essence and make it blossom in an ultimate sense she had not fore-
seen when she told Mesa aboard ship:

> There is no need that it be very loud, but if you call me by
> my name,
> By your name, by a name that you know and I don't, hear-
> ing it,
> There is a woman in me that will be unable to keep from
> answering you. (A, p. 1008)

This golden sound will reverberate so intimately through her whole
soul when it has attained its eternal bloom that the sound itself will
constitute her faculty of hearing, for she will vibrate like fine
crystal to her own secret note. This eternal harmony, purer than
the sound of brass and drum (le cuivre et la peau d'âne), will allow
an unending, most intimate duet with Mesa.

Could this ecstatic swansong have been inspired by Isolde's liebestod? Very probably, just as Mesa's canticle may have been partly

inspired by the lament of Amfortas in *Parsifal* (I, 2).[46] Claudel himself has told of his devout enthusiasm as a student for the first two acts of *Tristan und Isolde* ("like a First Communion memory") and of his emotion on leafing through the score containing Berlioz' "furious" notations, at the Bibliothèque nationale (*OPR*, p. 869). In each case there is a reprise of the voluptuous theme of the love duet of Act II, a sense of gradual dissolution and ecstasy incited predominantly not through sight but by a unique supernatural melody which accompanies the heroine's passage into the beyond, like cascading waves that penetrate and vibrate the whole being. On the other hand, and long before his explicit denunciation in 1938 of Wagner's poisonous music and the "dismal immorality of Tristan," "where the demons of pleasure and carnal tedium disport themselves," [47] Claudel thus turned the Tristan myth inside out by Christianizing it. Isolde's soul seems to become soaked up in a sea of nothingness as her personality melts away into a pantheistic universe ruled not by a personal God but by violent forces of nature, a chaos of infinite movement that promises liberation beyond the walls of her individuality. Her highest rapture comes with the absorption of her individual consciousness and personality into the surging cosmic forces of a Schopenhauerian Nirvana.[48] Ysé's dissolution is in diametrical contrast, for she mounts towards a personal God to show her husband the way to an eternal union in His company. This will be achieved not merely through liberation from the body but by an increase or accentuation of their own personalities and awareness. Their death together is a positive act, an affirmation of their past and of the destiny in which they hope. Their joy and optimism are in sharp contrast with the Wagnerian melancholy and pessimism. Death for Wagner is an eternal night of love, characterized by erotic escapism from the burdens of life and individuality into an ecstatic dissolution of being. Death for Claudel permits a purification and accentuation of the person in the light and love of God, even in the company of the lover whose eyes obliquely refracted these divine attributes.[49]

Ysé's adulterous past, then, enhances her new Beatrician role as a vertical Ophelia floating free of earth while inviting Mesa to follow her:

> Rise, fractured form, and see me as a listening dancer,
> Whose jubilant little feet are caught up in the irresistible tempo!
> Follow me, delay no more!
> Great God, here I am, rippling, rolling, uprooted, leaning on the very subsistence of light as if on the wing beneath the wave!
> O Mesa, this is the break of midnight, and I am ready to be liberated,
> The sign for the last time of these great tresses unfurled in the wind of Death! [50]

Insofar as Ysé beckons and incites Mesa to follow her to God, Beatrice is evoked.[51] To the extent that she is responsible for their dying, for riding out of this life on a midnight tide, Ophelia is suggested. The predominance in Claudel of the "water-dark-woman" group as associated with death has been demonstrated in detail.[52] Bachelard calls the water of death the Ophelia complex when it is a desired element and claims that an aquatic image is evoked as soon as a woman's hair undulates or waves.[53] Though she is no true suicide, Ysé lucidly embraces her death and with her floating tresses beckons Mesa to join her. She chooses to fulfill the presage she had early in Act II: "There is a certain death/ That I could give him. . . . Instead of growing old/ Tediously day by day, isn't it better not to age,/ To give all, in a single swoop . . . in a burst of laughter, in a triumphant generosity/ While I am young and splendid, and to perish with the one I cause to perish . . ." (A, pp. 1021–22). However, by the transposition of water into wind, with its suggestion of spirit and breath, Ophelia becomes Beatrice and her golden tresses become a token of their reunion hereafter, of the flames of their unquenchable love.[54]

Mesa looks with equal optimism to their reunion in the bright glory of God:

> Adieu, I've seen you for the last time!
> By what long, painful, still distant routes shall we,
> Still weighing on one another,
> Guide our souls in labor?
> Remember, remember the sign!

Mine is not one of vain hair blowing about, and a dainty
hanky,
But, all veils gone, myself, fine fulminous flame, the magnificent male in the glory of God,
Man in the splendor of August, the vanquishing Spirit in
the transfiguration of Noon! (A, pp. 1063–64)

His sign, complementary to Ysé's, is the more interior light of the
intellect, as she had just recognized: "O my shining light, O my
male sublime!" (A, p. 1056). Stripped of its veils of the senses and
removed from the dark night of faith, it will be their guide to recognition and their consolation along the purgatorial paths to God's
presence.[55] "For the shadows are exterior, the light is within./ You
can see only with the sun and know only with God in you" (OP,
p. 284). Because his faith and hope have remained alive like the
solitary sanctuary lamp that "keeps watch in the dark night/ And
the layers of shadows will not suffice/ To quench the tiny fire"
(A, p. 1062), the sun of passion and desire will be transfigured by
God into an eternal noon of the spirit.

Mesa's apotheosis in fire and divine glory is more explicitly
Christian than Tête d'Or's symbolic embrace of the sun, and their
common imagery of bedazzlement casts more of a religious aura
back on Tête d'Or than of a Nietzschian cloud on Mesa, despite
certain curious intimations to the contrary.[56] If the many biblical
expressions of the play are not convincing, the contemporary cita-
tions in his diary from the Bible and St. Gregory, involving gold,
light, stars, the moon, and the like, should be persuasive.[57] Finally,
the fact that an earlier manuscript contains "in the splendor of the
Mass of August" should remove all doubt.[58] Whatever Claudel's
reason for omitting "the Mass," his solar inspiration is clearly liturgical, not Nietzschian, and derives from the Mass of the Transfiguration, August 6, a feast celebrating the splendor of Christ, of
which Mesa and all Christians are coheirs. We can imagine the
significance he attached to this feast—it was also his birthday.

O'Brien has shown the complementary importance and range of
gold, sun, and water in Claudel, the first two elements signifying
male violence, intensity, and divine light but including a subconnotation of death. Conversely, water is associated with love,

desire, woman, darkness, death but includes a strong subconnotation of the sacramental life. Both elements thus serve to bridge the frontiers between the carnal and the spiritual dimensions, without confusing them. This "Rhinegold" yields both "self-knowledge and a divine talisman sunk in the darkness of the waters of love" and through the current of power the poet passes from passion to God.[59] Here, in the denouement of *Partage de midi*, the current of power is supplied both by the light waves of the undulating hair of the "listening dancer," which correspond to the "fine fulminous flame" of her sublime male, and by the sound waves of her pure chant, which echo in subdued tones the eschatological trumpet blasts evoked by Mesa:

> On the one hand, beyond the tomb I hear the Exterminator's bugle warming up,
> The summons of the judicial instrument in the incommensurable solitude,
> On the other, at the voice of the incorruptible brass,
> All the events of my life unfold at once before my eyes
> Like the fading sounds of a distant trumpet! (A, p. 1062)

What is significant here is that, although each partner is gliding from sensual to supernal use of sight and sound, the movement between the two poles parallels that between the animus and anima. The feminine element reflects, but in softened moonlit tones, the noonday glare and masculine brass of Mesa's animus. Each has his own unique yet complementary mode of embracing death, but the impetuosity of their generosity is identical: "We don't know how to give ourselves in moderation, Ysé! So let's give ourselves in a single swoop!" (A, p. 1032).

The theologically squeamish may squirm over the doctrinal implications of salvation attained under the impulse of passion, despite the Gospel disdain for the lukewarm. Nor is there any denying that "the voluptuousness of Claudel's religious concepts is staggering," as Agnes Meyer felt (CCC, VI, 198), and appalls many sensibilities. Still, when rightly read, the drama contains no serious theological flaw—just the appearance of heresy through dramatic exaggeration and bold metaphors. But neither is there, on the other hand, any high heroism of renunciation and mystic union here, such as will be found in two later masterpieces, *L'Annonce fait à Marie* and *Le Soulier de satin*.

This mediocre spirituality, however, is far outweighed by the psychological validity and intensity of these lovers facing death, by their transcendent confrontation of eros and thanatos. *Partage de midi* illustrates most profoundly the truth recently formulated by Dr. Rollo May, that love is not only enriched by our sense of mortality but constituted by it, that love is the cross-fertilization of mortality and immortality.[60] Claudel's genius is to suggest further that love cannot finally transcend death's darkness until it is transformed into agape.

V

L'Annonce faite à Marie:

Life and Death Reconciled

I nourish a certain pride at having been the first man of the theater to feel that the tragedies of Paul Claudel . . . were playable and that they would one day be taken for the gospel of a regenerated scenic art.[1]

With Ysé partially exorcised and her real-life double obviously inaccessible to the pursuing poet, Claudel painfully emerged from his season in hell during a lengthy visit in France. It culminated in marriage March 15, 1906, to a young lady of Lyons, and they set sail for China March 18, where he became consul at Tientsin. This new period was one of calm, undramatic happiness, expressed lyrically in certain Hymns and four more Great Odes. And yet, the shadow of death is constant: "O death of myself and of everything, in which I have to suffer creation!" (*OP*, p. 273). Just before his marriage, he had jotted in his diary: "First sounds of Death. Warning to destroy passion" (*J*, I, 34). Despite the continuing concern, the tone is calmer and more confident, however, and at the end of the fifth ode he turns at length towards the dead in fraternal compassion, pity, and communion (*OP*, pp. 291–292).

It was somewhat in this spirit that he returned to dramatic writing in late 1908 or early 1909 with *L'Otage* [*The Hostage*], the first and perhaps best play in his historical trilogy on nineteenth-century France; and with the medieval masterpiece, *L'Annonce faite à Marie* [*The Tidings Brought to Mary*], the first of his dramas to be staged and still the most popular. In fact, the motivation to

106

compose *L'Annonce*, which is a drastic revision of the second version (1900) of *La Jeune Fille Violaine*, came from a request by H. R. Lenormand and others associated with the Théâtre d'Art in Paris for permission to stage the 1900 *Violaine*. The request was transmitted by Gide in January 1909, but Claudel refused outright, considering it the least dramatic and stageable of his plays.[2] Yet only a week later Claudel wrote to Gabriel Frizeau that he believed he could make something "perfectly playable" out of it: "The role of Pierre de Craon will become very important, and the whole will have, I think, a rather grandiose character that was missing." [3]

What "grandiose character" did he so suddenly envision? The transposition of the action from the nineteenth to the fifteenth century? The resurrection miracle? Pierre's new stature? Perhaps it was the more basic concept of mystic substitution and expiatory suffering, obliquely operative in *L'Otage* and already visible in *Violaine* but central—and unto death—only in *L'Annonce*. Earlier, Claudel presented suffering and expiation as solely personal, whereas here Violaine offers herself for the sins of the world.[4] The doctrine of vicarious suffering, developed from that of the communion of saints, was a constant theme of Catholic writers of the period, and Claudel could have encountered it in such diverse works as Émile Baumann's *L'Immolé* (recommended to him by Frizeau in 1908), Bloy, Huysmans, Barbey d'Aurevilly or Péguy's *Mystère de la charité de Jeanne d'Arc* (sent him by Gide early in 1910).[5] In any event, he was apparently more occupied with *L'Otage* than *L'Annonce* until mid-1910, so that the January 1910 diary entry on St. Colette of Corbie assumes major significance as a guiding inspiration for the transformations in this 1911 version. The medieval atmosphere, the miracle, the character and significance of Violaine could all have sprung from this source:

St. Colette arrives on the scene at the end of the Middle Ages and finishes with the Hundred Years' War and the Western Schism. All over France she multiplies the sources of grace, the machinery for mercy. The violent situation ends, the Pope returns to Rome, and the King to Paris. Two women, the one a Dominican, the other a Franciscan, contribute to the end of the schism. . . .

[St. Vincent Ferrer] preaches with a cross of wood, but Colette receives from heaven itself a cross of gold. Her miracle is raising the dead to life. Over this whole time is spread the image of the Last Judgment. It is the period of grim sepulchers and dances of death.[6]

A dozen other entries in the *Journal* for 1909–1911 are more or less recognizable in *L'Annonce* but are extremely minor: impressions of the Rheims and Laon cathedrals, the fountain of La Doue, a pair of steeples, or images of a skylark or ivy.

The break with Ysé-Rosalie no doubt also explains some of the transformations. The earlier Aubin becomes a girl, Aubaine; Violaine's miraculous maternity and the analogy between her and the Virgin Mary no doubt offered a subtle source of consolation to the poet. And above all, Pierre, who formerly had renounced the world and love for religious reasons, is no longer immune to the fires of love and passion, which now war with his spiritual aspirations.

If Violaine has become to some extent a counterpoint to Ysé, this need not belie her possible original genesis as being the antitype of the author's sister, "audacious transposition, mystic transfiguration of the savage cruelty, of the purely pagan egocentrism of Camille Claudel." [7] The latter came to grief by refusing to renounce an illicit love,[8] whereas by renouncing a legitimate love Violaine serves as an instrument of grace. This does not, however, preclude the possibility of seeing in the new Violaine a new exploration of the mystery of death, especially in its relation to love. If Mesa could not truly survive the denouement of his human catastrophe to transform it into some meaningful new existence on earth, Pierre de Craon, on the other hand, once healed of his lust and leprosy by the innocent love and sacrifice of a generous peasant maiden, will prove a more practical exemplar for Claudel in his search for a significant vocation and spiritual reorientation.

It would be wrong, however, to exaggerate the possible biographical background of these characters. In the midst of composing *L'Annonce*, he wrote Gide that he had succeeded in checking his great enemy, lyricism, and in creating objective, exterior characters.[9] Looking back later, he felt that after 1909 his plays had become more objective, with composition dominating inspiration, and attributed this turning point in his dramaturgy "in great part to my interior pacification . . . to domination over the inner drama, which I had succeeded in calming" (*MI*, pp. 230–231). It will be useful, therefore, to study the theme of death not only for its spiritual sense but also for its place in dramatic technique in the 1911 version of L'Annonce, while substituting the 1938 stage version for the awkward 1911 Act IV, with its overblown lyricism, which Charles Dullin found so impossible. It was essentially this combination that Claudel had in mind when he said, "when I look at it from a constructor's point of view, I find that it is one of my best built plays, the best made to strike the public," though he still found the prologue and first act a bit too lyrical (MI, p. 240).

DEATH AS MOTIVE FORCE OF PLOT

In terms of its dramatic technique, death is used in L'Annonce as the primary force motrice or means for developing the plot and as the principal touchstone for the characterization of the various actors. Already in the opening lines of the Prologue there is present a vague atmosphere of death in the penitent consciousness of the master mason, Pierre de Craon, who is starting off from Combernon in the predawn to resume his construction work on the Church of St. Justitia at Rheims. He had been recalled to Combernon briefly to open a temporary passageway in the doorless cloister wall of the convent of Monsanvierge to permit the Queen Mother to retire from the world and join the recluses in their threshold of heaven on the mount above the village of Combernon. They are already dead to the world, and their only outlook is heavenward. Pierre is deeply impressed with this kind of seclusion as being a sort of antechamber to eternity. Reflecting on the approach of his own death, he foresees it in the guise of this imagery, as the moment when "through diaphanous walls on all sides appears darksome Paradise/ And when the censers of night mingle with the odor of the filthy wick as it expires!" (A, p. 17).

The architect's remorse and his preoccupation with death, however, have their roots only secondarily in his work of the previous day and in his reflections about the Queen's desire to offer herself in prayer for her defeated son and their lost kingdom. The primary grounds for his hasty early morning departure from the Vercors' barn at Combernon are the shame and leprosy that have grown on him since that evil hour a year ago when he scarred Violaine slightly with his knife after his failure to force his lustful attention upon her. This situation is doubly dramatic. On the one hand, Pierre is kept at a distance from Combernon and his old friends, the Vercors family, by the constant awareness of his leprous condition and by his uncertainty of their knowledge of, or reaction to, his attempted rape of the flower of the family. On the other hand, Violaine's reaction is unexpected and untypical.[10] She neither heaps abuse upon him nor panics at sight of him, but advances calmly and confidently to chide him gently over his hasty departure and excessive self-disparagement:

> I'm not afraid of you, mason! Not everybody can be wicked!
> It's not easy to get the better of me!
> Poor Pierre! You didn't even manage to kill me.
> With your wicked knife! Just a small slash on my arm, and no one noticed it. (A, p. 12)

She is not frightened by death—even in violent form—but somehow feels superior to it. Furthermore, she does not even know what leprosy is.

Death thus largely motivates and qualifies their morning meeting. Violaine seeks Pierre out to forgive his attempt on her life, while Pierre remains distant from her because of his more uncontrollable danger to her now, in the form of leprous contagion. Less concerned about dangers of body than of soul, however, she bestows a sisterly kiss on him out of compassion for his physical and moral isolation.[11] This naive but innocent act—in a sense, an affront to death—triggers the two principal events that bring about the downfall, humanly speaking, of Violaine and elevate her jealous sister, Mara. On the one hand, she contracts the living death of leprosy herself through the kiss; on the other, she unwittingly scandalizes and arms her spying sister with a mortal spite and scorn. But from the conjunction of these two evils will proceed the possibility of higher good.

Act One opens on a note of death, too, as Anne Vercors envisages the approaching end of thirty happy years before the hearth with his wife Elizabeth and their two daughters. The moorings of daily interest that ordinarily attach one to life seem severed for him, and not unlike the Queen Mother retiring from court to convent in the sunset of life, this minor patriarch is suddenly impelled to crown his earthly pilgrimage with a physical one to Jerusalem because "there is too much suffering in France" (A, p. 30). It is the thought of his own approaching death that goads him into this heroic folly, which will be a kind of rehearsal for permanent separation from the earthly hearth: "Soon I will be back./ Can't you have faith in me for a time, while I'm gone?/ Soon will come another separation" (A, p. 33). Thus does he choose to obey literally the biblical injunction to live as a stranger and pilgrim on this earth (I Pet. II, 11). Reflecting on the origin and meaning of *L'Annonce* in 1948, Claudel recalled the great influence the Psalms had had on him, "in particular that great Psalm CXIII of vespers, *In exitu Israel de Aegypto* which used to carry me away like the *Marseillaise*" (OC, IX, 298). Indeed, there is hardly a psalm which does not echo this one, for the memory of the great event of Exodus permeated all the religious history and liturgy of Israel, which, unlike the other Canaanite nations, no longer centered its cult on the return of spring but rather on the escape of their nation from Egypt. Although its primary meaning is that of a new birth through adoption by Yahweh as in a battle, the history of the people of God appears as an uprooting, a separation, a segregation, which is also a means of reassembling. Thus does the Exodus apply to the people itself the pilgrim principle that guided their patriarch Abraham (Gen. XII, 1) and that Christ will make the touchstone for his chosen disciples (Matt. XIX, 29). *Qualis pater, talis populus:* true life begins with a departure, a renunciation of terrestrial security which is also a liberation, however arduous, and thus prefigures the voyage to the beyond.[12]

As regards plot, Anne Vercors' decision to depart for Jerusalem is a very important catalyst, for it accelerates the whole drama. Before leaving, he must set his affairs in order and arrange for the continuity of Combernon, since he has no male heir. Hence his impulsive decision to arrange immediately for the marriage of his elder daughter, Violaine, in order to gain a dependable son-in-law, the neighbor boy Jacques Hury, whom he had helped raise (A, pp. 27–28). In this manner will he settle the problem of estate and inheritance but also inadvertently drive Mara, the jealous sibling, to desperate measures of intervention, such as her threat of suicide made to her mother: "Go tell him that she's not marrying him, or I'll kill myself!/ I'll hang myself in the woodshed,/ Where you found the cat strung up" (A, p. 34).

Act Two opens on a brief note of life and hope as we hear a nun singing the Salve Regina from one of the towers of Monsanvierge. Mara soon introduces her cankerous purposes by seeking out Jacques in order to calumniate Violaine with exaggerated gossip about "that clandestine kiss at daybreak" (A, p. 46) bestowed on Pierre. As Violaine and her fiancé meet by the melancholy Adoue fountain on this day of their engagement, Violaine's radiant beauty and colorful bridal-liturgical raiment all but overwhelm him. Still, he is disturbed mightily by the forebodings and intimations of mortality ("A moment suffices for dying, and death itself, the death of one of us in the other,/ Will not annihilate us any more than love. And who needs to live when he is dead?") which she pours forth, for his love is not substantial enough to embrace sacrifice, suffering, doubt:

> What are these strange words, Violaine, so tender and bitter? By what insidious and deadly paths are you leading me?
> I think you want to try me and make me a plaything because I am a simple peasant.
> How beautiful you are now, Violaine, and yet I am afraid when I see you in this garment!
> For it is not the raiment of a woman but the vestment of a deacon,
> Of the one who helps the priest. It leaves the sides open and the arms free. (A, p. 54)

And so when she reveals to him her great secret by slitting the left side of her blouse to show him the first spot of the dread disease, Jacques immediately believes the worst and jumps to the same insidious conclusion as Mara, rejecting her in violent terms: "Vile reprobate, damned of soul and flesh!" and calling her "daughter of the devil" (A, p. 56). The most he will do in this circumstance is to help her pretend to leave for a trip to visit his mother, in order to hide her retreat to the Géyn wilds and avoid scandal. This second departure, again triggered by the prospect of death, removes all obstacles to Mara's indomitable ambition to marry Jacques and inherit her family estate; indeed, it throws both into her lap.

Act Three takes place on Christmas Eve, eight years later, and brings us face to face with death in the guise of the cold, stiff corpse of Aubaine, the baby daughter and only child of Mara. Still convinced that Violaine had been corrupted by Pierre, Mara nevertheless brings the child into the wilds of the Chevroche forest in Géyn to seek out her leprous sister and demand a miracle. She claims that "it is easy to be a saint when leprosy serves as a bonus" (A, p. 72). The confrontation of the two sisters is highly dramatic even in their exploration of their past through Mara's accusations and Violaine's corrections and gentle explanations, but their encounter attains an apogee of tension when Mara demands her daughter back alive while her sightless sister, barely alive herself and now holding the little corpse to her bosom, protests with vigor that she is far from being a saint:

> Violaine: I swear and protest before God that I am not a saint!
> Mara: Give me back my child, Violaine!
> Violaine: Why don't you leave me in peace? Why come to torment me in my tomb?
> Am I worth anything? Do I have God at my disposal? Am I like God? (A, p. 78)

The echo of distant church bells summoning the faithful to Christmas midnight Mass calms them, and the remembrance of the Nativity is an invitation to pray together. Mara is persuaded to take up a breviary and read aloud three lessons from the Christmas Office. Each one has an admirable propriety and application to the situation. Thus in the first selection, taken from Isaias, she comes across this prophetic passage: "The people that walked in darkness have seen a great light: to them that dwelt in the region of the shadow of death, light is risen" (A, p. 79), but apparently she does not notice its applicability to either her moral or her physical situation. She next comes across the joyful summons of St. Leo the Great:

Indeed, there is no room for sadness when it is the birthday of life, which, having taken away the fear of death, fills us with the joy of a promised eternity. No one is excluded from a share of this happiness . . . since our Lord, the destroyer of sin and death, came to liberate everyone, as he found no one free of guilt. Let the saint exult because his palm is nigh; let the sinner rejoice because he is invited to forgiveness. (A, pp. 80–81)

Despite her obtuseness of spirit in matters of the supernatural, Mara now has a presentiment of the sublimity and actuality of this exhortation to trust in Christ, who has subjugated "this inventor of death, the devil," for she acknowledges: "Violaine, I am not worthy to read this book!/ I know I am too hard, Violaine, and I regret it. I wish I could be different."

Does her humility stem from a recognition of her need of pardon or from a hesitancy to entrust herself to the joy of the "promised eternity"? More likely, it stems from a vague shame at her selfish insistence upon an immediate miracle. Despite a trembling voice and a pause when overcome by emotion, she manages to read aloud the third lesson, a homily by St. Gregory the Great, which concludes with the appropriate remark: "He was not born in the house of his parents but on the roadside, doubtless in order to show, through the human nature that he donned, that he had been born in a foreign place" (A, p. 82). Far from reflecting that exiles like her father and sister may consequently be closer to the heart of the Nativity, Mara seems to remain as impervious to the significance of the third lesson as she had been to that of the first. In her grieving monomania, her dead daughter absorbs all her thoughts and only the miraculous restoration of life moments later by Violaine frees Mara from her fascination with death.

The crisis of dramatic tension attains both its peak intensity and its release with the resurrection of Aubaine, which is treated with such touching simplicity and understatement that the spectator's or reader's own emotions are automatically engaged to fill in the undeveloped, concealed ones of the two sisters. Claudel claims to have found the inspiration for this resurrection scene—so different from the restoration of sight in the first two versions (La Jeune Fille Violaine, 1893; 1900)—in the biography of some medieval

German mystic, "whose breast bloomed again." Thanks to the suggestion of this "miracle of milk" (at the end of the act, Mara notices a drop of milk on the infant's lips), Claudel found the means of dramatizing the interpenetration of the two worlds, the natural and the supernatural, by tying together "all those suspended elements of the plot of the play, which until then were dormant in my mind." [13] For Aubaine is in a sense now the daughter of both women, as Mara half-realizes on noting that "her eyes were black but now they are blue like yours" (A, pp. 84–85).

Act IV presents the denouement of the drama in the form of an elucidation of the earlier events and the enlightenment of all the characters when confronted with the death of Violaine. The extraneous lyricism and dithyrambic digressions of 1911, however, had to be pruned away and replaced by a dramatic denouement. The 1938 stage variant of Act IV, following cuts already made for the German production in Hellerau in 1913 [14] and according to the suggestions of Charles Dullin (Th., II, 1355), is but half as long and far more dramatic. The most apparent changes are the supression of Pierre de Craon (perhaps too obvious a counterpart to Mesa?) and of Vercors' rhapsodical reflections after Violaine's death, which concludes the revised drama.

If the emotional and spiritual resonances of L'Annonce are considerably deeper than those of the earlier versions of Violaine, this is due in large part to the introduction of death as the central element in the development of the plot and of the various characterizations. The gain is immense over the earlier versions, where only the blindness of Violaine and Aubin were at stake. Here, the two cases of leprosy and the two deaths raise the dramatic tension to a peak intensity, for, according to one well-developed theory, life is dramatic only because death is at the end, lurking in mystery and expressed in contradictions.[15]

DEATH AND CHARACTERIZATION

It has been suggested that the character Pierre de Craon may be a projection or thinly veiled personification of Claudel himself, who, "in the years 1895–1900, when he is elaborating the definitive outline of his play, develops and lives an intimate experience far more decisive for his spiritual destiny than the family conflicts of his childhood and the drama of his sister Camille." [16] Pierre makes his first appearance in the 1900 version of *Violaine*, where he is a wholesome, indeed sacerdotal, bridge-builder—a *pontifex*—with an overpowering sense of a universal vocation to be carried out in a spirit of renunciation, which his kiss communicates to Violaine. Despite Claudel's insistence that the essential change which he made in the 1911 version was the introduction of the miracle and the mystical maternity of Violaine (*MI*, pp. 232, 234), it seems equally tenable that the transformation of the whole drama is accomplished rather through the transformation of Pierre, whose leprosy introduces the motive force of death into the dramatic action. The intensified mortality of his new role deepens both the human truth or emotions of the drama and the spiritual reality of Violaine.[17] At the same time, we may well wonder whether this transformation does not contain as much biographical inspiration as the original creation. As suggested early in this chapter, the Pierre of 1911 may have reflected a different Claudelian direction for trying to sublimate the problem of illicit love by spiritualizing it in a medieval atmosphere through the healing intercession of a happier, holier Beatrice than Ysé had been. The Pierre of 1900, like the Chinese Emperor in *Le Repos du septième jour* (1896) [*The Seventh-Day Rest*] and Coeuvre in *La Ville* (1897), renounces the world and love for religious reasons, athirst for spiritual waters (*Th.*, I, 576–577). After 1900, Pierre undergoes a modification similar to the personal experience of his creator.

Now more susceptible to carnal desire, the master mason is also more sensitive to the weight of impending death. Indeed, his whole character seems etched and defined by his attitude towards death. This preoccupation is due primarily to his leprous condition and secondarily to his recent immurring of a new recluse at the Combernon convent. The living death that has been gnawing on him for a year dictates his isolation from the company of men. It also heightens his sense of guilt and awareness of his continuing danger towards women, or at least Violaine: "I'm not such a safe fellow, you know"; and again: "Just my simple presence can be fatal" (*A*, p. 12). He interprets everything in its relationship to death. Thus the rusty gate that Violaine insists on opening herself,

to show Pierre the short cut to Rheims, evokes for him the imminent gate of death that he expects to traverse shortly, and the
lovely one who opened it suggests to him the attractive tree that
led to Adam's downfall. On the other hand, Pierre is more resigned
than downcast, because the knowledge that he has preferred God
to a corruptible woman brings him the expectation of seeing his
guardian angel just beyond the last gate, and this sustains his hope:

> O young tree of the knowledge of good and evil, I am be-
> ginning now to draw away because I once laid a hand on you.
> Already my soul and body are being separated, like wine
> in the vat mingled with crushed grapes!
> What matter? I had no need of a woman. I have not pos-
> sessed a corruptible woman.
> The man who in his heart has preferred God sees when he
> dies the angel who guarded him.
> The time will soon come when another door will fade
> away.
> When he who has pleased few people in this life falls
> asleep, having finished his work, in the arms of the eternal
> Bird. (A, pp. 16–17)

Not only that. The resurrection of the body is also vaguely in his
mind as he perceives in the night beyond the opened gate the
countryside covered with meadows and harvests and as he alter-
nates with Violaine in the recitation of the Resurrection hymn,
Regina Caeli, on hearing the Angelus bell (A, p. 15). Nevertheless,
death remains for him repulsive and fearful. Even Paradise appears
somber and unclear when viewed from this side of the grave,
because the view is beclouded by the engrossing stench of the
decomposing body, even while the walls of earthly existence dissolve
to permit a diaphanous apparition of the beyond (A, p. 17). His
only consolation this side of the grave will be Violaine's forgiveness
and her encouragement to unite his sufferings with those of the
Lord.

The contrast of his somberness with Violaine's joy is almost
diametrical, as she sings, "How beautiful this world is and how
happy am I!" and he sighs, "How beautiful this world is and how
unhappy am I!" (A, p. 21). Sure of her simple destiny to prolong

the family fortune, she is happy over the innocence of her uncomplicated life and love. More than a contrast, her joy is a foil to his mortal sorrow: "Which is better, Pierre? That I share my joy with you, or that I share your grief?" By her joy, she hopes to lance and drain his hatred of her fiancé, but he is obdurately jealous of Jacques: "Another has taken Violaine from me and left me with this tainted flesh and stricken spirit!" There is the crux of his frustrations. The leprosy that devours his body impedes his normal human emotions and poisons his soul:

> It is hard to be a leper and carry around the foul sore and know you'll not be healed, for there is no remedy,
> But that every day it spreads and devours. Hard to be alone and to bear your own poison, to feel yourself decaying while still alive!
> To taste death not once only but ten times over, yet without foregoing even to the end any of the frightful alchemy of the tomb! (A, pp. 22–23)

There is a poisonous interaction between his soul and body, and the latter's rampant mortality does little to heal or relieve the inner poison: "I hate it. It was in me and still is, and this sick flesh has not cured my poisoned soul!" The reason is that the approach of death is robbing him of all hope of ever having his own hearth: "So many sublime spires! Shall I never see one over a little house of my own amid the trees?/ . . . . Am I never to design an oven or a children's room?" (A, p. 24).

Encouraged and chided by Violaine, however, Pierre finally forgets his personal troubles by concentrating on the supernatural aspect of his career: "Only this church, taken from my side like an Eve of stone in the sleep of sorrow, shall be my wife." She had urged him to be worthy of the flame that was consuming him and to radiate a glow from on high like the Paschal candle, and he promises to remain on high, to be a *holy* master craftsman. The threat of approaching death seems to stiffen his resolve and brighten his acceptance of her challenge to shed the maximum luster on earth of which his genius is capable by working with God: "What things remain for me to do and churches to raise up!" On parting with Violaine at dawn, his ambition to work for God is nearly boundless and is expressed in typically Claudelian terms of light and gold:

> I am taking your ring along.
> With this small circle I will make a seed of gold! . . . .
> And within the walls of Justitia I will embody the morning gold!
> Profane light changes but not the light I will decant under those vaults,
>
> .   .   .   .   .
>
> But the one I am going to build will be under its own shadow like condensed gold, like a pyx filled with manna!
>
> (A, p. 25)

Were his own death less imminent, Pierre would undoubtedly be less willing to forgo all distractions, to concentrate on constructing St. Justitia with such dedication. What he is here sublimating is human love, of course, but even more so his dread of death, especially a death with his destiny unaccomplished. Sublimating? More accurately, he is choosing to embrace his own death. And not just as a deserved penalty nor because it is inevitable but also in a spirit of altruistic, transcendent generosity.

The case of the master mason illustrates the dictum that death makes existence itself dramatic, not just the last minute of it. It is a reverse illustration, however. Ordinarily, the drama consists in suppressing the sight and thought of death, but this does not abolish a confused feeling of its threat.[18] In Pierre's case, though, the menace is precise and visible, and the dramatic tension is not between a "certain death" and an "uncertain hour" but derives rather from the inner reaction to it, from the hesitancy of the victim to renounce hatred and resentment and not so much to resign himself to it as to outstrip death by constructing a greater and more enduring edifice than he might otherwise have been content to do.

The exchange of disease and destiny brought about by the kiss that the compassionate Violaine bestows on Pierre paves the way for the crucial forest scene between the two sisters which culminates in the revival of the dead child, Aubaine. Faced with the leprosy of an admired friend, Violaine had been both humanly compassionate and spiritually lucid. Personally afflicted and shriveled into a sightless skeleton, she is even more spiritually lucid and sympathetic towards others' problems than before her own suffering and isolation, as Mara discovers. This is first apparent in her interest in Mara's comfort, her home life with Jacques, their mother's death, the farm (A, p. 71). So too is her spiritual lucidity in her humble and skillful parrying of Mara's accusing and sarcastic questions (A, pp. 72–74). In fact, she nearly convinces the younger woman that "love made suffering and suffering created love./ The wood we set on fire gives not only ashes but also a flame" and that "the male is the priest, but it is not forbidden women to be the victim" (A, p. 74). Without her living experience of death, Violaine would never have sounded such mystic depths as these phrases reflect: "Powerful is suffering when it is as voluntary as sin!/ . . . The cup of sorrow is deep, and whoever once puts his lips to it can no longer remove them at will!" The unifying principle and guiding light of her suffering is her belief in the value of vicarious expiation: "That is why my body is suffering in the place of Christendom as it dissolves" (A, p. 75).

Confronted with the corpse of her niece, Violaine's first thought concerns the infant's eternal happiness: "Her soul is alive in God. She is following the Lamb. She is with the blessed little ones." Her second movement is to obtain the mother's acquiescence to the harsh ways of God: "You've given me the body. Give the rest to God!" And she tries to comfort her: "Accept, submit/ . . . poor sister!" (A, p. 76).

Mara, on the other hand, shows absolutely no concern over her child's eternal welfare, only utter preoccupation with recovering its physical life. Only this wild hope draws her from home to pay a single visit to her suffering, disinherited sister after eight years of total neglect. Her motivation seems at least as selfish as maternal, for she has never felt completely sure of Jacques's love and is afraid of losing it as soon as he returns from Rheims and discovers their loss, especially since she is incapable of having another child. It is partly this fear of being held responsible by her husband, partly her accumulated disdain for her self-sacrificing sister that prompt her ironic questions, such as: "What do you know of an invisible God who appears nowhere?" (A, p. 72) and "What good is this blind fire which gives others/ Neither light nor warmth?" (A, p. 74). But these taunts are also a ruse for verifying Violaine's holiness before humbling herself by the revelation of her daughter's death and running the risk of ridicule when she importunes her to work a miracle. Thus the taunts and gradual revelation of her misfortune are also a means of probing and softening or preparing Violaine for her ultimate revelation and request. Request? It is more of an insolent demand that the distraught Mara makes on her sister:

> No—a thousand times no! You're not going to hoodwink me with your nun's talk! No, I won't let myself be appeased.
> The milk burning in my breast cries to God like the blood of Abel. (A, p. 76)

From violence she resorts to rhetorical questioning ("Are there fifty children to be taken from my body?") and then descends to soft pathos: "Violaine, it's so sweet and hurts so when that cruel little mouth bites you inside" (A, p. 76). Having trilled the whole octave of her emotions without producing the desired effect, Mara resorts to a final, dramatic stratagem to elicit her sister's compassion:

> Violaine, do you know what it means to damn one's soul?
> Deliberately and for all time?
> Do you know what's in your heart when you really blaspheme?
> While I was running here, there was a devil singing me a little song.
> Do you care to hear the things he taught me? (A, p. 77)

Violaine is of course horrified by this threat of self-damnation, and Mara takes advantage of this psychological moment of excitement to explode her bombshell explicitly: "Give me back the child I gave you!/ . . . Give it back to me alive!/ . . . I refuse to accept the death of my child" (A, p. 77).

It would be impossible to assess the various degrees of lucidity and calculation in this wide gamut of emotional display by Mara, but it is not difficult to imagine her more or less planning some such general strategy, perhaps subconsciously, as she hastened to

the Chevroche forest. Details and timing would be left to the
inspiration of the moment or improvised. This is not to accuse her
of insincerity, of course, of feigning false emotions. Rather, like
those who perform incredible feats of strength, often unconsciously,
in the face of mortal dangers, so are Mara's innate cleverness and
tempestuousness accentuated by her grief at her daughter's death.
Indeed, in the face of Violaine's orthodox rejoinder defending
God's inscrutable providence and her own powerlessness, she finally
loses all psychic control and lapses into near hysteria:

> I'm deaf and can't hear! I'm calling to you out of my
> despair. Violaine, Violaine!
> Give me back that child I gave you! Look, I yield and bend
> before you. Have pity on me!
> Have pity on me, Violaine, and give me back the child you
> took.
> / . . . . / So give her back to me. I know it's all your
> fault.
> No, all right, it's mine./ . . . . / You're lying, it's not
> dead! Oh, you lily-livered slut! If I had access to God like
> you,
> He wouldn't snatch my children away so easily!
>
> (A, pp. 77–78)

At this moment she is completely beside herself and out of control, this "hard head" "who does not give in and accepts nothing"
(A, p. 76). Possibly only Violaine's excited interjection, "Ask me to
re-create heaven and earth!" saves her from madness by acting like
a dash of cold water on her fever, for she murmurs, as if reciting
the Bible by rote or hypnosis: "But it is written that you can blow
on a mountain and cast it into the sea" (A, p. 78). Confronted with
her sister's controlled but firm insistence on her unsaintly condition,
Mara gradually recovers her self-possession while maintaining and
incessantly repeating her stubborn demand: "I'm only asking you
for my child" (A, p. 78). A certain calm comes to her as Violaine
exhorts Mara to pray with her and cease weeping:

> Pray with me. We haven't spent Christmas together for
> so long.

> Don't be afraid. I've taken on your suffering with mine.
> Look, what you gave me is hidden against my heart!
> Stop crying! This is not the time to cry, when the hope of
> all men has just been born. (A, p. 79)

The death of Aubaine thus brings about no drastic change in either her mother or aunt but serves as a dramatic catalyst to etch their characters in deeper relief through a most intimate encounter. The same traits that Violaine demonstrated earlier stand out here. She reveals almost all the theological and moral virtues, with perhaps humility and charity the most evident. Mara's reaction to this confrontation with death is equally in character, though of greater dramatic intensity. She has the more active role, being inwardly compelled to subdue temporarily her scorn and fear of her sister, to seek her help, no matter the cost in personal humiliation. The same stubborn, clever selfishness which she showed in dispossessing Violaine of husband and heritage are manifested more directly in her impulsive encounter here. Nor does she show the least qualms of conscience or compassion in regard to her sister or her own conduct, but rather barbs and baits her sister as bitterly as ever. Amid this morass of unpleasant characteristics, however, is gradually revealed a redeeming quality: her faith. Garish, because unmodified by any other virtue, even hope, it is more of an Old Testament faith than a Christian one, concerned almost exclusively with this life rather than guided by any light of eternity. Nevertheless, it is a deep and simple faith, even if manifested only in the face of death and for earthly motives, for Mara believes in God and in the possibility of His intervention in human affairs.

It is this unshakable faith even in the face of death that brings about the dramatic confrontation and conflict of the two sisters, pairing the one's restraint and resignation against the other's vitriolic violence. But since heaven can be taken by storm, vehemence wins this duel with humility by provoking a miracle. Claudel insisted that between the two sisters, so different in every way, there was an absolutely complementary relationship: that Violaine's holiness should serve her sister's exigency, and vice versa: "The Gospel tells us: 'Your faith has saved you'; the brutal, savage faith of Mara must serve some purpose, must serve to cause a miracle and to oblige God, so to speak, to perform a miracle. From this comes the powerful, vehement element that constitutes the whole force and intensity of *L'Annonce faite à Marie* and that makes of it, I think, an altogether human and superhuman drama" (*MI*, p. 235). If there is a kind of transcendent pragmatism in this inter-action of the two women, there is also a certain possibility of spiritual growth discernible in Mara's declaration of unworthiness while reading the sacred texts (A, p. 81), then in her humility and joy at her infant's rebirth (A, p. 84). Is there not also the chance that she will be tempted to pray again and perhaps ponder the sacred texts, either from curiosity or gratitude? In any event, as Claudel noted early in 1909, it is faith, not charity that moves mountains (*J*, I, 86).

Still, there will apparently always be many upright people, includ-ing critics and Catholics, who are genuinely shocked by the author's audacious analogies, by the violence suffered by the kingdom of heaven in Claudel, and by the success of the violent like Mara.[19] It is a proper problem, for Claudel's principal scriptural source (Matt. XI, 12: "From the days of John the Baptist until now the kingdom of heaven has suffered violence, and men of violence take it by force") is indeed highly ambiguous, susceptible of at least three interpretations: the historical (involving Jewish political Zealots), the ascetical (the violence to self in the renunciation and asceticism demanded by discipleship), and what might be called the catalytic, involving an evolutionary process beyond evil to good. What scandalizes so many is the way Claudel twists the notion so that holiness seems to *need* evil to be fulfilled and hence approves it for this purpose. Flannery O'Connor, Mauriac, and Bernanos have also dealt with this explosive theme, but in their more nuanced fictional approach it seems less dramatic, less shocking. For them all, the sinner is at the heart of Christianity, just as sin is at the center of redemption.

The problem is always oversimplified, of course, but even at this simple level it may be more paradoxical than unorthodox, if we think of God bringing good out of evil, as He did in Job's case (and indeed, for Claudel as for St. Augustine, He wouldn't be God if He couldn't). History is replete with instances of persecutions and crimes provoking sanctity and heroic achievement, of the death embraced by one for the lives of many.[20] This is at the heart of Christian drama, as Claudel tried to persuade Gide in 1909.[21] Does the saint need the sinner as a catalyst? Perhaps not always— but without this catalyst there is little or no drama. There is more dramatic tension in Judas' betrayal of Jesus than in the Sermon on the Mount, in Thomas à Beckett's murder than in Francis of Assisi's charity. As for the apparent approval of Mara's crime by Vercors and Violaine, it would seem more accurate to speak of mercy, since repentance and forgiveness are involved. Any analogy with Judas seems farfetched in view of the emphasis Claudel puts on Mara's faith and eventual self-accusation.

As for Violaine, her miraculous maternity is the culmination of such rapt prayer and angelic communication that she seems hardly aware of it and then reveals it only gradually and almost cryptically to Mara (A, p. 83). Her personal reaction is one of calm compassion ("Poor sister! You're crying. You've suffered too much too.") and of thanksgiving: "Glory to God. Peace on earth to men! She is alive and so are we. And the Father's face shines over the rejuvenated earth" (A, p. 84). But behind her self-effacing expressions, there are inner joy and gratitude at this divine confirmation of her hope and charity, at this seal set on her sacrifice of self.

The third encounter with death and its use in the characterization of those involved occurs in the fourth act. For reasons already noted, the stage variant of 1938 is preferable, where Claudel gives Mara her definitive importance. This is her act, he told Jean Amrouche: "Mara, in short, explains everything that happened and shows that from her point of view she acted according to the Faith." [22] From the point of view of dramatic technique, however, the scene of Violaine's death is of rather minor importance for the elucidation of character. Its principal function is really that of a denouement, an unwinding of the tension existing among the several protagonists. This release is accomplished by their recognition of God's design in their devious lives and by their reconciliation with one another and to their own inadequacies in coping with the divine design. From this operation derives the sense of catharsis experienced by the audience, suffused with that of pity, proper to tragedy, which is aroused by unmerited misfortune and released or purged by its integration into a higher design. This purgation is completed by the spectator's application of this exemplary interpretation to the chaos of his personal experience.[23]

FINAL DEATH SCENE

Nevertheless, dramatic elements are definitely engaged in this final death scene, and they do shed some additional light on each character. It is obvious that the scene would be considerably less dramatic if it were a question of the leprous outcast returning of her own accord to the family homestead to seek pity, revenge, or merely shelter. The fact that she has been waylaid by an unknown attacker for uncertain reasons, even though offstage, rewinds the tension that had been slacked by the miracle ending Act Three, especially since Mara is the one who announces it, coquettishly toying with Jacques. The suspense of the audience, which is minor, is less concerned with identifying the victim and the culprit, as Mara's ambiguity and sarcasm suggest (B, p. 117), than with her husband's density or apathy and his reaction to the eventual identification. Indeed, his characterization is the only one elaborated at any length in this final scene. The others merely affirm more fully their known personalities, although the violent, headstrong Mara performs a sudden volte-face that is crucial.

Jacques's evolution begins, and the tension quickly attains a plateau, when Anne Vercors enters bearing Violaine, unconscious, in his arms. Jacques is immediately resentful ("And what's that body in your arms?"), and when the old man digresses to muse on his own imminent death, he insists vigorously: "Father! What, may I ask, is this thing you've brought us in your arms? What is that corpse stretched out on the table?" (B, p. 118). With his typical circuitous answers, Vercors gradually reveals the identity in a series of clues, the better to soften and prepare Jacques for the blow of confronting his first love, whom Jacques still considers guilty of betraying him. He succeeds. Jacques sheds his resentment slowly, wondering whether she can hear them. However, when assured by the father that she had spoken of him during the night, Jacques bitterly, angrily asks if she also spoke of "Pierre de Craon! That thieving leper, that mason . . ." With acute sarcasm he inquires about "that chaste kiss she exchanged with him one May morning," as reported by Mara, whom he drags in by the wrist to make her confirm it. Heedless of the father's negation of her guilt, nearly in a frenzy ("I, I was her fiancé! She had never let me touch her!"), he is snapped out of it only by the shock of hearing that Pierre was cured. Or rather, he falls from his rage of indignation into a slough of despair: "He is cured and I am damned!" (B, p. 120), until reassured by Vercors. But even his sudden intuition that Aubaine may also owe her life to Violaine is not enough to still his recriminations against her for having given Pierre her mouth and his ring, when she was still so much in love with Jacques that May morn. He cannot grasp the father's explanation: "It was too wonderful! It was not acceptable" (B, p. 121). Full of tenderness for her holiness and acerbity for his obtuseness, Jacques finally apostrophizes the inert form in poignant oxymorons:

> O cruel Violaine, desire of my soul, you have betrayed me!
> O hateful garden! O spurned and useless love, o grief-planted garden!
> Sweet Violaine! Perfidious Violaine! O silence and profundity of woman!
> Can you say nothing to me? Can you give me no answer? Will you continue to keep silent?
> Having deceived me with lying words,
> Having deceived me with her bitter, charming smile,
> She is going off where I cannot follow her.
> I have to go on and live,
> With this poisoned arrow in my side! (B, pp. 122–123)

This poetic and dramatic crest shows a deep cleavage in Jacques's soul. This, and the uncertainty of his reaction towards his one-time fiancée, engage the onlooker's compassion for his conflict and evoke curiosity as to whether he will veer towards madness, rebellion, or resignation. This sense of conflict is transmitted through the accumulation of antithetical expressions. But the bittersweet reproaches reflect this realization: their separation might not have happened had she been less silent and mystic, or he more trusting. It exemplifies Gouhier's dictum of a "double paradox, signifying that we accord neither necessity nor legitimacy to death." [24]

Not without its dramatic value, too, is the uncertainty whether

Violaine will recover consciousness before dying and what exchange of sentiments there can be between her and the other three. When Mara speaks for the first time since her father's return, it is to show that she is the only one who can make herself heard, with "this same sister's voice that one Christmas day made itself felt deep within her." In so doing, she also reveals explicitly at last that Violaine had brought their daughter back to life:

> And Mara's call and cry, her screaming also became flesh in the bosom of this horror, in the bosom of this enemy, in the bosom of this woman in ruins, in the bosom of this abominable leper!
> From the depth of my being I cried so loud that I finally snatched away from her the child she had taken from me,
> I snatched it away from this living tomb. . . . (B, p. 124)

However, it is less in order to end her deception and speak the truth at her sister's deathbed than to justify herself and claim credit for the miracle: "You say that she did that? It was God, God who did it! I was the strongest, all the same! It was Mara who did it, Mara!" (B, p. 125). It is Jacques's sudden tenderness towards the dying sister that provokes Mara's confession and boast, and his violent reaction of pushing her aside to kneel at Violaine's feet intensifies his wife's effort to justify and exculpate herself as she releases a torrent of sarcasm on the whole house. Suddenly it dawns on her that she is the guilty one and what she owes her sister: "Father, my child was dead and she restored it to life!" This admission is her act of contrition, and she is absolved by her father who reconciles her with her sister in his heart: "I loved you both, and your hearts used to beat together as one with mine" (B, p. 126).

Only Violaine's return to consciousness, however, and her words of peace and pardon can restore equanimity to Jacques and bring him to resign himself to the situation and to his wife, as she speaks her love for Jacques, Pierre, and especially Mara: "And Mara loves me. She's the only one who believed in me!" Thanks to her sister's crude mixture of a violent self-interest and a radical faith, Violaine has experienced to the fullest the interpenetration of two worlds, the natural and the supernatural: "There are two, yet I say there is only one and that's enough and God's mercy is immense!"

Jacques's resentment, slowly subsiding but not subdued ("Happiness is ended for me" B, p. 127), is finally transmuted into resignation only by Violaine's conclusion, through and beyond suffering, in the immensity of God's mercy and by her assurance of reunion after death:

> What is one day from me? Soon it will be over.
> And then when your turn comes and you see the big door creak open,
> I will be on the other side, close by. (B, p. 127)

Jacques seems to be looking forward in hope to that reunion, and not merely recollecting a happy moment that never attained an earthly bloom, when he exclaims in reply: "O my fiancée through the flowering branches, greetings!" (B, p. 127). His reconciliation with his wife is told without words. While Vercors carries the unconscious Violaine out to the postern gate to die in ultimate poverty, Jacques turns slowly towards Mara, who makes the sign of the cross with their child, as if with a monstrance, in the direction of her departing sister, and husband and wife "exchange long and profound looks during the final notes of the angelus" (B, p. 129).

Jacques *appears* to dominate this third moment, the deathbed of Violaine. There are several reasons for this. He is the only one of the quartet who is still in the dark about Violaine's innocence, and his illumination provides the dramatic action as well as his characterization. Moreover, Mara, who had just been gaily pretending how smugly and triumphantly she would receive her father (whom she presumed dead) if he were to return (B, p. 117), was too shocked by his sudden appearance to utter a sound. Besides, her natural reaction was to conceal her fratricide by silence, until compelled to state a defense. The father is scarcely a protagonist in this scene, though his role is important as a foil to Jacques and as the all-knowing chorus that interprets the significance of the drama. Although Jacques evolves in this act from resentment, through compassion and momentary despair, to a resignation in hope, Mara in an important sense actually dominates the action. Her husband's final disposition is, after all, only a purified version of his reluctant consent to the loss of Violaine, whereas Mara at the end experiences a more radical conversion, from malevolent egomania to contrite gratitude. This death to self is perhaps deeper and more painful that the partial one her husband undergoes, though his lyric regrets and recriminations obscure this point. More important, however, is the fact that the dramatic action has been set in motion by her crimes and represents the undoing of her evil through the triumph of a higher good and the curing of the blight at the root. Thus her personality is ever present in everyone's thoughts, behind each utterance, like a secret motivation. Consequently, her one outcry, leading to admission of the miracle and eventually to recognition of her guilt, provides the climax of both the act and the whole drama. That is why Claudel called this Mara's act, for here she is given her definitive meaning in the context of Claudel's theology of evil, as being a necessary abrasive for the production of good, even within the sinner.

What is the reaction of Anne Vercors to his daughter's death and her sister's crime? Certainly there is little elaboration of character apparent in his Orphic utterances, and yet his function is not purely choral, as was more nearly the case in the preceding version.[25] Here, he exhibits less detachment and more sympathy, for he has also taken over the sacerdotal role of Pierre de Craon, now absent in Jerusalem. He prepares the death watch, supervises the domestic liturgy of reconciliation, and takes charge of the burial. The fact that he has spent the night comforting Violaine in the sand pit and learning what has occurred during his absence, plus the spiritual wisdom acquired on his seven-year pilgrimage, accounts satisfactorily for his calm, controlled attitude, although this prior enlightenment also precludes any development of his character on stage. The information that he brings about Pierre, his affirmation of Violaine's innocence and forgiveness and of Mara's pardon, are all important to the development of the action, but his explanation of the meaning of life and death provides the key to the mystery of Violaine's charity:

> My little Violaine was wiser!
> Is living the purpose of life? Are the feet of the children of
> God bound to this wretched earth?

The purpose of life is not to live, but to die! And not to construct the cross but to mount it and joyfully give what we have!

This is joy and freedom, this is grace and eternal youth!

.   .   .   .   .

What worth is the world by comparison with life? And of what value is life, if not to be used and given? (B, p. 122)

To this unworldly wisdom of the paternal pilgrim, Violaine brings a slight corrective when she recovers consciousness for the last time. It is all the more authoritative for being the final communication of the drama, offered by a saint who had already seemed swallowed up by death but has been granted a momentary resurrection [26] to set the interpenetration of the two worlds in proper perspective:

How beautiful is a great harvest!
Yes, even now I can remember how beautiful it is.
How beautiful it is to be alive, and how immense is the glory of God!/ . . . . /
But it is also good
To die when everything is over, when the darkness little by little
Spreads over us like a very dark shadow. (B, p. 128)

No doubt this legacy of serenity is also the author's, a serenity of faith and hope reflecting the reconciliation of life and death, as of human freedom and divine providence, in a design that transcends the individual and the natural order. Insofar as the play reflects a mingled atmosphere of human suffering and secret cause [27] and evokes a response of pity that so much evil was necessary to the attainment of wisdom and salvation, it has tragic aspects. Like the ancient Greeks, Claudel evokes the presence of the sacred and the absolute power of the supernatural over creatures but surpasses them in showing his characters being conducted despite themselves towards their salvation, as Henry Amer writes, adding: "The Claudelian God . . . is a god of love who draws from his most rebellious creatures the wherewithal to justify their redemption. Tragic Fatality thus reappears on the French stage metamorphosed into Providence." [28] And death is the catalyst for this metamorphosis and forms the most forceful intersection of the dramatist's art and his religion, for "Religion has not only put Drama into life, it has put at its end, in death, the highest form of drama which, for every disciple of our divine master, is *Sacrifice*." [29]

VI

Le Soulier de satin: *The Final Choice*

All the elements of my theater are reassembled here. I have made a blending especially of *Tête d'Or*, my first drama, of *Partage de midi* and of *Protée*. In a sense one witnesses their unexpected denouement, which is the total liberation of the human soul.[1]

I have just finished an enormous drama, *Le Soulier de satin*, which is both a masquerade and a resumption of all my old themes reunited in a probably testamentary ensemble.[2]

This drama, whose stage is not just the earth but the universe, was in gestation for more than five years, from May 1919 to December 1924. Curiously, it began as a kind of marine sketch meant to serve merely as a prologue or curtain-raiser to his two-act satyr comedy, *Protée* (1913; second version, 1926). It was to recount the story, as Claudel outlined it in March 1920, of an old conquistador, unhappy in love, who in revenge ravages Morocco and the Andes and ends up as a prisoner of one of his daughters. This evolved eventually into the fourth day (act) of *Le Soulier de satin* or *The Satin Slipper*, and retained as a subtitle "To Windward of the Balearic Isles" and such other Protean links as the playful seals, the idea of the sea as deliverance, and the frequently comic tone. But it soon outgrew this limited perspective in the author's creative imagination, which was sparked especially by a meeting in 1920 or 1921 with Ysé-Rosalie[3] that led to his final comprehension of the *Partage* crisis and a healing of its long-festering wound:

Le Soulier bears the mark of this alleviation. There is no longer the wound of something unexplained and without cause, which is perhaps

133

the most painful. What happened in *Partage de midi* I came to understand, and *Le Soulier de satin* . . . was only a kind of explanation of what had happened in two human hearts. (*MI*, p. 269)

By delving into his own experience of the mysteries of sin and grace, he elaborated anew his personal drama in an atmosphere of infinite expansion and found a more realistic and Christian resolution for Mesa's situation. He was no longer writing to exorcise a demon or to conquer peace but rather to explain how and why peace and joy are possible of eventual attainment even in an absurd world of separation, suffering, and death. Claudel is thus more personally committed and present in this dramatic testament than in his historical trilogy, composed between 1909 and 1916 and representing "a powerful effort at understanding that median age stretching between modern and contemporary history," [4] the first and second French empires. He had hoped to extend it into a tetralogy but could never find the inspiration for a fourth drama in the Coûfontaine-Turelure cycle. In retrospect, however, he considered that he had found "what one can call a solution, a consummation of the trilogy in *Le Soulier de satin*" (*MI*, p. 253), as the bitter, almost cynical, painful atmosphere gave way to a sense of joy in sacrifice.

Claudel's trilogy, as Henri Gouhier observes, is neither erudite history nor romanced history, like that of Dumas *père* and Sardou, but history poetically reflected upon, as in Shakespeare, and this explains Claudel's liberty in the creation of adventures and characters. [5] In the first and best of the series, *L'Otage* (*The Hostage*), Sygne de Coûfontaine is constrained to sacrifice her love for her cousin George and her family pride by marrying the detestable upstart revolutionary Toussaint Turelure in order to save the Pope, held hostage in France. But Sygne too is a prisoner, both of her ambitious husband and of her closed traditional views. Thus the play portrays not only a private agony but the clash between two lineages, between commoner and noble, both of which Claudel discerned in his ancestry. He treats both protagonists, consequently, with varying sympathy as he probes their dilemma, which is enveloped in violence and war and ends in a double murder, symbolizing the death of the old regime. George, in a revolt against man and God, tries to shoot Turelure but mortally wounds Sygne instead, who apparently tried to shield him, and is in turn the victim of Turelure's deadly aim. The ending is highly enigmatic, Sygne's state of soul uncertain. Turelure makes a final attempt to persuade her to pardon him and finally ratify their marriage in the depth of her heart, thus fulfilling the sacrifice to which she had consented. He asks her to give him her soul. In the original version she seems to refuse, but in a later variant she makes a gesture that could be interpreted as consent. Claudel's commentaries are themselves curiously ambiguous and vacillating, reflecting his more objective and realistic approach from the standpoint of human uncertainty.

Le Pain dur (Hard Crusts; 1913–14), set in the next generation under Louis-Philippe, depicts a world without God, where men are victims of their narrow visions and limited appetites. Turelure, grown old and prosperous, has also become despicable, resentful of the memory of Sygne, of their son Louis, who represents youth and adventure, and of the inanity of existence itself. And yet he is desperately attached to life by an inordinate fear of death, compounded of avarice, jealousy, obstinacy, and lust vis-à-vis his Jewish mistress Sichel and the young Polish countess Lumîr. The latter, in love with Louis Turelure but even more with Poland, persuades him to recover 20,000 francs she had lent his father and to kill him if necessary. Despite his fear of death, the old miser refuses to be intimidated by his son. In exasperation Louis finally shoots at him; both shots miss, but his father dies of a heart attack.

In the poignant separation scene (III, 2), the lovers sunder their ties not because of the parricide but because Louis refuses to accompany Lumîr to Poland, "the country of sadness, the fount of tears in the heart of her whom you love" (Th., II, 466), and she will not remain in France, an exile, as her vocation is to suffer and die for Poland, among her people in their dark night. In letting her depart alone, Louis seems to be both renouncing loyal love and rejecting its accompanying sorrows and death. Disinherited by his father and abandoned by Lumîr, he quickly overcomes his repugnance and marries Sichel, who comes to symbolize life, hope, the future. It is instructive that in her presence Louis denies being a parricide, perhaps because he feels he is righting his father's wrong to her, whereas with Lumîr, who represents death, despair, the past, he acknowledges full guilt. The apparently false resignation of the final movement and the unresolved contradictions present something of an anomaly in the dramatic development of Claudel, for Le Pain dur ends neither on a note of revolt, like L'Otage, nor on a real acceptance, like L'Annonce and Le Soulier, nor on a lyrical flight beyond, like Partage.[6] It presents, instead, a kind of temporizing compromise with this life.

Le Père humilié (The Humiliation of the Father; 1915–16), less dramatic than the preceding plays, is set in Rome (1869–71) and ostensibly concerned with Pope Pius IX and the demise of the papal states. But both he and the historical aspect remain quite secondary, limited to two scenes. The principal interest lies in the characterization of Pensée, Sichel's blind daughter (symbol of Israel), and of Orian, who is the nephew and adopted son of the Pope, as well as in the lyrical polarization of life and death, the future and the past, light and night. The question of Italy and Rome, of revolt and submission, simply highlight the basically moral theme, as Kempf and Petit have shown.[7]

Though a nominal Catholic, Pensée is in a state of revolt against the status quo: her blindness, the moribund society, the government, the Church. She wants light and needs love. She is attracted to Orian by his voice at a masked ball and he is attracted by her beauty, but he conceals his attraction because of a vocation and mission he has undertaken for the Pope. They quickly engage in a dialectic about life and death, joy and suffering. She is more interested in present joy, he in happiness hereafter, and he tries to transfer her affection from himself to his twin brother, Orso. Feeling that for him she is "danger, night, fatality" (Th., II, 527), not wanting to give her his soul or to share her night (p. 526), Orian departs for a year. On his return to fight for France, Orso persuades him to see Pensée before leaving for battle. In this familiar separation scene (III, 2) and their second meeting, the roles are reversed: he offers to remain with her but she finds the strength to send him to his destiny, which is to love her in death, beyond the flesh. But it is left to Orso to evoke the attraction of death in the next scene:

> It is good to be completely light, it is good to be freed of all the splotches of life. Gay, singing, your collar torn off your shirt. Yes, even among the spirits, I think one will recognize by their air those who died in their prime, in full bloom!
> How a twenty-year-old spirit flames in God's sun!
> It's such an easy thing to die and then not be bothered by anything else. To die as men instead of living basely as slaves, as specialists.
> Here are all dawns at once, the first ray of sun which kindles your window and your heart at a single stroke!
> That's why one pictures the dead with such handsome brows, they are like children looking.
> They regret nothing. To die for one's country is such a fine thing that it leaves them with a dazzled smile. (Th., II, 547)

Some months later Orso returns from battle to tell Pensée of Orian's death on the field of honor and to bring her her lover's heart in a basket of flowers, a scene inspired by Keats's poem, "Isabella, or the Pot of Basil." The two vie in cherishing the relic and memory of the fallen idealist, who like Mesa was incapable of moderation in happiness.

With such psychological, personal themes and lyricism re-emerging and dominating his so-called historical drama, it is no surprise that the Claudelian inspiration veered back to its source. That it blossomed in a final synthesis and resolution of his major motifs is due largely to the events already mentioned, to the assuaging of his long interior debate. This is already discernible in Le Père humilié, whose softened tone and looser, more open structure point to Le Soulier.[8]

The title of this masterpiece may have been inspired by a reminiscence of a poem by Baudelaire [9] and/or the party game called "Hunt the Slipper" that fostered Mesa's romance with Ysé en route to China in 1900.[10] Its reference in the play is to the early scene (I, 5) where Prouhèze, the beautiful young wife of old Don Pélagio, setting forth reluctantly to meet her husband, suddenly removes her slipper and places it in the hands of the Madonna, whose statue watches over the entrance of their house. Then she prays, in the presence of Don Balthazar, her guardian, with whom she had been discussing her love for Don Rodrigue, that she may never dishonor her house, that when she tries to rush towards evil, it will be with limping foot and crippled wing. Her prayer corresponds with one in the first scene made for Rodrigue by his dying brother, a Jesuit missionary lashed to the mast of a Spanish ship, *The Santiago*, which has been scuttled by pirates. His prayer and position serve as prologue to the major themes of the drama:

> It is true that I am attached to the cross, but the cross I am on is no longer fastened to anything. It is floating on the sea. (SS, p. 653)

He goes on to mention the freedom of the sea and its continuity with the sky, the old world and the new, disorder followed by "a great paternal peace," the beauty of the stars, the ease of sacrifice. He concludes by praying that, if Rodrigue desires disorder, may it be such that it involve the shaking and fissure of the walls around him that bar salvation, that the wound of love may open in him a longing, through separation on earth, for imperishable kinship in God.

This initial scene clarifies the scope of the ensuing drama: man's destiny, the ways of Providence in life, love, and death, and the communion of all creation. The love story of Prouhèze and Rodrigue is the heart of the play and consists of three movements. Until II, 4, she seeks to join her handsome hero, who has been wounded and lies at home in his mother's care, at death's door. Prouhèze arrives but is not allowed to see him, and eventually Don Pélagio persuades her to renounce this illicit love and accept the nobler, more challenging role of commandant of the Spanish outpost of Mogador in Morocco. There, Don Camillo, Pélagio's cousin and lieutenant, is in charge, but Camillo has Moorish ties and his loyalty is suspect. A wild adventurer, he is also madly in love with Prouhèze, has in fact already declared his passion to her and predicted that she would join him (I, 3), despite her repugnance for him. Like Tête d'Or, his soul is filled with the spirit of conquest and the breath of fire:

Others explore the sea, so why shouldn't I too plunge as far as it is possible to go, towards that other frontier of Spain, the fire!

.   .   .   .   .

As the Dutch live by the sea, so these people on the very frontier of humanity (not because the land ends but because the fire begins) live by the exploitation of the banks beyond the burning lake.

That's where I will carve out a domain for myself. . . .

(SS, p. 664)

The second movement, in a livelier cadence, consists of Rodrigue's pursuit of Prouhèze to Mogador and fills the rest of Act II. Ironically, he has been brought back from the edge of death not by his mother's devoted care or her prayers or even by the knowledge that Prouhèze was near, who could become for him only "that idol of living flesh," according to Pélagio (p. 729), but by the mere mention of the name of Camillo, his rival (p. 741). Rodrigue's ship almost overtakes hers, but a cannon shot from her frigate fractures his main mast just outside Mogador, forcing him to drift there for three days, during which he sees part of the prow of *The Santiago* float by. It is a reminder to him of the supernatural dimension of life and of the inevitability of death. When he finally gets to Mogador and tries to present Prouhèze with letters from Pélagio and the King advising her to return to Spain with him, she declines even to see him for fear of yielding and lets Camillo treat him with irony and derision. In the ensuing dialectic on love between the two arch rivals, Rodrigue becomes aware of the selfish and sinful aspect of his love and finds the strength, in imitation of Prouhèze's sacrifice of earthly happiness, to accept a higher call, the King's mandate to unite and rule America for him. This second day ends with two scenes (13, 14) of great lyricism that are the epitome of symbolist dramaturgy. In the moonlight the shadows of a man and a woman are projected on a wall and merge into one, which begins to speak. It represents the joining in eternity of the lovers so cruelly separated on earth except for this moment of reciprocal renunciation. Then the moon itself speaks, evoking the inmost reactions of each lover in a calm and compassionate monologue that recalls certain aspects of Mesa's canticle and duet with Ysé: the mingling of images of night, sleep, the Milky Way, the Cross, the Pool of Death. The following dream thoughts, attributed by the moon to Prouhèze, reflect a more mature mysticism and unselfish love than in any previous Claudelian character except Violaine:

> Yes, I know he will wed me only on the Cross, our souls each to each in death and in the night beyond all human grounds!
> If I cannot be his paradise, at least I can be his cross! For racking his soul and body I am quite as good as those two crossed pieces of wood!
> Since I cannot give him Heaven, at least I can tear him away from earth. Only I can provide him with an insufficiency commensurate with his desire!
> Only I was able to deprive him of himself. (SS, p. 765)

The third movement, after a lapse of ten years, during which Pélagio dies and Prouhèze marries Camillo and bears him a daughter named Seven-Swords, covers the whole third day and shows Rodrigue scurrying back to Mogador, after unifying America, in a new effort to rescue his beloved. Again (III, 8), as before their other encounter (I, 12), Prouhèze's guardian angel appears to instruct and strengthen her. This time she is in a state of suspension between life and death, like Mesa in his canticle or Newman's Gerontius. She learns that she is soon to die but that her soul and example will live on and that she will become a guiding star for Rodrigue. She thus consents to die, knowing that during her purification in Purgatory he will experience a similar cleansing here below (p. 811), as described in the fourth day. And again before Rodrigue's arrival, she is importuned by Camillo. The first confrontation (II, 9) had been a psychological stand-off, a mere introduction. In this one (III, 10), subtle and profound, he accuses her of perpetual spiritual adultery, of having always reserved her heart for Rodrigue. Jealous, despairing of his own salvation and dubious of hers in such a state, he taunts, cajoles, and browbeats her into renouncing Rodrigue even in the next life and giving her soul entirely to God. Despite her triple refusal, a glow on her face indicates her interior acquiescence. The total sacrifice, the gift of her soul, to which Sygne could not consent, is finally made by the more masculine Prouhèze. What Turelure could not provoke, Camillo succeeds in exacting, and with it the implication of his own conversion.

The high point of the long story of the separated lovers, not only in *Le Soulier* but in a sense in the whole theater of Claudel, occurs in the sole meeting of the lovers (III, 13), aboard the American Viceroy's flagship near the port of Mogador. To test Prouhèze's renunciation, the devilish Camillo arranged this ultimate temptation by sending his wife and child as envoys. In a tender but firm dialectic the lovers review their love and sorrows, and she explains her mission and destiny to Rodrigue. If she flees with Rodrigue now, these will be vitiated and their honor violated and Camillo's skepticism justified. "Dear Rodrigue, there is no other deliverance for me save through death" (p. 838). But before returning to share it with Camillo in the dynamiting of the fortress at midnight to keep the Moors from taking it, she bequeaths Seven-Swords to Rodrigue. Less generous and impetuous in self-renunciation, Rodrigue will have to die more slowly, wounded by the dart of death which was the sight of this angel: "Ah, it takes time to die and the longest life is not too long to learn to respond to this long-suffering call" (p. 840).

With this separation scene Claudel corrects or perfects many similar earlier ones. He experienced growing misgivings about the Wagnerian sophistry and romantic exultations of the final Mesa-Ysé duet, where they are preoccupied with themselves and their reunion in eternity, scarcely conscious of God.[11] Contrariwise, Prouhèze and Rodrigue slowly deflate and purify their unconsummated love through renunciation of each other even in the next life, so as to center their destiny on God. By having Prouhèze die in exile, like Ysé, in an explosion at midnight, but with her husband in a spirit of sacrifice instead of with her lover, and offstage instead of on, Claudel finally exorcises his noonday demon. He had attempted to do so, but never quite successfully, in each play of the trilogy, in curiously similar separation scenes (always Act III, Scene 2). Jacques Petit has shown that in every case the scene is dominated by three images: the illusion of the world, an explosion, and night.[12] In the earlier works these tend to reinforce a spirit of revolt; in *Le Soulier* they suggest rather a spirit of submission and resignation to a superior destiny. The deaths of Prouhèze and Camillo symbolize the liberation of Rodrigue from the fire of earthly love and desire or revolt. He is free now to grow in peace and understanding, to respond in old age to the long-suffering call of death through humiliation and prayer in the fourth day. For as we have seen from the start, Claudel tends to indulge in a subtle dichotomy of his own inner movements, pairing off his animus-anima in polarized characters: Simon-Cébès, Mara-Violaine, Turelure-Georges de Coûfontaine, Amalric-Mesa, Orso-Orian. In *Le Soulier*, for the first time, as J. Petit says, Claudel succeeded in "saving" both halves of his double personality.[13] Petit points out that this drama resolves the conflicts and struggles of *Tête d'Or* as well as of *Partage*. The profound duality attenuated, the inner debate appeased, there is therefore no more drama to write after *Le Soulier*.

The Camillo-Rodrigue pair recalls the psalmist's cry, "We went through fire and through water; yet thou hast brought us forth to a spacious place" (Ps. LXVI, 12). The image of fire is constantly associated with the violent Camillo, as he carves out his kingdom on Spain's fiery frontier (SS, p. 664) and finally with a sudden burst of belief releases his tortured soul in the midnight explosion, in a form of martyrdom. The similarity with his violent predecessors is striking: Tête d'Or, Turelure, Mesa; and Avare in *La Ville*. What is instructive, however, is that we are not present or involved directly in the catapult into eternity. Instead, the whole affair is relegated to an offstage incident and an almost offhand remark. This is Claudel's subtle, ironic rebuttal of his many previous lyrical and explosive denouements. The moment of death is no longer enlarged and examined under either a romantic or a religious microscope. And why? One reason is that the exploration of the meaning of death has been completed in the preceding encounters, especially Prouhèze's with the angel and her two suitors. Another is that Claudel has attained a deeper view of death, no longer centered on the last moments of life but expanded to include the slow progression towards death. Exorcised of his youthful turbulence in the first three days of *Le Soulier*, he can spend the fourth day elaborating Rodrigue's, and his, daily dying—not in the fire of violence and glory, but on the waters of purification and peace.

This concentration on the principal themes and characters involves, of course, a gross and unfortunate falsification of such a richly textured tapestry as *Le Soulier*. Dona Musica, the Viceroy of Naples, the Chinese servant, Almagro, and the host of other characters serve frequently as important, sometimes ironic, counterpoints and help elucidate the dramatist's mature world view, half in a serious vein, half in one of gay buffoonery. Thus the joyful Musica, happy in love and marriage with a lesser viceroy, is a foil for the sorrows of Prouhèze, and Almagro is a delightful parody of Tête d'Or, Rodrigue, and ultimately of the author himself. The Viceroy's commission to Almagro (III, 3) is in fact a light lampoon of all dreams of a grandiloquent death: "I do not want you to die in a bed, but cut to the heart by some good blow, alone, on the roof of the world, on some inhuman peak, under the black sky full of stars, on the great plateau whence all rivers descend. . . ./ And no one will ever know where Almagro's body lies" (SS, p. 790). A "real bleating muttonhead" (SS, p. 814), he will fail through cowardliness, and he lacks the slightest tragic dimension.[14]

This wealth of counterpoint and minor characters, the interweaving and synthesis of all his themes, and especially the new variety of tones ranging from the most solemn to sheer burlesque, keep *Le Soulier* from seeming like a repetition or mere revision of *Partage*, despite their similar structure and central theme. Technical innovations, especially the casual beginning (repeated for Act III in the stage version), perhaps derived from Pirandello's *Six Characters in Search of an Author* and/or Goethe's *Faust*, are likewise noteworthy. But the most important of all in this respect, as well as in the treatment of the theme of death, is the startling originality of the final act, the fourth day.

THE FOURTH DAY: SEA, STARS, SALVATION

The last act, subtitled "To Windward of the Balearic Isles," with its ninety pages and thirty-three characters, is actually almost another play,[15] though of course an integral sequel and indeed key and crown to the first three days. It was conceived and partly composed, as we have seen, before the rest of the drama, and its atmosphere of self-pacification and ironic detachment permeates the whole play. "The word detachment might not be exact; it would be rather a separation of things from me, the creation of a wider and wider empty space," wrote Claudel on leaving Japan, just two months after completing Le Soulier. "I have great difficulty finding my place in this world which is no longer made for me. Hence this penchant for buffoonery" (J, pp. 656–657). Rodrigue, as the editor notes, experiences a similar deliverance. Essentially, it is a shift from concern with this world to concern with the next.

All the characters who introduce this irony, this movement of the creator making fun of his drama, of the lover who relives his love with sadness and detachment, sprang from this fourth day, which originally, says J. Petit, included the Chinese servant, the Neapolitan servant, and Camillo.[16] There may seem to be less concern with death in such an atmosphere. In reality, however, the scope of Claudel's concern is broader: the paradox of death, seen in the humiliation of the hero, which brings joy and deliverance. For Claudel, death alone gives a meaning to life, as only the Last Judgment gives a meaning to the history of men. This growing conviction will culminate in the dramatic device of opening his two operatic plays, Le Livre de Christophe Colomb (1929) and Jeanne d'Arc au bûcher (1934) with the death scene and using flashbacks of life. His ultimate hero and his ultimate heroine discover the sense of their lives and struggles only on the threshold of death, from the perspective of eternity.[17]

The most important difference between Le Soulier and the earlier plays may well be in the lighter, mocking tone, in the familiar, comic, even joyous view of death—and consequently of life. Assured of his immortality, man can have a more profound sense of humor:

> Laugh, immortal one, at seeing yourself amid these perishable things!
> Make sport and look at what you took seriously! For they pretend to be there but they are passing on. (OP, p. 269)

Little by little Rodrigue is able to heed this advice of the muse, to finally appreciate if not quite imitate the playfulness of Musica and Seven-Swords. For Claudel came to view the comic spirit and farce as the extreme point of lyricism, inspired by joy (*MI*, pp. 274, 285–286), and early characterized his masterpiece as an "enormous drama in four days, an incongruous mixture of buffoonery, of passion, and of mysticity." [18] In a 1909 letter to Gide he summed up tragedy as the struggle between the visible and the invisible (*MI*, p. 270). To the extent that this struggle is resolved, the possibility of tragedy declines and that of comic joy arises.

Rodrigue's purification and attainment of joy were slow and tortuous. Another ten years have elapsed, and the fourth day finds the hero disgraced, maimed, antiquated, reduced to selling huge holy pictures from his old boat, but still proud. These "Feuilles de saints," painted by his Japanese servant, evoke Claudel's collection of poems by the same title and Rimbaud's *Illuminations*, a parallel underlined by Rodrigue's loss of a leg, which occurred in an abortive attempt to conquer Japan, and was followed by years of imprisonment.

Despite its apparently looser structure, the fourth day is as skillfully constructed as its predecessors. The opening scene immediately evokes the burlesque, Protean tone of the whole day and the great leitmotiv of the sea: "All Spain is there, dancing on the pretty sea. The people have finally perceived that you can't really live anywhere but on the water" (*SS*, p. 850). At the same time it introduces almost all the remaining episodes: the burlesque fishing expedition for the mysterious bottle (Scenes 1, 5), Rodrigue's reincarnation as a holy-card merchant (Scenes 2, 11), the floating Court of the King of Spain (Scenes 4, 6, 9), where Rodrigue is baited and ridiculed, and even the Armada and Lepanto.[19] Scenes 3, 8, 10 evoke the presence of Prouhèze through her daughter, Seven-Swords, and Scene 7 offers a bourgeois parody of the first three days.

There are many minor references to death in this last act: Seven-Swords' readiness to die with Don Juan, who knows he will not live to be thirty; the drowning of her companion, La Bouchère; the King's magic crystal ball, a translucent Mexican skull, which reveals the naval disaster; the weary fatalism of the King, whom "no disaster can sate" and whose heart is open only to the "call of catastrophe" (*SS*, p. 870). But these are merely adjuncts and atmosphere for the very core of the fourth day—Rodrigue's slow dying, his delayed acquiescence to self-surrender, as he relinguishes his love, rank, ambition, pride, self-esteem, all human comfort.

Prouhèze and Rodrigue fulfill their sacrifice in three stages. She first forsook him when she accepted Pélagio's offer of Mogador (II, 4); she made a second renunciation to her guardian angel (III, 8); and she consummated her sacrifice when she renounced Rodrigue even in the next life (III, 13). Rodrigue's renunciation follows a similar but slower path: at Mogador (II, 11), then the great encounter with Prouhèze (III, 13), and finally his slow self-surrender in the twilight of life. Only in this third stage is love transformed into charity, though the first one had already produced great good on two continents and completed the cleansing of self. The process of purification involves the humiliation of being hood-winked by an actress, who makes him believe she is Mary Stuart escaped from Queen Elizabeth and inviting him to take over England for her (IV, 6); of being held up to mockery by the whole Spanish Court (IV, 9); and of being enslaved to the King's chamberlain, who sells him to his valet, who fobs him off on a soldier. Rodrigue must bear the soldier's insults and insolence about Prouhèze and Seven-Swords, and the rumor that the latter drowned, but his calm resignation and awareness of the beauty of the night signify that deliverance is nigh: "I have never seen any-thing so magnificent! It is as if the sky were appearing to me for the first time. Yes, it is on this beautiful night that I am finally cele-brating my engagement with freedom!" (SS, p. 928).

This release is possible because the purification is almost com-plete: "My soul is empty. Because of her who is not here, teeming tears, my tears, could nourish the sea" (SS, p. 900). The sea and the stars, always highly symbolic for Claudel, have invaded every-thing in this fourth day, submerging the mirage of the first three days and fulfilling the promise of Prouhèze's dream when she prayed to the angel: "He asked but a drop of water, but help me give him the ocean, brother" (SS, p. 808). The imagery of these two elements, of sea and stars, symbolizes the dual process of salvation—purification and liberation.

Claudel's fascination with each element was enduring. A 1909 entry in his *Journal* reads: "The sea like a view onto God" (*J*, p. 101). He compared wine and water to life and eternity (*J*, p. 284). He considered water a kind of paradisiac element and planned to write a treatise on its biblical symbolism. In the Tokyo earthquake of September 1, 1923, he lost not only the original third act of *Le Soulier* but two preparatory studies on water (*J*, p. 606). In September 1924, just as he was finishing the fourth day, he observed in a ten-line entry on baptism: "To be baptized, to vanish, to be swallowed up" and "Baptized, water over the head, this Head which is Christ" (*J*, p. 642). He was fascinated by the phenomenon of a luminous, milk-white sea; in the play he has the moon evoke "la Mer de Lait" (*SS*, p. 764; *cf. J*, p. 705). He associated the sea with living things and God, in contrast to Maurice Barrès' motto of "the Land and the Dead" (*J*, p. 621), and looked on it as "the horizon, the mirror of the sky," "the inexhaustible reservoir of possibilities," or like "an eternal temptation to embarkment and adventure" (*OC*, **XXV**, 34, 182).

In *Le Soulier*, the sea is essentially unlimited freedom and vital movement, with a constant, regular rhythm like breathing. Its majestic flux and reflux suggests a strong but hidden life. The poverty of description, in contrast with the rich, pagan, passionate images in *Partage* reflects the deliverance of Rodrigue and his creator from earthly pomp and pleasure, evoking an impression of calm and security. In the fourth day, the rhythm becomes lively and liberated. Seven-Swords adapts to it quite naturally, while Rodrigue does so gradually, with the result that his purification is implicitly imaged more by sonic vibration than by washing. Those who cannot adapt to its life find the sea ridiculous and inconsistent, but they themselves become incongruous and implausible, subject to disintegration and decomposition.[20] This is especially true of the unrhythmical, disjointed Spanish Court (*SS*, pp. 908, 910).

Rodrigue is associated with the sea, then, as thoroughly as Camillo was with fire. Master of two oceans for Spain, he has spent most of his life on the water and is loath to leave it even to serve Mary Stuart in England: "Must I be yanked off the sea I have so long felt living under my heart and which for so long has been my bed companion, the imperial couch under my body?" (*SS*, p. 892).

He is just as attuned to the profound interior life of "the free sea" as his Jesuit brother on his floating cross (SS, p. 653) and through him is plunged vicariously into a cleansing watery grave.

Although Prouhèze, dreaming, hears "the sea breaking ceaselessly on these eternal shores" (SS, p. 799), eternity is not to be found in the sea itself but in those "eternal waters" of heaven which it symbolizes and toward which the guardian angel pulls his fish. Mediating between the two are the regenerative waters of baptism, that effervescent spring that dissolves and recomposes all of Prouhèze's members, the nothingness she drowns in each instant, with God on her lips reviving her (SS, pp. 801, 807). A critic who cared enough to count found the image of the sea (called "the chief actor in the drama") used over thirty times—more frequently than that of the prison (about twenty times), which opens and closes the drama.[21] The two themes are closely entwined, of course, and one often evokes the other, at least implicitly.

The sensation of eternity as such is accorded less to the incessant and circular movement of the sea than to the celestial movements mirrored in it.[22] When the angel promises to make Prouhèze into a star to guide Rodrigue, he explains:

> No longer your body, but your reflection on the bitter waters of exile,
> Your reflection on the moving waters of exile endlessly vanishing and reforming. (SS, pp. 806, 809)

With his imaginative intuition, Rodrigue had already dimly divined this in his conversation with his Chinese servant. After comparing the new world to a star sprung up from the sea and from darkness, he evokes Prouhèze several times as a star, concluding in these terms:

> I know that this union of my being with hers is impossible in this life, and I will have no other.
> Only the star that she is
> Can slake this awful thirst in me. (SS, pp. 680–685)

One whole scene (II, 6) is devoted to the majestic appearance and monologue of the constellation Orion, also known as Saint James

(Santiago), a thread of light that guided Columbus. He is reflected in the ocean and serves to unite in the heavens those lovers separated on earth. The moon symbolizes the mercy of God bathing all men (SS, p. 763), while the order in the sky points to that of Paradise, and the multiplicity of golden stars suggests to Rodrigue the inexhaustible riches of God (SS, p. 906).

Many entries in his *Journal* attest to Claudel's constant fascination with the firmament: reflections on the nebulae at the frontiers of creation (J, pp. 39, 49), the Pleiades and other constellations, the numbers of stars, the ellipses of planets, Kepler's laws, the evening star, the morning star, data about Mars. In mid-1909 he pasted in a two-page picture of the antarctic aurora borealis.[28] An undated entry summarizes Taoist beliefs about the stars (J, p. 138), including their incarnation.

Perhaps the greatest characteristics of the cosmos for Claudel are its immensity and continuity: "Wondrous enlargement of the world. Nebulae 1,400,000,000 years away! Room to breathe! We are contemporaries of all Eternity" (J, p. 767). The beatific Seven-Swords assured Rodrigue, disconsolate over "this essential absence" of Prouhèze, that "the soul of the dead penetrates our heart and our brain like the air we breathe" (SS, p. 900). After a final bout of despair, he at last attains to this faith and freedom himself, under the spiritual direction of Friar Leo:

> Don Rodrigue: She is dead, dead, dead! She is dead, Father, and I shall never see her again! She is dead and never will she be mine! She is dead, and I am the one who killed her!
> Friar Leo: She is not so dead that this sky around us and this sea under our feet should not be yet more eternal!
> Don Rodrigue: I know. That was what she had come to bring me with the sight of her!
> The sea and the stars! I feel it under me, I gaze on them and cannot have my fill!
> Yes, I feel we cannot escape them and that it is impossible to die! (SS, p. 930)

Rodrigue's purification and pacification are completed, fittingly, in the dark but hope-filled conjunction of the sea and stars. The concluding episode of the gleaning nun, who is persuaded by the sailors to take Rodrigue along to wash the convent pots, is largely anticlimactic as far as Rodrigue's salvation is concerned but provides a clever device for disposing of the decrepit old conquistador in his last days. It may also be a personal tribute to certain Carmelite nuns and perhaps to Isabel Rimbaud, who went down to Marseilles to assist her dying brother and whose lengthy letter to her mother about Arthur's edifying death Claudel copied into his *Journal*.

The ending of *Le Soulier* is more genuinely autobiographical than any of Claudel's other plays, since the hero is brought only to the very threshold of death here and given the chance to "breathe in God" while doing something useful for the deliverance of souls before crossing the Holy Frontier. We can imagine Rodrigue sharing Claudel's own desire and fear of death: "O God, You know I have an immense desire to see You as well as a frightful fear of it!" (OC, XX, 120).

In a seminal study of Claudelian dramaturgy, Jean Rousset has shown that Claudel always works from the basic paradox of presence in absence. Dramatically, this is frequently transposed into poignant scenes of confrontation in which the principals are separated by some sort of a screen or meet only to part.[24] From our observations on the importance of the problem of death in Claudel's life, thought, and works, we are inclined not only to agree with this analysis of Claudel's fundamental dramatic technique but to add, moreover, that this constant structure is rooted in his existential anguish over the mystery of death. It is a natural, logical outgrowth of his metaphysical and theological struggles with the mockery death makes of man's aspirations and ambition for perfecting and perpetuating his existence. Since no lasting love or union is possible in this life, although love by its very nature and definition seeks to eternalize itself, the scandalous obstacle of death must be faced and its enigma resolved.

The shadow of mortality hovers over even man's most effective and intensive weapon against death, human love, leaving perfect happiness unattainable this side of the grave. That is why all of Claudel's intensely passionate characters are so wary of finding satisfaction on earth and consciously or subconsciously seek it in the hereafter. Most of his plays have one lover, usually the heroine, inviting the other to a communion in life beyond the grave: the Princess and Tête d'Or, Ysé and Mesa, Violaine and Jacques, Lumîr and Louis, Orian and Pensée, Prouhèze and Rodrigue. It is not an incapacity to love that induces this chthonic orientation but rather a preceding and prevailing obsession that alerts them to the insufficiency of human love in the face of death. Hence the series of separations and thwarted loves, the images of prison and the thirst for deliverance and freedom.

Death itself, then, is ultimately the screen or partition and stands not only between characters but most fundamentally between eros and agape. It is impervious to the first but penetrable by the second, reflecting eros back on itself but admitting agape into a new existence. The Christian paradox of life and death also inspires other stylistic devices for Claudel—the oxymoron and the chiasmus. "The most dangerous form of violence is patience," he wrote in 1948, and "L'Annonce faite à Marie is the fruit of fifty-six years of furious patience" (Th., II, 1356). In 1908 he had noted: "Chiasmus —cross in the shape of an X in order to disapprove" (J, I, 70).

The choice of deaths, for Claudel, means much more than the last act or attitude. It includes the kind and quality of life from which the final act springs. "Each free act involves an interpretation of oneself and one's life, and death is the final interpretation we give our whole life." [25] By eventually renouncing the autonomous dying of the secular hero and submitting to the ambiguities of death as an ultimate act of believing, hoping, loving, the later Claudelian heroes consummate their passion and desire for immortality. "Happy the man who in seeking Paradise. . . proceeds to the beyond by passion and desire" (OP, p. 625), as he exclaimed of Theresa of Avila. They see death not as extinction of self but as fulfillment, as entry into total freedom by union of a finite will with an infinite will. The vision of this freedom leads to joy and to the idea that our clothes and flesh are uncouth hindrances "to satisfying the unique duty of life, which is to dance." Whence the dance of the naked Negress (SS, p. 696) and Claudel's interest in Holbein's and Niklaus Manuel's Dance of Death at Basle in 1934.[26]

Even the violent, impetuous Tête d'Or was seeking in his revolt against death an unlimited light and life, and the point of his failure and agony is surely that each person must explore and encounter his own death and choose his form of salvation with lucidity, courage, and hope. With Mesa and Ysé the intimate relationship of love with death is explicitly explored and resolved in a Christian context full of romantic overtones. Violaine's serene resignation to death reflects a reconciliation of life and death in a mystic design transcending the natural order—and also the author's spiritual state, if not his aspirations. The ambivalence and hesitation of the Coûfontaines and Turelures in the trilogy reflect Claudel's own incomplete comprehension or acceptance of the ultimate sacrifice, but the optimistic tone and joy that characterize Orian and the Pope in *Le Père humilié* point to Rodrigue's eventual acceptance and renunciation:

> Make them understand that they have no other duty in the world but joy!
> . . . make them understand that it is not a vague word, an insipid sacristy commonplace,
> But a horrible, a superb, a dazzling, a poignant reality! And that all the rest is nothing beside it.
> Something humble and material and poignant, like the bread you desire, like the wine they find so good, like the water that makes you die if they give you none, like the fire that burns, like the voice that resurrects the dead!"
> (*Th.*, II, 528; cf. 510)

But it is only Rodrigue's own gradual discovery of joy and liberty through abandonment that signals the real resolution of Tête d'Or's revolt and marks the end of Claudel's quest, begun in proud despair, completed in humble hope. Or rather, the joy and sorrow, the hope and despair are entwined from first to last in a double helix, with joy and hope gradually gaining ascendancy.

Besides this evolution in his outlook on death, there are also some underlying constants. One recurring phenomenon is the panoramic vision of the past at the moment of death. Tête d'Or, Mesa, Ysé, and Violaine all experience this, while Rodrigue seems to anticipate it. Claudel was in fact so intrigued by its probability that he copied Bergson's explanation of it into his *Journal* in 1919 (I, 458).[27] It is particularly in this privileged instant of supreme lucidity, too, that his heroes find the wisdom and power to die in full freedom, to embrace their death as their very own in their final and supreme act of freedom—thus anticipating certain recent speculations.[28] Another important constant is the idea of freedom and expansion of the self after death. This is perhaps best epitomized, albeit negatively, by Prouhèze when she complains to the angel after her dream-ecstasy: "Ah, it's as if you were putting me back into a coffin. My limbs are corseted once more in narrowness and weight. I am yoked again by the finite and accidental" (*SS*, p. 808). A corollary of this is the solidarity and relationship of the separated soul with the cosmos, including the sun, moon, stars, and other spirits. Another corollary is the transmortal influence of the dead, such as Prouhèze exercises on Seven-Swords and Rodrigue on the fourth day, or such as Violaine promises to Jacques. This view of death as only a veil interposed between two worlds is neatly evoked in a little 1923 scenario, "La Femme et son ombre [The Woman and her Shadow]":

> Friend! Just as there is a shadow of bodies, so there is a reflection of voices.
> The voice that sings, beyond this visible world, does not cease being propagated in successive waves. (*Th.*, II, 644)

This encouraging voice singing of hope and joy beyond the grave, the many visions of a gallery of characters exploring the mystery of death, may well be Claudel's principal legacy to literature. Certainly in no other playwright has the exploration of this dark mystery been so pervasive or its resolution so profound.

Claudel's own death could hardly have been better chosen or more appropriate to him. He had attended the gala inaugural of *L'Annonce faite à Marie* at the Comédie Française on February 17, 1955. After a good Mardi Gras meal on February 22, he was stricken while reading a new book on Rimbaud, received the last rites fully conscious, and died before dawn on Ash Wednesday. His last words were, "Let me die alone. I'm not afraid." No doubt he experienced then what he had once expressed to a friend: "When

I'm on my deathbed, it will be sweet to think that my books have not added to the frightful sum of darkness, of doubt, of impurity that afflicts humanity, but that those who read them have found only reasons to believe and to rejoice and to hope." [29] Pierre Claudel relates that towards the end of his father's life he attained a child's curiosity about his death and said one day, "I am thrilled when I think of it," eager as a child to tear open a Christmas package.[30] No wonder André Maurois found "an admirable serenity" on his deathbed countenance. "If ever a man entered upon the last sleep with confidence, it was Paul Claudel." [31]

Notes

CHAPTER I

1. André Suarès, "Notes sur deux livres," *La Grande Revue*, 10 Oct. 1908, quoted by Robert Mallet, ed. Suarès-Claudel, *Correspondance*, 9th ed. (Paris: Gallimard, 1951), pp. 21–22.

2. Rollo May, *Love and Will* (New York: Norton, 1969), p. 109.

3. Frederick J. Hoffman, *The Mortal No* (Princeton, N.J.: Princeton University Press, 1964), p. 25.

4. Cf. Pierre-Henri Simon, *L'Homme en procès* (Neuchâtel: La Baconnière, 1950), pp. 32–35.

5. See Claude Vigée, "La Mort comme épreuve du réel dans les romans d'André Malraux," *MLN*, LXXXIII (May, 1968), 513–514, and Serge Gaulupeau, *André Malraux et la mort* (Paris: Lettres modernes, 1969), pp. 32–35.

6. As predominant as this basic theme is in Claudel's work, critics have seemed curiously unaware of it. Only Albert Béguin has written of it. A recent monumental book on the aesthetics of death makes only one reference to Claudel—to his very minor "Danse des morts." A study of some hundred images and the lyric elements in *L'Annonce* equally ignores the presence of death. See Michel Guiomar, *Pour une esthétique de la mort* (Paris: Corti, 1967), and Monique Parent, "Les Éléments lyriques dans *L'Annonce faite à Marie*," *Revue d'histoire du théâtre*, XX (1968), 261–274; see especially pp. 264–265.

7. Cf. Paul-André Lesort, "L'Amour et la vallée de larmes," in *Entretiens sur Paul Claudel*, ed. Georges Cattaui and Jacques Madaule (Paris: Mouton, 1968), pp. 103, 90–92.

8. Quoted by Albert Béguin, *Poésie de la présence* (Neuchâtel: La Baconnière, 1957), p. 243.

9. Quoted by Henri Mondor, *Claudel plus intime* (Paris: Gallimard, 1960), p. 61.

10. Quoted in *Paul Claudel 1868–1955*, ed. Étienne Dennery (Paris: Bibliothèque nationale, 1968), p. 35, item 122.

11. Ibid., p. 78, item 290.

12. Quoted by Jacques Petit, "Une Nature barbare," *Le Monde*, July 27, 1968, p. 4 (supplement).

13. Jacques Guicharnaud, *Modern French Theatre*, rev. ed. (New Haven: Yale University Press, 1967), p. 77.

14. This pessimistic side of Claudel has been best treated by André Espiau de la Maëstre. See especially *Das göttliche Abenteuer, Paul Claudel und sein Werk* (Salzburg: Otto Müller, 1969); and "Job et le problème du mal dans l'oeuvre de Claudel," *Entretiens sur Paul Claudel*, pp. 301–327.

15. From "The Ship of Death," *The Complete Poems of D. H. Lawrence*, ed. Vivian de Sola Pinto and F. Warren Roberts (New York: The Viking Press, 1964), II, 957.

16. See Hoffman, *The Mortal No*, p. 317.

17. Gaulupeau, *André Malraux*, p. 7.

18. Josef Pieper, *Death and Immortality*, trans. Richard and Clara Winston (New York: Herder and Herder, 1969), p. 77. See also Jacques Choron, *Death and Western Thought* (New York: Collier-Macmillan, 1963), pp. 234–240.

19. "Paul Claudel et le mythe grec," *La Table ronde*, no. 194 (Mar., 1964), p. 91.

20. Henri Guillemin, "Claudel jusqu'à sa 'conversion,'" *Revue de Paris*, LXII (April, 1955), 30.

21. Ibid., p. 23.

22. *OPR*, pp. 17, 19. The couplet is from "L'Horloge," which concludes with the verse, "Where everything will say to you: Die, old coward! It's too late! [Où tout te dira: Meurs, vieux lâche! il est trop tard!]" Charles Baudelaire, *Oeuvres complètes*, ed. Y.-G. Le Dantec and Claude Pichois (Paris: Gallimard-Pléiade, 1961), p. 77. One thinks of Tête d'Or's slaughter of the King. On the extent of this influence, see Jacques Madaule, "Baudelaire et Claudel," *Europe*, nos. 456–457 (April-May, 1967), pp. 197–204.

23. Frédéric Lefèvre, *Les Sources de Paul Claudel* (Paris: Lemercier, 1927), p. 164. Jean-Louis Barrault defined the three plays as "his sap, his test, his synthesis [sa sève, son épreuve, sa synthèse]" and as "his youth, the age of his greatest ardor, his flowering [sa jeunesse, l'âge de

sa plus grande ardeur, son épanouissement]." *Une Troupe et ses auteurs* (Paris: J. Vautrain, 1950), p. 83.

Chapter II

1. Gabriel Marcel *et al.*, "Vie et mort de Tête d'Or," in *Controverses: théâtre, roman, cinéma*, ed. R. Abirached (Recherches et débats, no. 32; Paris: A. Fayard, 1960), p. 28.

2. "Un Questionnaire au sujet de Tête d'Or," *Bulletin de la société Paul Claudel*, no. 4, pp. 12–13.

3. Stanislas Fumet, "Claudel lutteur réfléchi," *Cahiers de la compagnie Renaud-Barrault*, no. 27 (Oct., 1959), p. 38. This was the choice of Barrault for his 1959 and 1968 productions.

4. "If you only knew how ridiculous I appeared to myself! I have just reread *Tête d'Or*, which I have rewritten almost entirely, and how grateful I would have been to have my friends tell me all the ill they thought of it!" Letter to Marcel Schwob, July 12, 1894, *CPC*, I, 168. He expressed similar sentiments in a letter a fortnight later to M.-G. Byvanck, *CPC*, II, 271, and in 1911 to André Gide, *Correspondance: 1899–1926*, ed. Robert Mallet, 36th ed. (Paris: Gallimard, 1949), p. 171.

5. For an elaboration of this tendency in the young dramatist, see Petit's introduction to his critical edition of *La Ville* (Paris: Mercure de France, 1967), especially pp. 19–23 and 33–34.

It is ironical that the May, 1968, student uprisings that shook the strongest French government of the century followed a very successful revival of *Tête d'Or* at the Théâtre de France.

6. Number "C" comes immediately to mind, with its beginning:

> The maid with the big heart who made you so jealous—
> Now fast asleep beneath a modest lawn—
> We really ought to take her some flowers.
> The dead, the poor dead, have such great sorrows.

> [La servante au grand coeur dont vous étiez jalouse,
> Et qui dort son sommeil sous une humble pelouse,
> Nous devrions pourtant lui porter quelques fleurs.
> Les morts, les pauvres morts, ont de grandes douleurs].

It goes on to commiserate the dead "devoured by gloomy reveries/ Without a bedfellow, with no more pleasant chats [dévorés de noires songeries,/ Sans compagnon de lit, sans bonnes causeries.]" Cf. Baudelaire, *Les Fleurs du mal*, ed. Antoine Adam (Paris: Garnier, 1961), p. 112.

7. Consider these lines, for instance:

> Her sunken eyes are made of void and shadows,
> And her skull, artfully adorned with flowers,
> Upon her feeble skeleton limply sways.

> [Ses yeux profonds sont faits de vide et de ténèbres,
> Et son crâne, de fleurs artistement coiffé,
> Oscille mollement sur ses frêles vertèbres.] (Ibid., p. 108)

8. Ibid., p. 39.

9. Cf. A, p. 70: "That bark disappearing on the horizon flying my colors." For an interesting psychoanalytic interpretation of such imagery, see Gaston Bachelard, *L'Eau et les rêves* (Paris: J. Corti, 1947), pp. 104–108. On his first ocean voyage, Claudel related the watery vastness with the notion of death: "The water of the open sea is black . . . and this immense space takes on a sepulchral aspect . . ." (*CPC*, I, 72).

10. Thus Eugène Roberto writes: "The night exalts the significance of every created thing. It is not a symbol but a symbolic context that emphasizes what everything means. For night is an absence. But this absence situates everything by relationship to What is. Night underscores the interval needed by each thing to be fulfilled and the distance, needed for faith, which separates each creature from God." *Visions de Claudel* (Marseilles: Leconte, 1958), p. 29.

11. "The refusal of woman, the refusal of place (*lieu*) [the birthplace, with its charms of sleepiness and its temptations to rest] . . . , are probably only the expression and metamorphosis of the more essential refusal of death. The imagination ceaselessly intermingles these three terms, these three themes." Jean-Claude Morisot, "Tête d'Or ou les aventures de la volonté," *Revue des lettres modernes*, VI (1959), 127–128. Cf. pp. 128–142, *passim*.

12. "In the face of this calling (this 'tiding brought to' himself), he trembles at first and backs away, then he plunges forward." André Blanchet, S.J., *La Littérature et le spirituel*, III: *Classiques d'hier et d'aujourd'hui* (Paris: Aubier, 1961), p. 309. Cf. André Vachon, *Le Temps et l'espace dans l'oeuvre de Paul Claudel* (Paris: Seuil, 1965), pp. 57–67.

13. Blanchet, *La Littérature*, I: *La Mêlée littéraire* (Paris: Aubier, 1959), 307–308. Earlier, Charles Du Bos had written: "A non-Christian Claudel would have been a sun child who, like his Tête d'Or, at the moment of death would have called on the sun as a father, would perhaps have invoked it as a God, would in any case have no more admitted

that death is darkness than he had ever conceded that death is an end."
Approximations (1935; rpt. Paris: Fayard, 1965), p. 1199.

14. For a good résumé of the principal interpretations and possible sources of this expression, see Suzanne Bernard (ed.), Rimbaud, *Oeuvres* (Paris: Garnier, 1961), pp. 503–504. For a convenient listing of the first publications of the Rimbaud poems, see the bibliography established by Rolland de Renéville and Jules Mouquet in Arthur Rimbaud, *Oeuvres complètes* (Paris: Gallimard-Pléiade, 1954), pp. 810–813.

In a recent masterly article, André Blanchet details Claudel's changing critical appraisal of Rimbaud and concludes that the Rimbaud of his 1912 article is a subconscious double of Claudel himself in the throes of conversion between 1886 and 1890, as represented in *Tête d'Or*. "L'Élaboration par Claudel de son article sur Rimbaud," *Revue d'histoire littéraire de la France*, LXVII (1967), 759–775.

15. Cf. items 22 and 62 in the Renéville and Mouquet bibliography. There are other possible sources for the hero's strange appellation. Vachon (p. 124, n. 40) makes a very plausible case for Claudel's having read Daniel II, 38, where the prophet, interpreting Nabuchodonosor's dream about the statue with the golden head, tells the king, "Thou art this head of gold." He adds that Claudel's hero seems to share other traits of Nabuchodonosor, both being proud conquerors whose glorious careers end in total defeat.

16. Ernest Friche, for instance, analyzing the role of analogy in the two poets, remarks that all of Claudel's work seems to be a commentary on the following Rimbaud intuition: "Elle est retrouvée./ Quoi?— L'Éternité./ C'est la mer allée/ Avec le soleil." *Études claudéliennes* (Porrentruy: Portes de France, 1943), p. 110, n. 4. Indeed, it even appears from Claudel's early interest in Verlaine that "L'Éternité" may have been his very first contact with Rimbaud, through Verlaine's *Les Poètes maudits* (Paris: Vanier, 1884). Cf. Friche, pp. 80–81. But years later, Claudel quoted it sarcastically in his commentary of Romain Rolland's study of Hindu mystics. See *Emmaüs*, 13th ed. (Paris: Gallimard, 1949), p. 20.

17. "Ma Conversion," *Revue de jeunesse*, October 10, 1913; reprinted in OPR, pp. 1008–1014.

18. Blanchet, *La Mêlée*, p. 312. In an interview on October 6, 1942, Claudel confided to Fr. Blanchet that during this period he read the entire *Moralia* of St. Gregory the Great "with delight" and some St. Augustine, among other Fathers of the Church. Letter to the author, February 6, 1964.

19. Hugo Rahner, S.J., *Greek Myths and Christian Mystery*, trans. Brian Battershaw (New York: Harper & Row, 1963), p. 147. For an engaging scholarly analysis of this whole question, see all of Part I, Chapter 4, pp. 89–176: "The Christian Mystery of the Sun and the Moon."

20. *Journal intime*, quoted by Henri Guillemin, "Claudel jusqu'à sa 'conversion,'" *Revue de Paris*, LXII (April, 1955), 22.

21. These quotations are from *The Layman's Missal* (Baltimore: Helicon, 1962), using the Ronald Knox scriptural translations. Perhaps the most luminous synthesis of this whole light liturgy is the rapturous and recurrent hymn, Jesu, Redemptor omnium.

22. *MI*, p. 51. Cf. Blanchet, *La Mêlée*, p. 305. It is worth insisting on this source of Claudel's analogical tendency, in order to temper the view that his whole poetic method stems from Mallarmé and the symbolists. Cf. Henri Guillemin, "Claudel avant sa 'conversion,'" *Revue de Paris* (May, 1955), p. 97.

23. *Patrologia latina* (ed. Migne), LVII, 361.

24. See Erich Fromm, "Creators and Destroyers," *Saturday Review*, January 4, 1964, pp. 22–25.

25. *Paul Claudel interroge l'apocalypse* (Paris: Gallimard, 1952), pp. 112–113.

26. Ibid., p. 116.

27. Cf. Guillemin, "Claudel avant sa 'conversion,'" p. 94, as well as his dramatic re-creation, spliced with fitting quotations, of Claudel's mentality at that time, p. 93.

28. Cf. ibid., p. 91. After many years in an asylum at Montfavet, near Avignon, this talented sister died in October, 1944.

29. *The Layman's Missal*, p. 1037. The sole biblical usage of the Greek term "Tartarus" (II Peter II, 4) is to designate the abode of the fallen angels, held in an abyss of darkness. For Homer (*Iliad* VIII, 13), it lay as deep beneath Hades as the earth is beneath the sun.

30. Cf. Fromm, "Creators and Destroyers," *passim*.

31. *Les Fleurs du mal*, p. 36.

CHAPTER III

1. Roland de Vaux, *Ancient Israel: Its Life and Institutions*, trans. John McHugh (London: McGraw-Hill, 1961), p. 56. Cf. José Ferrater Mora, *Being and Death* (Berkeley and Los Angeles: University of California, 1965), pp. 218–219. For a fuller treatment, see Edmund F. Sutcliffe, *The Old Testament and the Future Life*, 2d ed. (London: Burns Oates, 1947).

2. See Robert Gleason, S.J., *The World to Come* (New York: Sheed & Ward, 1958), pp. 50–52.

3. Gabriel Marcel *et al.*, "Vie et mort de Tête d'Or," in *Controverses: théâtre, roman, cinéma*, ed. R. Abirached (Paris: A. Fayard, 1960), p. 33.

4. André Blanchet, *La Mêlée littéraire* (Paris: Aubier, 1959), p. 307.

5. Gabriel Marcel *et al.*, "Vie et mort de Tête d'Or," pp. 37–38.

6. Thus Claudel himself refers to Lâla in *La Ville* as a multiple symbol of Wisdom, Grace, and the Church, adding that all his feminine creations share this symbolism. *MI*, p. 91.

The Church symbolized by the Princess is much less the exterior or visible one with its earthly and Roman roots (*pace* S. Fumet) than the visionary and invisible Bride of Christ evoked in the Apocalypse (XII, 1): "a woman clothed with the sun, and the moon under her feet." Here again, however, it is not a question of a clear distinction between two unrelated entities but rather of their interpenetration, like the biblical and patristic use of type and antitype, for the woman clothed with the sun must also flee into the wilderness and suffer persecution. And perhaps both aspects of the Church can already be detected in the Princess' announcement of her temporary personality: "She who has closed her eyes and is going to wake up from a long silence" (*B*, p. 200).

7. *J'aime la bible* (Paris: A. Fayard, 1955), p. 8. For a fuller treatment of this question, see Blanchet, *La Mêlée*, pp. 305–308, especially p. 306: "But whatever form she puts on, she will always be that unexpected apparition that upsets one's life, because she 'announces' Beatitude and makes one leave all to follow her."

8. Cf. Jean-Claude Morisot, "Tête d'Or ou les aventures de la volonté," *Revue des lettres modernes*, VI (1959), pp. 170–171.

9. *Paul Claudel interroge l'apocalypse* (Paris: Gallimard, 1952), p. 86.

10. For a brilliant, but overly erotic, psychoanalytical interpretation of this curious scene and several allied ones, see Conor Cruise O'Brien, *Maria Cross* (Fresno, Calif.: Academy Guild, 1963), pp. 226–233.

11. On the complex relationship between human passion and the sublimest forms of love, see Martin C. D'Arcy, *The Mind and Heart of Love* (New York: Meridian, 1956) and Ignace Lepp, *The Psychology of Loving*, trans. Bernard B. Gilligan (Baltimore: Helicon, 1963).

Eugene Roberto has discovered a possible source of inspiration for this curious scene in the pathetic encounter between the explorer Camillus Douls and a Moorish girl, as related in *Le Tour du monde*, no. 1, 1888. *CCC*, IV, 59–61. In view of Claudel's early infatuation with Wagner, it is also quite possible that he was inspired by the reconciliation and transfiguration of Siegfried and Brünnhilda. See Jacques Moscovici, "Paul Claudel et Richard Wagner," *La Nouvelle Revue française,* 140 (August, 1964), p. 326.

12. See Hugo Rahner, S.J., *Greek Myths and Christian Mystery,* trans. Brian Battershaw (New York: Harper & Row, 1963), pp. 160–161, for an elucidation of the Christian symbolism of the moon in relation to Mary and to the Church.

13. Morisot, "Tête d'Or," p. 177, has also observed this, stating that we must not overlook her "sweet and twenty" side, that she senses her affinity with the flowers and fruit of the garden while at the same time exhaling an unearthly fragrance.

14. Roberto has suggested a resemblance between the double figure of Simon and Cébès and the Hindu androgyne Siva, half man and half woman. *CCC,* IV, 58. But it seems more probable that their names and attitudes—if not their characters—may have been inspired by the two principal interlocutors of Socrates in Plato's *Phaedo,* Simmias and Cebes, with their arguments about the immortality of the soul. Claudel's first acquaintance with them may well have been through Édouard Charton's *Le Tableau de Cébès, souvenirs de mon arrivée à Paris.* The book appeared the year Claudel himself arrived in Paris (1882), where he soon became an avid reader (*MI,* p. 25) of Charton's semiannual travel encyclopedia, *Le Tour du monde.* Cf. Roberto, *CCC,* IV, 61, and André Tissier, *"Tête d'Or" de Paul Claudel* (Paris: Société d'édition d'enseignement supérieur, 1968), pp. 103–106.

15. "For Claudel, the altogether first and capital question is always the 'Where am I?' and the following questions, the 'How far have I come?' and even the 'Who am I?' are conditioned by the first. . . . It is because they are moving in the midst of the fog that the incredulous, the indifferent, and the blind walk without knowing where they are and who they are, and it is because they do not know *where* they are that they do not know *who* they are." Charles Du Bos, *Approximations* (1935; rpt. Paris: Fayard, 1965), pp. 1174–1175.

16. Much of this naturalistic description may have been prompted by the depressing hospital and prison section of Paris, "the fetid Mouffetard Street," where the Claudels lived at this period. Cf. Henri Guillemin, "Claudel avant sa 'conversion,' " *Revue de Paris,* LXII (May, 1955), 91.

17. Jacques Madaule, *Le Drame de Paul Claudel,* 4th ed. (Paris: Desclée de Brouwer, 1947), p. 14. Cf. André Blanchet, *Classiques d'hier et d'aujourd'hui* (Paris: Aubier, 1961), p. 308.

18. Marcel *et al.,* "Vie et mort de Tête d'Or," p. 36.

19. Ibid., pp. 31–32. Alain Cuny, the actor who created the title role in 1959, felt that "the woman of the prologue, loved by both of them, could be considered as only the instrument by means of which they give a conventional aspect to feelings condemned by a conventional, imperative society."

20. For a good elucidation of Claudel's view of this natural and human duality, see D'Arcy, *The Mind and Heart of Love*, pp. 195–230, e.g., p. 207: "Each person has an animus and an anima, each is in different proportions masterful or clinging and submissive, fierce or gentle, hard or soft, Apolline or Dionysiac, intellectual or emotional, selfish or devoted." See also Jacques Madaule, *Le Génie de Paul Claudel*, 2d ed. (Paris: Desclée de Brouwer, 1933), pp. 227–230.

Although Lucretius and Tertullian are possible sources for Claudel's parable of animus and anima (which first appeared in the October and November 1925 issues of *La Nouvelle Revue française* in "Réflexions et propositions sur le vers français" [OPR, pp. 3–45]), Louise Allen reached the conclusion that it has no fixed literary source at all and that "its background is as general as the whole concept of the Rational and the Irrational." "The Literary Background for Claudel's *Parabole d'animus et anima*," *Modern Language Notes*, LXII (1947), p. 319.

From a strictly chronological point of view, it is of course possible that Claudel could have been familiar with some of Jung's early use of these terms, but there is no evidence of this either, and their two conceptions differ somewhat. For Claudel, they both exist in each sex, somewhat after the manner of cognitive and affective faculties, whereas Jung restricts the anima ("an irrational feeling") to the masculine subconscious and the animus ("irrational understanding") to the feminine subconscious. Cf. C. G. Jung, *Problèmes de l'âme moderne* (Paris: Corrêa, 1960), pp. 56, 313. As Jolan Jacobi stated, "the archetypal figure of the soul-image stands for the respective contrasexual portion of the psyche, showing partly how our personal relation thereto is constituted, partly the precipitate of all human experience pertaining to the opposite sex. In other words it is the image of the other sex that we carry in us, both as individuals and as representatives of a species." *The Psychology of Jung*, trans. K. W. Bash (New Haven: Yale University Press, 1947), pp. 104–105. Despite his unfamiliarity and differences with Claudel, it is interesting to note that Jung found the anima "strongly linked to an outline of the idea of reincarnation, under the form of an irrational feeling." *Problèmes*, p. 59.

21. D'Arcy, *The Mind and Heart of Love*, p. 208.

22. For the four levels or uses of anima, see ibid., p. 209. D'Arcy finds three levels of activity above the dark one explored by Jung.

23. As noted on pp. 13–16 of this study, the death of Cébès was darker and more pessimistic in the first version. There, the emphasis was on their bond of brotherly love, rather than on hope in a future life and on a voluntary adieu to this one. In "A" he does not relinquish himself and earth as in "B" but remains subject to worldly gravity, to the pull of mortality.

24. Consequently, it is only in a provisional or intentional sense, and not as a final judgment, that Morisot can say ("Tête d'Or," p. 170) that after Cébès' death Tête d'Or closed himself to all possibility of exchange in order to construct a destiny which would permit him to exorcise death by forgetting it.

25. "La 'Conversion' de Paul Claudel," Les Études classiques, XXV, 42. Cf. Morisot, "Tête d'Or," p. 171: "One hardly understands Tête d'Or if he does not sense in it this kind of long debate between the feminine voice and the masculine."

26. On the question of friendship and sex, Lepp, The Psychology of Loving (p. 197) and D'Arcy, The Mind and Heart of Love (p. 234) are enlightening.

27. Blanchet, Classiques d'hier et d'aujourd'hui, p. 308.

28. Quoted by Guillemin, "La 'Conversion' de Paul Claudel," Les Études classiques, XXV, 31–32.

29. G. Marcel et al., "Vie et mort de Tête d'Or," p. 36.

30. Quoted by Guillemin, "Claudel jusqu'a sa 'conversion,'" Revue de Paris, LXII (1955), 28.

31. See, for example, Morisot, "Tête d'Or," pp. 135–136.

32. "Chant à cinq heures" (second version of dedication), Th., I, 1157.

33. Morisot, "Tête d'Or," pp. 159–162.

34. Ibid., p. 195.

35. Jacques Rivière, Correspondance, 1907–1914 (Paris: Plon, 1926), p. 98.

36. Du Bos, Approximations, p. 1199.

37. "La 'Conversion' de Paul Claudel," pp. 37–39.

38. Tête d'Or ou l'imagination mythique chez Paul Claudel (Paris: Collection de l'École normale supérieure de jeunes filles, 1967), p. 65.

39. Blanchet, Classiques d'hier et d'aujourd'hui, p. 315.

CHAPTER IV

1. Suarès-Claudel, Correspondance: 1904–1938, ed. Robert Mallet, 9th ed. (Paris: Gallimard, 1951), p. 89.

2. Claudel-Gide, *Correspondance: 1899–1926*, ed. Robert Mallet, 36th ed. (Paris: Gallimard, 1949), pp. 67–68. Cf. the ecstatic comment of Alain-Fournier in a January, 1907, letter to Bichet: "How divine, pure, frighteningly beautiful it is—asceticism and ecstasy: Mesa is not accepted by God until he has suffered from life, loved life, suffered from woman, loved Ysé." *Lettres au petit B.* (Paris: Émile-Paul, 1930), p. 119.

3. Rivière, *Correspondance: 1907–1914* (Paris: Plon, 1926), p. 184.

4. The third edition (Gallimard, 1949) was used for the English translation: *Break of Noon*, trans. Wallace Fowlie (Chicago: Henry Regnery, 1960). Until Gérald Antoine's critical edition appears, some idea of the three incomplete drafts that preceded the 1906 edition may be obtained from Moriaki Watanabé's perceptive article, "Le 'Don,' ou la logique dramatique de *Partage de midi*," in *Revue des lettres modernes*, nos. 180–182 (1968), pp. 25–57. See especially p. 52, n. 3.

5. OC, XI, 310. Mauriac was particularly incensed over the vulgarization of Ysé in the new versions, asking why Claudel had to add to her role such vulgarities and even oaths, almost blasphemies, which never figured in the original text. P. 311.

6. "Le Réalisme de Claudel," *La Table ronde*, no. 194 (March, 1964), p. 151.

7. François Varillon, *Claudel* (Bruges: Desclée de Brouwer, 1967), p. 63. Her bearing and appearance must have been like that of Edwige Feuillère, the actress who created the role in 1948, as Claudel remarked on the striking resemblance. "Une Lettre de Paul Claudel à Edwige Feuillère," *Plaisir de France*, no. 352 (February, 1968), pp. 28–31.

For a 1929 American appreciation of Rosalie's personality and role in the affair, see Agnes Meyer's diary, CCC, VI, 163, 184–185. For a glimpse of Claudel's confusion at her flight in 1905, see his *Journal*, I, 126–127.

8. For instance, *Les Cinq Grandes Odes*, especially the first two odes; "Ténèbres," "Obsession," "Ballade," "Dissolution"; *La Cantate à trois voix* (1911); *Cent Phrases pour éventails* (1925); and nearly all his subsequent dramas, especially *Le Soulier de satin* (1919–24).

9. For the sense of the title and the names of the characters, see Fowlie, *Break of Noon*, pp. xii–xiii. The mythic proportions in the genesis and character of Mesa and Ysé are adroitly elaborated in two recent articles. Eugène Roberto (CCC, IV, 195–204) suggests that Claudel may well have found the name in the Bible (II Kings), the ancient history of Palestine, or in Victor Hugo's *La Légende des siècles* and shows that the Mesa of *Partage* has some features of all three presentations of the Moabite king, especially Hugo's.

Moriaki Watanabé, "Le Nom d'Ysé: le mythe solaire japonais et la genèse du personnage," *Revue d'histoire littéraire de la France*, LXIX (1969), 74–92, after studying Claudel's treatment of the Japanese legend in his prose poem, "The Deliverance of Amaterasu" (*OP*, pp. 109–114), concludes that the name Ysé is derived partly at least from a remembrance of this myth, "of the retreat and deliverance of the Great Solar Goddess, with whom the name of Isé is originally associated. The solar attribute of Ysé is the element that links her directly to Yseult the blond and to the legend of Amaterasu." P. 92.

10. Suarès-Claudel, *Correspondance*, p. 89.

11. See Watanabé, "Le 'Don,'" p. 35.

12. The French version of the whole canticle of Mesa follows:

CANTIQUE DE MESA

Monologue

1.   Me voici dans ma chapelle ardente!

Et de toutes parts, à droite, à gauche, je vois la forêt des flambeaux qui m'entoure!

Non point de cires allumées, mais de puissants astres, pareils à de grandes vierges flamboyantes

Devant la face de Dieu, telles que dans les saintes peintures on voit Marie qui se récuse!

5.   Et moi, l'homme, l'Intelligent,

Me voici couché sur la Terre, prêt à mourir, comme sur un catafalque solennel,

Au plus profond de l'univers et dans le milieu même de cette bulle d'étoiles et de l'essaim et du culte.

Je vois l'immense clergé de la Nuit avec ses Évêques et ses Patriarches.

Et j'ai au-dessus de moi le Pôle et à mes côtés la tranche, et l'Équateur des animaux fourmillants de l'étendue,

10.   Cela que l'on appelle Voie lactée, pareil à une forte ceinture!

Dialogue with Stars

Salut, mes soeurs! aucune de vous, brillantes!

Ne supporte l'esprit, mais seule au centre de tout, la Terre

A germé son homme, et vous, comme un million de blanches brebis,

Vous tournez la tête vers elle qui est comme le Pasteur et comme le Messie des Mondes!

15.   Salut, étoiles! Me voici seul! Aucun prêtre entouré de la
pieuse communauté
Ne viendra m'apporter le Viatique.
Mais déjà les portes du Ciel
Se rompent et l'armée de tous les Saints, portant des
flambeaux dans leurs mains,
S'avancent à ma rencontre, entourant l'Agneau terrible!

Interrogation of Christ
20.   Pourquoi?
Pourquoi cette femme? pourquoi la femme tout d'un
coup sur ce bateau?
Qu'est-ce qu'elle s'en vient faire avec nous? est-ce que
nous avions besoin d'elle? Vous seul!
Vous seul en moi tout d'un coup à la naissance de la Vie,
Vous avez été en moi la victoire et la visitation et le
nombre et l'étonnement et la puissance et la merveille et le
son!
25.   Et cette autre, est-ce que nous croyions en elle? et que le
bonheur est entre ses bras?
Et un jour j'avais inventé d'être à Vous et de me donner,
Et cela était pauvre. Mais ce que je pouvais,
Je l'ai fait, je me suis donné,
Et Vous ne m'avez point accepté, et c'est l'autre qui nous
a pris.
30.   Et dans un petit moment je vais Vous voir et j'en ai effroi
Et peur dans l'Os de mes os!
Et Vous m'interrogerez. Et moi aussi je Vous interrogerai!
Est-ce que je ne suis pas un homme? Pourquoi est-ce que
Vous faites le Dieu avec moi?
Non, non, mon Dieu! Allez, je ne Vous demande rien!
35.   Vous êtes là et c'est assez. Taisez-Vous seulement,
Mon Dieu, afin que votre créature entende! Qui a goûté
à votre silence,
Il n'a pas besoin d'explication.

Dawning of Understanding
Parce que je Vous ai aimé
Comme on aime l'or beau à voir ou un fruit, mais alors
il faut se jeter dessus!
40.   La gloire refuse les curieux, l'amour refuse les holocaustes
mouillés. Mon Dieu, j'ai exécration de mon orgueil!

Sans doute je ne Vous aimais pas comme il faut, mais pour l'augmentation de ma science et de mon plaisir.

Et je me suis trouvé devant Vous comme quelqu'un qui s'aperçoit qu'il est seul.

Eh bien! j'ai refait connaissance avec mon néant, j'ai regoûté à la matière dont je suis fait.

J'ai péché fortement.

45.   Et maintenant, sauvez-moi, mon Dieu, parce que c'est assez!

C'est Vous de nouveau, c'est moi! Et Vous êtes mon Dieu et je sais que Vous savez tout.

Et je baise votre main paternelle, et me voici entre vos mains comme une pauvre chose sanglante et broyée!

Comme la canne sous le cylindre, comme le marc sous le madrier.

Et parce que j'étais un égoiste, c'est ainsi que vous me punissez

50.   Par l'amour épouvantable d'un autre!

Chastened Comprehension of Love

Ah! je sais maintenant

Ce que c'est que l'amour! et je sais ce que Vous avez enduré sur votre croix, dans ton Coeur,

Si vous avez aimé chacun de nous

Terriblement comme j'ai aimé cette femme, et le râle, et l'asphyxie, et l'étau!

55.   Mais je l'aimais, ô mon Dieu, et elle m'a fait cela! Je l'aimais et je n'ai point peur de Vous,

Et au-dessus de l'amour

Il n'y a rien, et pas Vous-même! et Vous avez vu de quelle soif, ô Dieu, et grincement des dents,

Et sécheresse, et horreur et extraction,

Je m'étais saisi d'elle! Et elle m'a fait cela!

60.   Ah, Vous Vous y connaissez, Vous savez, Vous,

Ce que c'est que l'amour trahi! Ah, je n'ai point peur de Vous!

Mon crime est grand et mon amour est plus grand, et votre mort seule, ô mon Père,

La mort que Vous m'accordez, la mort seule est à la mesure de tous deux!

Acceptance of Death
　　　Mourons donc et sortons de ce corps misérable!
65.　　Sortons, mon âme, et d'un seul coup éclatons cette dé-
testable carcasse!
　　　La voici déjà à demi rompue, habillée comme une viande
au croc, par terre ainsi qu'un fruit entamé.
　　　Est-ce que c'est moi? Cela de cassé,
　　　C'est l'oeuvre de la femme, qu'elle le garde pour elle, et
pour moi je m'en vais ailleurs.
　　　Déjà elle m'avait détruit le monde et rien pour moi
70.　　N'existait qui ne fût pas elle et maintenant elle me dé-
truit moi-même.
　　　Et voici qu'elle me fait le chemin plus court.
　　　Soyez témoin que je ne me plais pas à moi-même!
　　　Vous voyez bien que ce n'est plus possible!
　　　Et que je ne puis me passer d'amour, et à l'instant, et non
pas demain, mais toujours, et qu'il me faut la vie même, et
la source même,
75.　　Et la différence même, et que je ne puis plus,
　　　Je ne puis plus supporter d'être sourd et mort!
　　　Vous voyez bien qu'ici je ne suis bon à rien et que
j'ennuie tout le monde
　　　Et que pour tous je suis un scandale et une interroga-
tion.
　　　C'est pourquoi reprenez-moi et cachez-moi, ô Père, en
votre giron! (A, pp. 1051–1054)

13. Georges Poulet, *The Metamorphoses of the Circle*, trans. Carley
Dawson and Elliott Coleman (Baltimore: The Johns Hopkins Press,
1966), p. 326.

14. Cf. Marius-François Guyard, *Recherches claudéliennes* (Paris:
Klincksieck, 1963), p. 89. In his 1910 letter on Patmore, Claudel wrote:
"The world is not infinite. It is inexhaustible, which is quite different,
inexhaustible like the jar of the widow of Sarepta." *OPR*, p. 531.

15. Guyard, *Recherches*, pp. 87–89. This idea permeates his fifth great
ode, "La Maison fermée." See especially *OP*, pp. 284–285.

16. Cf. "Art poétique," *OP*, pp. 167, 168.

17. Cf. Poulet, *Metamorphoses*, p. 324; *J*, I, 142–146.

18. Claudel, unpublished text quoted by Jean-Claude Berton, *Shakespeare et Claudel* (Geneva: La Palatine, 1958), p. 217.

19. Poulet, *Metamorphoses*, p. 328. He goes on to make this interesting comparison: "The strange thing is how difficult it is for Proust to realize what Claudel achieves with such ease." P. 329.

20. Cf. Pierre Teilhard de Chardin, *The Phenomenon of Man*, trans. Bernard Wall (New York: Harper, 1959), *passim*, e.g., 180–183 or 299–301. Although they met once, neither writer was familiar with the other's work. Cf. *J*, II, 617, 740.

21. See Poulet, *Metamorphoses*, p. 335.

22. In the last entry for 1905 in his *Journal*, Claudel copied two pages of extracts from a French translation of Newman's poem, with a reminder to see what he says about angels. *J*, I, 31–32; 1061–1062. A few weeks later, early in 1906, he wrote to Gabriel Frizeau to recommend "The Dream of Gerontius," calling it an "admirable psychagogic poem" and adding, "There are some surprising encounters between certain parts of this poem and some of my own works and ideas." *Correspondance: 1897–1938*, ed. André Blanchet, 4th ed. (Paris: Gallimard, 1952), p. 82.

A recent edition of the poem can be found in *A Newman Reader*, ed. Francis X. Connolly (Garden City, N.Y.: Doubleday-Image, 1964), pp. 450–477.

23. Cf. Poulet, *Metamorphoses*, p. 335: "There is, on Claudel's part, a sort of final withdrawal of the whole being toward the mysterious Point which is that of all of birth and all of death."

24. Claudel, forty-three years later, was pitiless in excoriating Mesa, calling him miserly, egotistic, a sugar-coated tough nut, narrow-minded, occupied uniquely with himself, utterly unconcerned with his neighbor. However exaggerated this retrospective scorn, the essential point is clear: "The adventure of the road to Damascus [the earlier conversion of Mesa-Claudel] . . . worked no essential transformation in him. It simply accentuated his feeling of difference and superiority. . . ." *OC*, XI, 305.

25. *Les Cinq Grandes Odes de Claudel* (Paris: Lettres modernes, 1959), p. 36. Cf. p. 37: "Every time, the repetition of the *and's* is accompanied by a display of other resources belonging to the same stylistic domain: repetitions of sounds, constructions, rhythmic units." For the biblical influence (especially of the Psalms and Job) on the canticle, see Elfrieda Dubois, "Some Reflections on Claudel's *Verset*," in *Claudel: A Reappraisal*, ed. Richard Griffiths (London: Rapp & Whiting, 1968), pp. 122–125.

26. *Linguistics and Literary History* (Princeton: Princeton University Press, 1948), pp. 206 ff.; cf. also p. 226, n. 28.

27. See Spitzer, *Linguistics*, p. 235, for an analysis of Claudel's symbolism of numbers in terms of the week.

28. This impression of movement backwards or of a redescent into an unwanted position is a sort of negative counterpart of the usual, fivefold forward or re-creative movement and meaning implied in the typical Claudelian *re*-cluster. Instead of a "semantic expansion," line 43 here connotes a vortical contraction. Cf. Spitzer, *Linguistics*, pp. 228–229.

29. Martin D'Arcy, S.J., *The Mind and Heart of Love* (New York: Meridian, 1956), p. 173.

30. Émile Capouya, review of Wayland Young, *Eros Denied: Sex in Western Society* (New York: Grove, 1964), in *Saturday Review*, June 6, 1964, p. 42.

31. Gérald Antoine, "L'Expression tragique dans *Partage de midi*" in *Le Théâtre tragique*, ed. Jean Jacquot (Paris: Centre national de la recherche scientifique, 1962), p. 449.

32. Cf. Watanabé, "Le 'Don,' " pp. 46–47.

33. But then, as we know, the real-life Ysé never returned, to the constant chagrin of Claudel who always remained baffled and piqued, inventing pretexts why she should have come back. Less than a year before his death he explained her stage-version return in this fashion: "She just got the idea like that of bringing her heart back to this abandoned wretch. She was going to leave, to let herself be carried away by the current, anywhere, to the devil. But suddenly she was smitten by the sun, so to speak, or by the starry sky. And she came back, rather unaware of what she was doing. She knew only that she was the stronger." *OC*, XI, 328.

34. On the importance of the name as a key and talisman to the personality of another, see Louis Bouyer, *The Meaning of Sacred Scripture* (Notre Dame, Ind.: University Press, 1958), p. 22; also, Wallace E. Caldwell, "Names," in *Studies in Honor of Ullman*, ed. Lillian B. Lawler *et al.* (St. Louis: University Press, 1960), pp. 29–34. Rollo May is particularly perceptive in *Love and Will* (New York: Norton, 1969), pp. 167–177.

35. Antoine, "L'Expression tragique" (p. 450), asks for instance if Mesa is joking ("raille-t-il?") but can only decide in the negative.

36. See, for instance, Georges Gargam, *L'Amour et la mort* (Paris: Seuil, 1959), p. 163; Roger Pons, *Procès de l'amour* (Paris: Castermann, 1955), pp. 115–125; Joseph Chiari, *The Poetic Drama of Paul Claudel* (New York: P. J. Kenedy & Sons, n.d.), p. 69. Insistence on their black-and-white extremes would tend to wash away the twilight zone of poetic suggestivity, not to mention the possibility of redemptive repentance.

37. Bernard Howells, "The Enigma of *Partage de midi*: A Study in Ambiguity," in *Claudel: A Reappraisal*, ed. Richard Griffiths (London: Rapp & Whiting, 1968), pp. 19–33.

38. Ibid., pp. 31–32.

39. Ibid., p. 28. Nor is it exact to say that the definitions she gives of herself are always definitions of Mesa's feelings towards her (p. 28). She is no servile foil but a highly independent character. As Watanabé says in "Le Nom d'Ysé," p. 89, she is not simply the object of desire but is herself a desire that jealously covets Mesa's soul.

40. Cf. André Vachon, *Le Temps et l'espace dans l'oeuvre de Paul Claudel* (Paris: Seuil, 1965), p. 255, and Watanabé, "Le 'Don,' " p. 46.

41. Quoted by Vachon, *Le Temps et l'espace*, p. 55. See also pp. 193, 249, 253, 255.

42. Marianne Mercier-Campiche, *Le Théâtre de Claudel* (Paris: Pauvert, 1968), pp. 149–150.

43. See Jean-Claude Morisot, "Tête d'Or ou les aventures de la volonté," *Revue des lettres modernes*, VI (1959), 136.

44. For a résumé of these notions, see D'Arcy, *The Mind and Heart of Love*, pp. 80–82.

45. In his otherwise astute study of water and gold in Claudel, Conor Cruise O'Brien gives the perplexing, if not ludicrous, interpretation that the soul's own "golden sound" serves as the ears of God. Furthermore, he falls into too easy a dichotomy when he claims that "this spiritual exaltation is at the same time an orgasmic cry." Cf. "The Rhinegold of Paul Claudel," *Maria Cross* (Fresno, Calif.: Academy Guild, 1963), p. 162. This mischievous half-truth comes from neglecting the passage of time (and Ysé's conversion)—a frequent fault in thematic studies, which too often reduce complex nuances to one-dimensional simplicity in the present tense. In this case, it is more correct to speak of a spiritual rhapsody with a strong sensual overtone, for her past carnal conduct is not now the object of a renewed delectation, but rather the memory of it serves as a symbol of her imminent death and transfiguration, and also as a spur to donate herself more generously to this impending destiny.

As a matter of fact, Ysé herself explicitly distinguishes between her irrational, sinful past ("I've been pliant flesh under you . . . and like a beast that is not impelled by reason") and her new nature, now on the threshold of eternal fulfillment: "See her now unfolded, Mesa, the woman full of beauty unfurled in greater beauty!" (*A*, p. 1063). The fact that platonic and mystic love so often have recourse to a terminology and imagery borrowed from sense experience does not prove any identity between an orgasm and a genuine ecstasy but simply that the "categories of human experience are erected on the basis of sense experience." Cf. Ignace Lepp, *The Psychology of Loving*, trans. Bernard B. Gilligan (Baltimore: Helicon, 1963), pp. 217–218, and Claudel, *OP*, p. 199. The identification of the two on the basis of metaphoric similarity is gratuitous and destructive of symbolism.

46. Mercier-Campiche, *Le Théâtre de Claudel*, pp. 157–158.

47. "Le Poison wagnérien," *OPR*, p. 368. Already in 1913 he had exclaimed to Rivière: "How ridiculous the romantic vapors of purely carnal love and the brayings of that great ass Tristan seem to me!" Rivière, *Correspondance: 1907–1914*, p. 262.

48. See Leo Spitzer, "Three Poems on Ecstasy," *Essays on English and American Literature*, ed. Anna Hatcher (Princeton: Princeton University Press, 1962), pp. 171–179.

For a résumé of the Schopenhauerian philosophy of nature and death, see Jacques Choron, *Death and Western Thought* (New York: Collier, 1963), pp. 163–185. The gist of his view is that death destroys only consciousness and intellect, without affecting man's true nature—the will—which remains at one with the inner essence of the world.

49. Cf. Jacques Duron, "Le Mythe de Tristan," *La Nouvelle Revue française*, September, 1955, pp. 550–551, and *Entretiens sur Paul Claudel*, ed. Georges Cattaui & Jacques Madaule (Paris: Mouton, 1968), pp. 19–20. By contrast, other critics think there is less question of reaction than influence in the early dramas, including *Partage*. See André Espiau de la Maëstre, "Claudel et la musique," *Les Lettres romanes*, XIII (1959), 162, 171; Jacques Moscovici, "Paul Claudel et Richard Wagner," *La Nouvelle Revue française*, no. 140 (August, 1964), pp. 332–333. Werner Oswald, "Die symbolischen Bezüge in P. Claudel's *Tête d'Or*," *Die Neueren Sprachen*, Feb. 1963, pp. 61–72, seems closer to the truth in holding that Claudel's early drama is already so inspired by Christianity that Wagnerian thematic influences have been essentially changed and Christianized.

50. *A*, p. 1063. Whatever the exact sense of this lyrical explosion, its imagery was almost certainly inspired, as Alain-Fournier remarked to Rivière in 1907, by Camille Claudel's *The Dance* and *The Conversation*. See Mercier-Campiche, *Le Théâtre de Claudel*, p. 152, n. 1.

51. On Ysé as Emma Bovary as well as Beatrice, see Ernest Beaumont, *The Theme of Beatrice in the Plays of Claudel* (London: Rockliff, 1954), pp. 31–43.

52. O'Brien, *Maria Cross*, pp. 169–176.

53. Gaston Bachelard, *L'Eau et les rêves* (Paris: J. Corti, 1947), pp. 117–118.

54. Although Ysé herself evokes no image of fire here in the moonlight, but only her feminine charm, Mesa will soon do so, complementing midnight with noon and water with fire. A more explicit shifting between water and fire, but without any spiritual overtones, as metaphors for the hair of the beloved occurs in Claudel's evocation of Erato a year earlier, at the end of "Les Muses," *OP*, pp. 232–233. The fact that *there* the blond hair was undulating "in the wind of the sea," prior to waving in "the wind of Death" here, substantiates O'Brien's and Bachelard's views on the group "water-woman-death." See also Mercier-Campiche, *Le Théâtre de Claudel*, p. 153.

55. Claudel probably had in mind both *The Divine Comedy* and "The Dream of Gerontius," although he has pointed out that Mesa's swan song is a nearly literal quotation of the ending of his early "Fragment d'un drame," except that there Henri declines Marie's invitation to join her in death. See *MI*, pp. 29–30.

56. See, for example, Mercier-Campiche, *Le Théâtre de Claudel*, p. 155, and Espiau de la Maëstre, "Claudel et la musique," pp. 162, 171.

57. *J*, I, 9–11, 16, for instance. By contrast, the sparse mentions of Nietzsche are invariably derogatory and linked with such Claudelian *bêtes noires* as Voltaire, Rousseau, Renan, and Ibsen. Claudel wrote Agnes Meyer in 1929 that he had never read Nietzsche and was horrified by his anti-Christian position. *CCC*, VI, 106.

On the significance of noon for Claudel, see Vachon, *Le Temps et l'espace*, p. 255, n. 36. The elaboration of the same imagery at the end of the fourth ode (1907) clarifies its meaning considerably:

> After the abundance of April and the superabundance of
> summer,
> Behold the work of August, the extermination of Noon,
> Behold the seals of God broken open as He comes to judge
> the world by fire!
> From the destroyed heaven and earth He now makes but a
> single nest in the flame,
> And the untiring cry of the cicada fills the deafening
> furnace!
> Thus the sun of the spirit is like a cicada in the sun of God.
> (*OP*, p. 276)

58. Watanabé, "Le 'Don,' " 1968, p. 46. The seven-line entry on the Transfiguration in his diary at this time attests to the feast's fascination for him. *J*, I, 25.

59. O'Brien, *Maria Cross*, pp. 164–165; 174–176; 185.

60. Rollo May, *Love and Will*, p. 102.

CHAPTER V

1. H. R. Lenormand, quoted by Robert Mallet, ed., in Claudel-Gide, *Correspondance: 1899–1926*, 36th ed. (Paris: Gallimard, 1949), p. 287.

2. Claudel-Gide, *Correspondance: 1899–1926*, pp. 97–99.

3. Claudel-Jammes-Frizeau, *Correspondance: 1897–1938*, ed. André Blanchet, 4th ed. (Paris: Gallimard, 1952), p. 151.

4. See Richard Griffiths, "Liberté, souffrance et expiation chez Claudel," in *Entretiens sur Paul Claudel*, pp. 240–243.

5. For background on this doctrine and period, see Chapter VIII, "Vicarious Suffering," in Richard Griffiths' *The Reactionary Revolution* (New York: Ungar, 1965), pp. 149–222. As for Griffiths' promotion of Huysman's *Sainte Lydwine de Schiedam* (1901) as a direct influence, it seems unlikely in view of Claudel's denial. (See Harold A. Waters, "Possible Sources for Claudel's Violaine," *Renascence*, XXII [Winter, 1970], 105.) Still, he had seen Huysmans a couple of times at Ligugé in 1900 (*J*, I, 644) and undoubtedly heard about him from their mutual friend and director, l'abbé Fontaine, to whom Huysmans bequeathed all his books upon his death in 1907. In 1915 Claudel quoted copiously from Huysman's annotated copy of St. Theresa of Avila's *Life* (*J*, I, 308). Although he may have seen or at least heard of it on his visit to France in 1909 (September–November), en route to his new post in Prague, there is no mention of this book or saint in his *Journal* or published correspondence.

6. *J*, I, 114. For further information on St. Colette, as well as other possible sources for Violaine, see Waters, "Possible Sources for Claudel's Violaine," pp. 99–107. He does not cite this passage from the *Journal*, however, which would seem to clinch the case for Colette. Curiously, two lives of St. Colette were published in Paris a year *after* Claudel's entry in his *Journal*.

Eugène Roberto offers two more possible sources, referring to Claudel's favorite periodical in his youth, *Le Tour du monde*. CCC, IV, 63–64.

7. André Espiau de la Maëstre, "*L'Annonce faite à Marie*," *Les Lettres romanes*, XVI (1962), 15.

8. Namely, for Rodin. On his return to Paris in 1909, Claudel found her quite crazy, living amid horrible filth and speaking incessantly in a metallic monotone. He had to commit her to an asylum in 1913. See his *Journal*, I, 103–104; 247; 1112.

9. Claudel-Gide, *Correspondance*, p. 157.

10. This conflict between lust and grace has a special poignancy for the modern reader familiar with the story of the Italian girl, Maria Goretti, who, stabbed to death by a trusted farm hand in the throes of passion, forgave him on her deathbed in 1902. Her assailant, after some years in prison, was allowed to retire to a monastery as a lay worker and died there in 1970. Claudel does not seem to have been aware of this contemporary overtone, even at the time of the gala performance of *L'Annonce* at the Comédie française in 1955, several years after Maria's canonization.

11. The emotional, human resonance of the 1911 version of this scene of the kiss gives way in the definitive form of 1948 to an almost liturgical act, "the visible sacrament of a providential destiny." This spiritual osmosis may owe something to the recollection of Wagner's *Parsifal* by Claudel, "who, to the scene of the temptation kiss that threatens to paralyze Parsifal in the arms of a seductive and unhappy Kundry, opposed the redemptive kiss of Violaine and Pierre de Craon." Espiau de la Maëstre, "*L'Annonce*," p. 161.

12. See Louis Bouyer, *The Meaning of Sacred Scripture* (Notre Dame, Ind.: University Press, 1958), pp. 35–39.

13. *MI*, p. 234. See above and n. 6. The "blooming breast" legends seem to have been rather rife in late medieval hagiographies.

14. See Annie Barnes, "*L'Annonce faite à Marie* at Hellerau (October, 1913)," in *Claudel: A Reappraisal*, p. 38.

15. See Henri Gouhier, *Le Théâtre et l'existence* (Paris: Aubier, 1963), pp. 76–84.

16. Espiau de la Maëstre, "*L'Annonce*," p. 153.

17. Cf. Paul-André Lesort, *Claudel par lui-même* (Paris: Seuil, 1963), p. 84.

18. See Gouhier, *Le Théâtre*, pp. 80–82.

19. Cf., most recently, Marianne Mercier-Campiche, *Le Théâtre de Claudel* (Paris: Pauvert, 1968), pp. 99, 205–206, 259–260.

20. For some controversial contemporary examples, see Francine Du Plessix Gray, *Divine Disobedience: Profiles in Catholic Radicalism* (New York: Knopf, 1970).

21. Claudel-Gide, *Correspondance*, pp. 106–107.

22. *MI*, p. 239. Cf. Espiau de la Maëstre, *"L'Annonce,"* p. 250. He characterizes this attitude as "the simplistic starkness of Jewish religious faith." He also suggests that Claudel is here endowing Mara with the same intense sense of triumph over the horror of death that he himself experienced upon his conversion.

It is interesting that Claudel usually found the role of Mara better served on stage than that of Violaine—even when an outstanding actress tried both roles. Thus, at Hellerau, he found Maria Dietrich more out-standing as Mara than as Violaine. *CPC*, V, 131. He preferred, for the role of Mara, someone big in stature, with the energy of a lioness.

23. Pursuant to these problems, useful material will be found in the following: Louis L. Martz, "The Saint as Tragic Hero," *Tragic Themes in Western Literature,* ed. Cleanth Brooks (New Haven: Yale, 1960), pp. 150–178; Richard B. Sewall, *The Vision of Tragedy* (New Haven: Yale, 1959); William Chase Greene, *Moira: Fate, Good, and Evil in Greek Thought* (New York: Harper, 1963); *Hegel on Tragedy,* ed. Anne and Henry Paolucci (Garden City, N.Y.: Doubleday, 1962); Walter Kaufmann, *Tragedy and Philosophy* (Garden City, N.Y.: Doubleday, 1969); Max Scheler, "Le Phénomène du tragique," *Mort et survie* (Paris: Aubier, 1952).

24. "When death comes, we have the feeling that it could have been otherwise: here is the paradox of an inevitable that always takes on the appearance of the accidental.

"When death comes, we have the feeling that it ought not to have been: here is the paradox of an inevitable that always takes on the appearance of a fraud." Gouhier, *Le Théâtre,* p. 77.

In the first version (1911), both Violaine (p. 88) and Jacques (p. 91) explicitly muse that she might have been healed and spared if he had believed in her.

25. In the 1911 version, Vercors' detachment seemed so aloof and unmotivated as to border on the scandalous, since he seemed more in-terested in reminiscing over the seasons and the changes in Combernon and Monsanvierge. His disappointment on finding the convent empty was reminiscent, there, of Perceval's failure to recognize the Fisher-King and holiness when he first saw it, or to relocate his previous hearth happiness. These lyrical outbursts are nearly all excised from the later versions in favor of a more direct, dramatic denouement.

A useful comparison of the several versions will be found in Joseph Boly, *L'Annonce faite à Marie: étude et analyse* (Paris: L'École, 1957), pp. 13–43.

26. The final resurrection/glorification of Violaine was suggested in the 1913 Hellerau production by lighting and stage effects. Three planes, superimposed on stage, served to highlight simultaneously several motifs of the drama. Below, a dark space for the tomb of Violaine; above, the four living characters; above them, on a third plane, Violaine appears at the end, clothed in gold and veiled, framed by a kind of luminous Gothic arch which had glowed during the miracle scene. See Annie Barnes, "L'Annonce," p. 36, and Claudel's letter to Lugné-Poe, plus a sketch, in *Claudel homme de théâtre, CPC,* V, 128–130.

This hope-filled ending is in marked and deliberate contrast to the desolate, hopeless one of *La Porte étroite* [*Strait Is the Gate*], of which Claudel complained to Gide in 1909: "The desolate death of your noble Alissa between four spic-and-span walls constricts my heart." Claudel-Gide, *Correspondance,* p. 102.

27. Cf. Martz, "The Saint as Tragic Hero," pp. 153, 158, 176; Gouhier, *Le Théâtre,* pp. 34, 42, 48–59.

28. "Le Hasard, l'homme et les dieux dans le théâtre de Corneille, Racine, Claudel," *La Nouvelle Revue française,* no. 147 (March, 1965), pp. 427, 428.

29. Paul Claudel, "Religion et poésie," OPR, p. 65.

CHAPTER VI

1. Letter to Stanislas Fumet, cited in *Littérature française,* II, ed. Antoine Adam *et al.* (Paris: Larousse, 1968), 267.

2. Letter to Gabriel Frizeau, January 17, 1925, *Correspondance: 1897–1938,* ed. André Blanchet, 4th ed. (Paris: Gallimard, 1952), p. 306. Cf. his letter of August 17, 1926, to Eve Francis: "I know I should add a final drama to the three Coûfontaine ones, but my interior voice remains mute, and I do not want to write something artificial. Besides, *Le Soulier de satin* is my sentimental and dramatic testament, and my only interest now is in the things of God." *Figaro littéraire,* February 13–19, 1964, p. 19.

3. On preceding details, see Pierre Brunel, *Le Soulier de satin devant la critique* (Paris: Minard, 1964), pp. 26–28; and Jacques Petit, *Pour une explication du Soulier de satin* (Paris: Minard, 1965), pp. 9–11.

4. Henri Gouhier, "La Trilogie," *Revue des lettres modernes,* nos. 150–152 (1967), p. 40.

5. Ibid., p. 41.

6. See Jean-Pierre Kempf and Jacques Petit, *Études sur la "Trilogie" de Claudel: 2. Le Pain dur* (Paris: Minard, 1967), p. 25.

7. Kampf and Petit, *Études: 3. Le Père humilié* (Paris: Minard, 1968), pp. 42–45.

8. Ibid., p. 46.

9. Jean-Noël Segrestaa, "Une Source du *Soulier de satin:* 'A une madone' de Baudelaire," *Bulletin de la société Paul Claudel*, no. 33 (1969), pp. 11–12.

10. Witold Leitgeber, "Poland in the Life and Works of Claudel," in *Claudel: A Reappraisal*, ed. Richard Griffiths (London: Rapp & Whiting, 1968), p. 141.

11. His anti-Wagnerian reaction had set in by 1921. Cf. Petit, *Pour une explication*, pp. 11, 41.

12. "Trois scènes de la 'Trilogie,'" *Revue d'histoire du théâtre*, XX (1968), 256.

13. "*Le Soulier de satin*, 'somme' claudélienne," *Revue des lettres modernes*, nos. 180–182 (1968), p. 110.

14. Ibid., pp. 103–104.

15. In fact, in observance of the Claudel centennial, Jean-Louis Barrault had scheduled a performance of just the fourth day for July 17, 1968, in Lyons, but the destructive spring strikes that wrecked his Odéon-Théâtre de France prohibited it.

16. *Pour une explication*, p. 49. He adds that one might define the drama with Nietzsche's words: "The great synthesis of the creator, of the lover, and of the destroyer," insofar as derision is destruction. In this case, however, the irony is destructive of an obsession and productive of a release in joy.

17. Cf. Jacques Petit, "L'Histoire dans la lumière de l'Apocalypse," *Revue des lettres modernes*, nos. 150–152 (1967), p. 88.

18. Quoted by Gérald Antoine, "L'Art du comique chez Claudel," *CPC*, II, 143. This whole volume is devoted to humor in Claudel.

19. Cf. Jean-Noël Segrestaa, "Regards sur la composition du *Soulier de satin*," *Revue des lettres modernes*, nos. 180–182 (1968), pp. 73–76.

20. Cf. Raymond Bernard, "La Description de la mer dans *Partage de midi* et *Le Soulier de satin*," *Revue des lettres modernes*, nos. 134–136 (1966), pp. 40–46; Michel Autrand, "Les Enigmes de la Quatrième Journée du *Soulier de satin*," *Revue d'histoire du théâtre*, XX (1968), 323–324.

21. Barbara Selna, "Paul Claudel: Prison and the Satin Slipper," *Renascence*, VII (1955), 172. On this important theme, see also Michael Wood, "The Theme of the Prison in *Le Soulier de satin*," *French Studies*, XXII (1968), 225–238.

22. Odile Vetö, "La Mer comme symbole de l'espace," CCC, IV, 91.

23. The picture was an illustration for E. A. Poe's *Arthur Gordon Pym*. Such paste-ups in his diary are rare but include a photo of a painting of Poe's wife, Virginia, and one of the death mask of Keats.

24. "La Structure du drame claudélien: L'Écran et le face à face," in his *Forme et signification* (Paris: J. Corti, 1962), pp. 171–189.

25. Robert Ochs, *The Death in Every Now* (New York: Sheed & Ward, 1969), p. 61.

26. See Albert Béguin, *Poésie de la présence* (Neuchâtel: La Baconnière, 1957), pp. 240–241; *Littérature française*, ed. Antoine Adam *et al.*, II (Paris: Larousse, 1968), 267.

27. "The panoramic vision of the past (at the moment of death) is therefore due to a brusk *disinterestedness in life*, born of the sudden conviction that one is going to die right away. Until then, the brain had been occupied as the organ of memory, in order to rivet attention on life, to shrink the field of consciousness for pragmatic purposes." Henri Bergson, *L'Énergie spirituelle* (Paris: Presses universitaires de France, 1919), p. 82.

28. See Josef Pieper, *Death and Immortality*, trans. Richard and Clara Winston (New York: Herder and Herder, 1969), pp. 98–99.

29. Quoted by Henri Mondor, *Claudel plus intime* (Paris: Gallimard, 1960), p. 313.

30. *Paul Claudel* (Paris: Bloud & Gay, 1965), pp. 58–61.

31. *Choses nues* (Paris: Gallimard, 1963), p. 208.

A Selected Bibliography

Additional, but less useful or significant, titles may be found in the foot-notes and in the mushrooming bibliographical sections of the *Bulletin de la société Paul Claudel* (since 1956), of *PMLA* (since 1955) and of *Revue d'histoire littéraire de la France* (since 1953). For editions of Claudel's works used in this study, see the page of abbreviations in front.

Alter, André. *Paul Claudel*. Paris: Seghers, 1968.

Antoine, Gérald. "L'Expression tragique dans *Partage de midi*," *Le Théâtre tragique*. Ed. Jean Jacquot. Paris: C.N.R.S., 1962.

Autrand, Michel. "Les Énigmes de la quatrième journée du *Soulier de satin*," *Revue d'histoire du théâtre*, XX (1968), 309–324.

Bachelard, Gaston. *L'Eau et les rêves*. Paris: Corti, 1947.

Barjon, Louis. *Paul Claudel*. Paris: Éditions universitaires, 1953.

Baudot, Alain. "Le Soulier de satin est-il une anti-tragedie?" *Études françaises*, V (May, 1969), 115–117.

Beaumont, Ernest. *The Theme of Beatrice in the Plays of Claudel*. London: Rockliff, 1954.

Béguin, Albert. "Grandeur de Claudel," *Poésie de la présence*. Neu-châtel: La Baconnière, 1957, pp. 225–243.

Berchan, Richard. *The Inner Stage: An Essay on the Conflict of Vocations in the Early Works of Paul Claudel*. East Lansing: Michigan State University Press, 1966.

Bernard, Raymond. "La Description de la mer dans *Partage de midi* et *Le Soulier de satin*," *Revue des lettres modernes*, Nos. 134–136 (1966), pp. 39–48.

Berton, Jean-Claude. *Shakespeare et Claudel*. Paris: La Palatine, 1958.

Blanchet, André. "L'Élaboration par Claudel de son article sur Rim-baud," *Revue d'histoire littéraire de la France*, LXVII (1967), 759–775.

——. *La Littérature et le spirituel.* 3 vols. Paris: Aubier, 1959–61.

Boly, Joseph. *L'Annonce faite à Marie: étude et analyse.* Paris: L'École, 1957.

Broilliard, Jacqueline. "La 'réhabilitation' de Mara," *Revue des lettres modernes*, Nos. 114–116 (1965), pp. 73–93.

Brunel, Pierre. *L'Otage de Paul Claudel ou le théâtre de l'énigme.* Paris: Minard, 1964.

——. *Le Soulier de satin devant la critique.* Paris: Minard, 1964.

Cattauï, Georges, et Jacques Madaule, eds. *Entretiens sur Paul Claudel.* Paris: Mouton, 1968.

Chaigne, Louis. *Paul Claudel: The Man and the Mystic.* Trans. Pierre de Fontnouvelle. New York: Appleton, 1961.

Choron, Jacques. *Death and Western Thought.* New York: Collier, 1963.

Claudel, Paul et André Gide. *Correspondance: 1899–1926.* Ed. Robert Mallet. 36th ed. Paris: Gallimard, 1949.

——. *Francis Jammes, and Gabriel Frizeau. Correspondance: 1897–1938.* Ed. André Blanchet. 4th ed. Paris: Gallimard, 1952.

Claudel, Pierre. *Paul Claudel.* Paris: Bloud & Gay, 1965.

Cornell, Kenneth. "Claudel and the Greek Classics," *Yale French Studies*, No. 38 (1967), pp. 195–204.

Cunneen, Joseph E. "Present State of Claudel Criticism," *Thought*, XXVII (1952), 500–520.

D'Arcy, Martin. *The Mind and Heart of Love.* New York: Meridian, 1956.

Dennery, Étienne, ed. *Paul Claudel 1868–1955.* Paris: Bibliothèque nationale, 1968.

Du Bos, Charles. *Approximations.* Paris: Fayard, 1965, pp. 1159–1267.

Emery, Léon. *Claudel.* Lyons: Les Cahiers libres, 1967.

Espiau de la Maëstre, André. *Das göttliche Abenteuer, Paul Claudel und sein Werk.* Salzburg: Otto Muller, 1968.

——. "Paul Claudel, *L'Annonce faite à Marie.* Étude critique," *Les Lettres romanes*, XVI (1962), 3–26; 149–171; 241–265.

Fowlie, Wallace. *Paul Claudel.* London: Bowes & Bowes, 1957.

——. trans. *Two Dramas,* by Claudel. Chicago: H. Regnery, 1960.

Fragonard, Marie-Madeleine. *Tête d'Or ou l'imagination mythique chez Paul Claudel.* Paris: Collection de l'École normale supérieure de jeunes filles, 1967.

Friche, Ernest. *Études claudéliennes.* Porrentruy: Portes de France, 1943.

Fumet, Stanislas. *Claudel.* Paris: Gallimard, 1958.

Gargam, Georges. *L'Amour et la mort*. Paris: Seuil, 1959.

Gatch, Milton McG. *Death: Meaning and Mortality in Christian Thought and Contemporary Culture*. New York: The Seabury Press, 1969.

Gouhier, Henri. *Le Théâtre et l'existence*. Paris: Aubier, 1963.

——. "La Trilogie," *Revue des lettres modernes*, Nos. 150–152 (1967), pp. 31–42.

Griffiths, Richard, ed. *Claudel: A Reappraisal*. London: Rapp & Whiting, 1968.

——. *The Reactionary Revolution*. New York: Ungar, 1965.

Guillemin, Henri. "Claudel jusqu'à sa 'conversion,'" *Revue de Paris*, LXII (April, 1955), 20–30; "Claudel avant sa 'conversion,'" *Revue de Paris*, LXII (May, 1955), 89–100.

——. "La 'Conversion' de Paul Claudel," *Les Études classiques*, XXV (Jan. 1957), 5–64.

——. *Le "Converti" Paul Claudel*. Paris: Gallimard, 1968.

Guyard, Marius-François. *Recherches claudéliennes*. Paris: Klincksieck, 1963.

Hoffman, Frederick J. *The Mortal No*. Princeton: Princeton University Press, 1964.

Hoppenot, Henri. "Claudel et sa conversion," *Revue de Paris*, April, 1969, pp. 54–61.

Ince, W. N. "The Unity of Claudel's *Le Soulier de satin*," *Symposium*, XXII (1968), 35–53.

Kempf, Jean-Pierre and Jacques Petit. *Études sur la "Trilogie" de Claudel*. 3 vols. Paris: Lettres modernes, 1966–68.

Lefèvre, Frédéric. *Les Sources de Paul Claudel*. Paris: Lemercier, 1927.

Lesort, Paul-André. *Paul Claudel par lui-même*. Paris: Seuil, 1963.

Lioure, Michel. "Claudel et la notion du drame," *Revue d'histoire du théâtre*, XX (1968), 325–336.

Madaule, Jacques. *Claudel et le langage*. Paris: Desclée de Brouwer, 1968.

——. *Le Drame de Paul Claudel*. 4th ed. Paris: Desclée de Brouwer, 1947.

Marcel, Gabriel. *Regards sur le théâtre de Claudel*. Paris: Beauchesne, 1964.

May, Rollo. *Love and Will*. New York: Norton, 1969.

Mercier-Campiche, Marianne. *Le Théâtre de Claudel*. Paris: Pauvert, 1968.

Mondor, Henri. *Claudel plus intime*. Paris: Gallimard, 1960.

Morisot, Jean-Claude. "De *Tête d'Or* au *Repos du septième jour*: Dieu et la 'peur de Dieu,' " *Revue des lettres modernes*, Nos. 180–182 (1968), 7–24.

———. "Le Mythe et l'histoire dans *Tête d'Or*," *Revue des lettres modernes*, Nos. 150–152 (1967), 7–29.

———. "*Tête d'Or* ou les aventures de la volonté," *Revue des lettres modernes*, VI (1959), 115–196.

Moscovici, Jacques. "Paul Claudel et Richard Wagner," *La Nouvelle Revue française*, No. 140 (August, 1964), pp. 323–334.

O'Brien, Conor Cruise. "The Rhinegold of Paul Claudel," *Maria Cross*. Fresno: Academy Guild Press, 1963, pp. 155–186.

Ochs, Robert. *The Death in Every Now*. New York: Sheed & Ward, 1969.

Oraison, Marc. *Death—and Then What?* Trans. Theodore DuBois. New York: Newman Press, 1969.

Paoletti, Floriane. "*Tête d'Or* 1889–1894," *Revue des lettres modernes*, Nos. 114–116 (1965), pp. 25–45.

Petit, Jacques. *Pour une explication du Soulier de satin*. Paris: Minard, 1965.

———. "Trois Scènes de la 'Trilogie': Évolution de la structure dramatique et du style," *Revue d'histoire du théâtre*, XX (1968), 255–260.

Peyre, Henri. "The Drama of Paul Claudel," *Thought*, XXVII (Summer, 1952), 185–202.

———. "A Dramatist of Genius," *Chicago Review*, XV (Autumn, 1961), 71–78.

Pieper, Josef. *Death and Immortality*. Trans. Richard and Clara Winston. New York: Herder & Herder, 1969.

Poulet, Georges. *The Metamorphoses of the Circle*. Trans. Carley Dawson and Elliott Coleman. Baltimore: The Johns Hopkins Press, 1966.

Rivière, Jacques et Paul Claudel. *Correspondance: 1907–1914*. Paris: Plon, 1926.

Roberto, Eugène. *Visions de Claudel*. Marseilles: Leconte, 1958.

Rousset, Jean. "La Structure du drame claudélien: l'écran et le face à face," *Forme et signification*. Paris: Corti, 1962, pp. 171–189.

Scheler, Max. *Mort et survie*. Paris: Aubier, 1952.

Segrestaa, Jean-Noël. "Regards sur la composition du *Soulier de satin*," *Revue des lettres modernes*, Nos. 180–182 (1968), pp. 59–81.

Suarès, André et Paul Claudel. *Correspondance: 1904–1938*. Ed. Robert Mallet. 9th ed. Paris: Gallimard, 1951.

Tissier, André. "*Tête d'Or*" de Paul Claudel. Paris: Société d'édition d'enseignement supérieur, 1968.

Vachon, André. *Le Temps et l'espace dans l'oeuvre de Paul Claudel.* Paris: Seuil, 1965.

Varillon, François. *Claudel.* Bruges: Desclée de Brouwer, 1967.

Watanabé, Moriaki. "Le 'Don,' ou la logique dramatique de *Partage de midi*," *Revue des lettres modernes*, Nos. 180–182 (1968), pp. 25–57.

————. "Le Nom d'Ysé: le mythe solaire japonais et la genèse du personnage," *Revue d'histoire littéraire de la France*, LXIX (1969), 74–92.

Waters, Harold A. "Justice as Theme in Claudel's Drama," *Renascence*, XVII (1964), 17–28.

————. "Possible Sources for Claudel's Violaine," *Renascence*, XXII (Winter, 1970), 99–107.

Wood, Michael. "A Study of Fire Imagery in Some Plays by Paul Claudel," *French Studies*, XIX (April, 1965), 144–158.

Index

187

About the Author

Dr. Watson received his B.A. from St. Benedict's College, attended St. Benedict's Theologate for four years, won an M.A. from the Université Laval, a Diplome de langue et de littérature (Fulbright) from the Université de Lyon, and a Ph.D. from the University of Colorado. He has chaired the Modern Language Department at St. Benedict's College for five years and is currently Associate Professor of French at Memphis State University. He has written for the *Romanic Review*, the *French Review*, *America*, and other periodicals.